The Two Wo

Wellesley Tudor Pole

Gerry Fenge

The Two Worlds Of Wellesley Tudor Pole

Copyright © 2010 by Gerry Fenge

All rights reserved, including the right to reproduce
this book, or portions thereof, in any form.

Book Design by Jeremy Berg

Starseed Publications
2204 E Grand Ave.
Everett, WA 98201

ISBN-13: 978-0-9791700-6-5

Fenge, Gerry
The Two Worlds Of Wellesley Tudor Pole/ Gerry Fenge

First Edition December 2010

Printed in the United States of America

0 9 8 7 6 5 4 3 2 1

www.lorian.org

For my father, Frederick Maitland:
'carrying on where he left off.'

Acknowledgements

Wellesley Tudor Pole was no ordinary person and this has been no ordinary project, spanning eleven years and drawing on help, materials and moral support from diverse people. I particularly wish to thank the following:

David Spangler for resuscitating a project that had been quietly dozing; every book needs a good reader, and he was that reader.

Jeremy Berg for giving life and form to that project; every book needs a good publisher, and he is that publisher.

Lady Carroll, Jean (TP's daughter) for her quiet and alert personality, for her hospitality, and for her help with letters and photographs until her passing in 2003.

William Carroll (TP's grandson) for supplying many family photographs and for continuing interest.

Kate Harris (née Tudor Pole) (TP's great granddaughter) for lively and perceptive support.

Ed Tudor Pole (TP's grandson) for stimulating letters and 'He's got a moustache'.

Patrick Benham (author of The Avalonians; recommended read) for generous and friendly access to his private researches, including permission to quote from private letters.

Lynne and Michael Orchard (resident guardians at Chalice Well around 2000) for aiding my research and for unfailingly cheerful welcomes.

Martin Oliver (former editor of the 'Chalice Well Messenger') for supplying transcripts of the Walburga correspondence and for stimulating exchanges of view.

Dr Norman Reid (keeper of manuscripts and muniments at St Andrews University Library during my visits) for deploying his cheerful staff – whom I also heartily thank – to transport endless boxes of Russell Trust material to and from my desk in the bowels of the library.

Cecilia Russell (of the Russell Trust) for the photograph on page 65, for many other useful materials, and for lively interest sustained over a decade.

Meic Pierse Owen (archivist at St Andrews University Library) for heroic quantities of photocopying, for amiable coffee breaks, and for 'much light'.

Michael Leveaux and his wife, Eve, for elegant hospitality while allowing access to the archives of Frederick Leveaux.

Alick Bartholomew for very brief access to the Rosamond Lehmann archives in 2000.

Anna O'Connor (friend of TP's niece Monica) for posting materials from Ireland, including Mary's painting of The Cup.

Maggi Fielder (long time editor of Gatekeeper News) for printing my articles on TP and for consistent support.

Erica Leith (of George Ronald publishers) for generous emails and enclosures.

Farhad Naderi for image of Abdul Baha at the Clifton Guest House on page 57

Pam Roberts for sending fascinating items, especially a copy of the 'matinee idol' photo of TP (on the front cover of this book and on page 7).

Sylvia Moss for much interesting correspondence.

Sue Burke for being a valuable reader as chapters emerged.

But the largest thanks of all must go, as ever, to:

Christine, my wife, trusty pal on all jaunts and expeditions, wise and discriminating editor, all-round sustainer of existence, and aesthetic medium through which 'the rays of the noumenal can filter into the phenomenal'.

THE FOLLOWING HAVE KINDLY GIVEN
PERMISSION FOR USE OF THEIR MATERIAL:

The Trustees of Chalice Well for extracts from TP's writings, most notably his letters and his books: The Great War, Private Dowding, The Silent Road, and Writing On The Ground, as well as Rosamond Lehmann's collection of his letters My Dear Alexias. I thank them also for permission to use the photographs on the title page and page 24.

Random House for an extract from A Man Seen Afar by Wellesley Tudor Pole, published by C W Daniel; reprinted by permission of The Random House Group Ltd.

The Imperial War Museum for the photographs on pages 92 and 97.

Michael Leveaux for extensive use of the Frederick Leveaux archives.

Every effort has been made to trace relevant copyright holders. If any have been inadvertently missed, I would be grateful if they could contact they me so the situation can be rectified in any future edition.

Books By Wellesley Tudor Pole

The Great War: Some Deeper Issues (G. Bell and Sons, 1915)
With a foreword by Stephen Graham.

Private Dowding (John M. Watkins, 1917)
(Fifth expanded edition 1943; Sixth Edition, Neville Spearman, 1966; Seventh edition, Pilgrims Book Services, 1984)

The Cosmic Touch (1926, unpublished)

The Silent Road (Neville Spearman, 1960)
(Sixth impression, C.W. Daniel, 1987)
With an Introduction by the Hon. Brinsley le Poer Trench.

A Man Seen Afar (Neville Spearman, 1965)
(New Edition, C.W. Daniel, 1983)
Written in collaboration with Rosamond Lehmann, with a foreword by Sir George Trevelyan, BT. M.A.

Writing On The Ground (Neville Spearman, 1968)
(New Impression, Pilgrims Book Services, 1984)
Written in collaboration with Walter Lang, with a foreword by D.F.O. Russell.

My Dear Alexias (Neville Spearman, 1979)
Letters from Wellesley Tudor Pole to Rosamond Lehmann, edited by Elizabeth Gaythorpe, with a foreword by Rosamond Lehmann.

Contents

Introduction

As I grew up in the early Sixties I was taught that all the important spiritual action had happened two thousand years ago, and the only thing left for us, stranded as we were in the wastes of the twentieth century, was obedience to authority. I could never reconcile myself to that depressing verdict. I felt as if something transcendent, glorious, fulfilling was only just out of reach. If pressed to specify, I might have said it was like the sun searing its way through clouds, firing their edges with golden hosannas. If pressed further, I might have suggested something ethereal yet powerful was breathing its way through the world. However that, as I say, was not the prevailing teaching.

As the Sixties progressed, though, some remarkable intimations entered Western awareness. At first they emerged in the form of sitars on Beatles records, or a giggling Maharishi on news bulletins. Then a friend – my dad in fact – passed me a copy of Autobiography of a Yogi (Paramhansa Yogananda), and suddenly I realised the transcendent, glorious, fulfilling thing could happen right now. Only not here, not in the West. You'd have to go to India for that, follow the hippy trails and maybe buy an Afghan coat en route. If marooned at home, you could at least try sitting in a lotus posture, changing your name to something Sanskrit, and wearing a kaftan.

However, something else happened in the Sixties. There was an old, much travelled man by name of Wellesley Tudor Pole – often just 'TP' – who published a book called The Silent Road in 1960, following it up with a couple more as the decade progressed. His writings created only a small stir, and it probably wasn't until some time in the Seventies that The Silent Road found its way into my hands, but suddenly I realised the transcendent, glorious, fulfilling thing could happen right here, as well as right now. No need for priests or authority. No need for lotus postures or kaftans. You could wear what you wanted, sit how you wanted, even keep your own name if you were really fussy about the matter.

That wasn't all. TP had arranged the purchase of Chalice Well, reckoned by some to be a 'thin place', that is a place where the veil between this world and the next is particularly slender, tenuous, insubstantial. As the Sixties wore on visitors to Chalice Well could experience this for themselves. Indeed, looking back, I try to remember my own first involvement, but such is the selective memory of fatherhood that I need Chris, my wife, to remind me how our kids used to totter around the gardens – it must have been the late Seventies then – until, on repeating visits and with longer legs, they managed more of a scamper.

In amongst all this, of course, one has to earn a living, and my profession, schoolteaching, was an exportable one, taking me and the family abroad. Things went well, but not invariably, and as I lay dying (although apparently not quite) in the Aga Khan Hospital Nairobi in 1990, I kept a copy of The Silent Road by my bed. I'm not sure what for. I doubt if I was capable of any genuine thought by that stage, but I may have felt – in a vague and pre-discarnate sort of way – that an experienced guide to the Beyond might be a handy neighbour.

Then, at the end of the Nineties, and back in England, I was recovering from some more surgery, less drastic this time, so I could take my time enjoying the convalescence. Maybe I enjoyed it too much because I got one of those surges of well-being that accompany returning health, and decided to write a biography of TP. Ah, the optimism of youth! (I was just under fifty.) I set to work, investing time, energy and a few thousand pounds into research, collation of research, editing of research, sewing together of research and eventual sending out of sewn-together research. And – guess what – the first agent I tried said yes.

But this wouldn't be a book about TP if everything happened so smoothly. I've not yet mentioned the obstructions and frustrations he encountered. He encountered lots. So if this was truly to be his biography, then it would need its own obstructions and frustrations. The agent retired, the book languished, and by 2008 I thought I may as well place some extracts on the net – at wellesleytudorpole.com

And that's what did it. In September 2010 I received an email from David Spangler – a practical mystic not unlike TP himself – who had spotted the website and wanted to arrange publication.

Consider the timing – 2010 – exactly fifty years from the start of the Sixties, exactly fifty years since the publication of The Silent Road, a volume of anecdotes and ideas in which TP, amongst other things, left plenty of gaps for a biographer to fill. Such anniversaries can have special resonance. With the onward circling of time, we have arrived at a moment to fill some of those gaps, and this volume covers the first half of his very full life.

How about the other half? Well, the decade is yet young. Volume two hovers in potential, as might many other things in these potentially crucial times. Soon it will be fifty years from sitars and Maharishis. Soon it will be fifty years from the realisation – in some of us – that the important spiritual action was not locked away in a two thousand year old vault. Soon it will be fifty years from a suspicion – in some of us – that further crucial events might be just around the corner.

Right here, right now.

It's a good time for keeping our eyes and ears open. It's a good time for getting Wellesley Tudor Pole back into print.

1. Meeting TP—Impressions

Picture to yourself a London businessman, conventional of suit, measured of speech, 'a plain-looking man, suggesting in dress and appearance the English tradesman.'

Then picture the same man crawling and scraping through underground tunnels in Constantinople as he searches for lost manuscripts. Picture him in the forefront of a cosmic battle, reorienting soldiers as they 'die' in the chaos of war. Picture his own life preserved from certain death as a spirit guide intervenes, and a bullet passes right through him..

Welcome to the Two Worlds of Wellesley Tudor Pole.

Don't stop yet. Climb aboard his Egyptian houseboat in World War One and listen to him ponder the future of the Near East with General Allenby or Chaim Weizmann. Press your ear to a door in the House of Commons in World War Two as he warns Churchill about psychic spying. Listen too at his London office between the wars as he advises the casualties of peace: the starving ex-officer who cannot support his family, the baffled relatives of a man possessed and committed to an asylum, the distressed family of a girl abducted by occultists.

Who was he, this 'confidant of the great and lowly, the rich and the poor'? Who was he, this plain looking businessman, this spiritual adventurer, this man known as TP? At one time he thought the celebrated novelist Rosamond Lehmann might write his biography, so he gave her his instructions:

> *Avoid grandiosity. Depict one who lives mundanely, brings up a family, soldiers, engages in industry, travels, risks his life when the object justifies it, starts and runs the Big Ben Minute; takes over the Chalice Well property and administers a boys' school; writes and lectures, studies Nature's secrets.*
>
> (Letter to Rosamond Lehmann, 2.7.64)

That might have been what he wanted, but after his departure in 1968 (not 'death': he considered 'death' a misleading and destructive concept) there were many who failed to 'avoid grandiosity'.

Major General L.L. Hoare, for instance: 'T.P. appeared to be quite selfless and devoted to helping suffering humanity.'

Squadron Leader Peter Lovatt too: 'A great man, whose work and example has long gone unrecognised.'

Major Oliver Villiers D.S.O.: 'T.P. was undoubtedly one of the most spiritually evolved men of our time.'

Richard St. Barbe Baker: 'For me Glastonbury will always be a Holy Land and the Chalice Well a place of pilgrimage, thanks to W.T.P.'

The Chalice Well Trust was set up by TP, and in the Sixties it published its own quarterly magazine, The Messenger of Chalice Well. So when he moved on, the following issues were full of testimonies, many with an international flavour.

Simone Saint Clair (France): 'The world owes him a debt that will never be repaid.'

Helen Degler (Germany): 'He was one of God's Messengers, entrusted with a holy Mission on our planet.'

Rey d'Aquila (Holland): 'TP's life was glorified simplicity as a reflection of the Master's life.'

Ann Moray (America): 'W.T.P. is a beacon before us, and a path for our wandering feet.'

Some went further. Sir George Trevelyan, the New Age pioneer, described him in *Operation Redemption* (1981) as 'Undoubtedly one of the great seers and adepts of this epoch.' And Rosamond Lehmann, lapsing at last into 'grandiosity', let it slip in *My Dear Alexias* (1979) that 'Obviously he was a Master.'

But perhaps we should hear from TP himself. In 1960 he published The Silent Road a collection of ideas and incidents from the life of a well travelled 76 year old, as he was by then. We can dip in and try to catch the tone of a man of two worlds as he tells one of his tales, even if, typically, he presents himself as just an ordinary sort of person—someone who might catch a train home, miss a bus, then worry about a phone call.

On a wet and stormy night in December 1952, I found myself at a country station some mile and half from my Sussex home. The train from London had arrived late, the bus had gone and no taxis were available. The rain was heavy and incessant. The time was 5.55 p.m. and I was expecting an important trunk call from overseas at 6 p.m. at home. The situation seemed desperate. To make matters worse, the station call box was out of order and some trouble on the line made access to the railway telephone impossible. In despair I sat down in the waiting-room and, having nothing better to do, I compared my watch with the station clock. Allowing for the fact that this is always kept two minutes in advance, I was able to confirm the fact that the exact time was then 5.57 p.m. Three minutes to zero hour! What happened next I cannot say. When I came to myself I was standing in my hall at home, a good twenty minutes' walk away, and the clock was striking six. My telephone call duly came through a few minutes later. I should have explained that I had set out that morning minus both coat and umbrella. It had been a fine morning but by early evening the downpour had become almost tropical. Having finished my call, I awoke to the realisation that something very strange had happened. Then, much to my surprise, I found that my shoes were dry and free from mud, and that my clothes showed no sign of damp or damage. My housekeeper looked at me somewhat strangely at supper that night, but no word was said. Indeed what 'word' was there to say?

(The Silent Road, 1960, p.23)

Much of the book has this tone: a tone of 'much to my surprise' and 'what happened next I cannot say'—as though he is simply the decent sort who leaves his umbrella at home but manages to get away with it. This, of course, was calculated: he didn't want to put people off with too much 'grandiosity'. Throughout his life he had stories like this to tell, sometimes domestic, sometimes quite otherworldly. For instance, forty three years earlier he found himself with an unexpected companion.

On Monday, 12th March 1917, I was walking by the sea when I felt the presence of someone. I looked round; no one was in sight. All that day I felt as if someone were following me, trying to reach my thoughts. Suddenly I said to myself, 'It is a soldier. He has been killed in battle and wants to communicate!'

(Private Dowding, 1917)

And so TP settled down to a conversation between the worlds, publishing the results in Private Dowding, a volume of massive interest to people suffering the anxieties and bereavements of World War One. Many enquiries resulted, which TP could not personally answer, having been posted to the front. However, his friend, David Russell, was able to respond and here is what he told one enquirer:

My dear Sir,

Your letter of the 26th April addressed to W.T.P. has been forwarded to me. I should in the first place explain that during his absence abroad I am dealing as far as I can with his correspondence. He at present has the rank of Captain in the British Army and holds an important staff appointment.

W.T.P. has from the age of 16 or 17 had abnormal vision, but since leaving school he has, until he joined the army, led a strenuous business life, and the development of his psychic powers has been natural.

Since the outbreak of war he has come into touch with many soldiers killed in battle. Practically all his experiences have been in the homes of friends or of a personal nature, and the vision is direct and he seldom makes written records of experiences. Speaking generally, he lives a perfectly normal life and sees abnormally while in a perfectly normal state. He has never so far as I am aware been in a trance condition.

(Letter from David Russell to James S. Hyslop, May 1918)

We might notice here TP's facility for contacting 'killed' soldiers in a state of normal consciousness. This places him in a different category from the trance mediums, table-turners and ectoplasm exuders who, round about this time, would extract snorting dismissal from fierce sceptics. TP appears, on the contrary, to communicate as if people have just popped in for a chat. Russell continues:

He works as many others do during the period of sleep and can bring back clear memories of his experiences. In normal life he can guide and help people by telling them simply what he sees in their lives. He is a man of much business ability and to him, the Private Dowding experience was, although in some respects unusual, of a perfectly genuine nature.

With regard to his intellectual interests, he is primarily a man of business. He has visited Egypt and the Near East on several occasions. He has had no special training and he is as much at home conversing with a Professor of Science as with authorities on social and religious subjects.

(Letter from David Russell to James S. Hyslop, May 1918)

There are more notable details here: for instance, TP's capacity to 'work' during sleep. There again: 'In normal life he can guide and help people by telling them simply what he sees in their lives.' But if we are discussing 'normal life' we ought to seek the opinions of those who lived with him. What, for instance, did Florence, his wife, think of her unusual husband? Children can often be good witnesses and TP's daughter, Jean (later Lady Carroll), recalled some of her younger days in the 1920's like this:

> *My mother supported WTP in everything he did and frequently had*
> *psychic experiences herself. They entertained a lot and there seemed to be*
> *a constant stream of visitors, either people down on their luck, refugees*
> *from Russia, struggling pianists and so on, as well as people interested*
> *in spiritual matters. All this made for a lot of work for Florence, but she*
> *enjoyed it and her parties were famous.*
>
> *My father was a very good host and to use a commonplace phrase, was*
> *the life and soul of the party.*
>
> ('Florence Tudor-Pole', by Jean Carroll, short ms sent to the present author,
> 20.6.02)

'Life and soul of the party.' There, in all likelihood, we have a vital
component of Two-Worlds spirituality. Few would be able to withstand the
strange challenges without a sense of fun as safety valve. So let us pause in
the mid twenties to see him tell a funny story in a letter to David Russell. It is
headed, Grand Hotel du Parc, Chatel-Guyon, and is dated September 1926:

> *Everyone here is an invalid and the waters are for the 'Intestins' I*
> *understand. A Spaniard speaking little French casually addressed me*
> *and enquired gently after my 'Intestins'. I thought he was referring to*
> *some make of car (he spoke vile French) and so I said I hadn't got one. He*
> *seemed very shocked and said: 'Mon Dieu! Quel operation.' Being still*
> *at sea, I said one could get on very well in England without one. 'Diable.*
> *Quel Pays!' He then entered into a description of his own insides and I*
> *thinking still he referred to a car, and as he spoke in the plural, enquired*
> *how many he had? It was only then that I tumbled to the situation. I*
> *fled. But I am sure I am now known throughout the hotel as the strange*
> *Englishman without an inside!*
>
> (Letter from TP to David Russell, Sept 1926)

TP's humour is at its most evident in a book published after his passing,
My Dear Alexias (1979), a selection from the letters he wrote to Rosamond
Lehmann. She mentions a touch of his bantering style in the Foreword as well
as another, more disturbing, sort of liveliness:

> *I first met him in 1963; and it was my great privilege to become his*
> *close friend and collaborator during his last six years.*
>
> *I still remember his amusement when I told him that our meeting had*
> *been foretold by a numerologist at the College of Psychic Studies' Christmas*

Fair in 1962. A gentleman, she told me, about seventy-eight years old, was shortly coming my way and would change my life. Elderly gentlemen, did I not agree, could be such wonderful companions? Dubiously and with strong if tacit reservations, I agreed. This was a story he particularly relished — pressing me to admit that it had been a spot-on prediction.

When I first came face to face with him, which was over coffee in the St. Ermin's Hotel, I experienced a distinct sense of shock. I don't know if this was due to some subconscious stir of recognition, or to a deeper, one might say spiritual malaise. I was in the presence of someone quite formidably awake; and my nerve ends got the message which his old-fashioned courtesy and shield of banter tried to mask. Then and later he gave me a sense... a tingling electric sense, as of being lightly showered with fiery particles - and sometimes lightly stung by them.

('My Dear Alexias', 1979, pages 2 & 3)

He did not always switch on his charisma so obviously. If we meet him again, this time in the company of Walter Lang, we find him ensconced in his more mundane, unspectacular persona. Lang was the collaborator on the last book TP published in his lifetime, *Writing On The Ground* (1968), so his observations have a quality of summation:

The first impression you got of T.P. was his ordinariness: this whether you met him at a friend's house, in his own home at Hurstpierpoint or in his panelled eyrie in Ivorex House in the City.

He was an ordinary, sound chap, you felt; good company, literate and astute but withal ordinary. He was of medium height and straight, with a formidable jaw, a most direct gaze and a deep resonant voice, the precision of which was further accentuated by a slightly formal choice of words.

The vast un-ordinariness of T.P. revealed itself only gently and slowly to a few, and even then, only if he chose to reveal it. You would notice a deliberation about something he said and you would get the impression of an old-time elocutionist over-making a point; and insist on doing it, moreover in the third person, as though T.P. was somebody not in the room at the time.

If you resisted the temptation to pass this over as mere eccentricity you would begin to catch the glint of something under the surface.

('The Messenger of Chalice Well', number 9, Spring 1969)

Reading between the spiritual lines we might guess that some of the qualities stressed by Walter Lang may have been necessities for TP: the straight posture, formidable jaw, direct gaze, strong voice, even the precise choice of words. To be a man of two worlds, he would need a method of staying stable.

Let us see how he managed. It is time to begin his story and discover the Two Worlds of Wellesley Tudor Pole.

TP in the 1920s

2. Early Years: 1884-1902

Something very odd was afoot in the nineteenth century. In March 1848, the Fox sisters in New York State started hearing knocks and raps, and Spiritualism thereby began its bumpy journey into Western consciousness. In August 1852, in Connecticut, Daniel Dunglas Home began levitating and went on to baffle people in Britain and Europe for the next thirty years. In November 1875, in New York City, Madame Blavatsky and Colonel Olcott founded the Theosophical Society. In February 1882, in London, Sidgwick, Barrett, Myers and Gurney founded the Society for Psychical Research. Whatever was going on?

We might play sociologists and say that it was all caused by the cravings of a society baffled by the Victorian Crisis of Faith. However, let us pause and ask where this Crisis of Faith came from. In 1859 Charles Darwin published The Origins Of Species and suddenly human beings were all descendants of apes, nothing divine to our ancestry, certainly no Garden of Eden, and any bishop who dared suggest otherwise — such as Bishop Wilberforce in 1860 — would be 'eaten for breakfast' by T.H. Huxley (Darwin's Bulldog).

Darwin, however, was not the first to write down the theory of natural selection. That was achieved in 1858 by a certain Alfred Russel Wallace in a letter from the jungles of the Malay peninsula posted to Darwin. This raises a fascinating question. Suppose the theory of natural selection had been Wallacism and not Darwinism? Would that have made a difference? Quite a lot: Wallace became a pioneer Spiritualist. Bishop Wilberforce might not have been eaten for breakfast, and—who knows—Western thought could have been spared a century and a half of angst-ridden scepticism.

Overstating the case? Well, maybe, but the whole episode demonstrates what a divided world young Wellesley Tudor Pole was born into in 1884. All the sonorous certitudes of Victorian Britain were under threat, but at the same time, like a bizarre Anglo-American cavalry galloping to the rescue, Spiritualism, Theosophy and Psychical Research (though not, as it happened, Wallacism) were offering alternatives.

Family Background

As for young Wellesley's family, they had a considerable pedigree of uncanny events, some of which pre-date even the Fox sisters and Daniel Dunglas Home. Try this story, probably from the 1810's (Jane Austen time, Napoleon time). The person telling the story is Mary, TP's older sister.

The Tudor Poles come of Welsh ancestry on their mother's side, as her great grandfather, Squire Tudor of a village in Pembrokeshire, prided himself on his direct descent from the famous Owen Tudor who was the fierce old Welsh rebel and patriot who did all in his power to prevent the English from conquering Wales in the reign of Henry II.

Our grandmother vividly remembers the story her mother told her how, one never-to-be-forgotten day, Squire Tudor strode into the Hall in his hunting attire of scarlet coat ready for the hunt, but in a towering rage after a row with his men servants. He looked so wild with anger that his wife thought he should take a quiet walk to calm himself. So he set off, whip in hand, on his favourite route across the fields, but still fuming with rage. As he reached the first stile, to his amazement and horror, facing him on the other side, was the living image of himself, scarlet coat and all, but with such an awful face that he thought it must be a Devil clad in his own clothes! He came rushing back home, pale and shaken, and said to his wife: 'I have had the greatest fright of my life! How this came about I cannot imagine, but all that I can say (after describing what he had seen) is that if anger makes me look as awful as that, I'll never lose my temper with anyone again to the end of my days'. And to her surprise and delight he kept his word!

Our mother often wondered if the meaning of the very old English saying: 'To be beside oneself with rage' signified 'To be outside oneself with rage'? Who knows?

(Mary Bruce Wallace, in 'The Messenger of Chalice Well', number 9, spring 1969)

Mary came up with another strange tale in the next edition of *The Messenger of Chalice Well*. We ought to have a look at this one as well, because it further demonstrates the sort of family TP was heading into. This story concerns his uncle.

Our Welsh grandmother's eldest son was christened 'Tudor' as his first Christian name, and as she had been left a widow with four young children, this boy, as he grew up, was a great comfort, and helped her financially too, when he became a traveller in our father's business firm in Bristol. However, at only twenty-eight he died tragically, to all the family's sorrow.

At that time our father had a man in his office who said that he was a 'medium' and could receive messages from the Unseen, so father decided to test him. The man produced two school slates, placed one on top of the other, and put an end of slate pencil loose between them. He then tied them securely with a string and holding his hands about four inches above them, shut his eyes and said a short prayer. Almost at once, some unseen spirit responded, for father heard clearly the slate pencil, scratching between the slates. When they were taken apart, there, to his astonishment was a letter, in the most characteristic slanting handwriting of Uncle Tudor, signed with his name, asking his dear ones on earth not to grieve for him, as he was so very happy in the Higher World; and it ended: 'Tell darling Mother I shall always be with her still in prayer at 9 o'clock of night'. When she heard this, she exclaimed: 'Only Tudor and I knew that when he was away on his travels, we always met in prayer by thought at 9 o'clock at night'.

Mother had this slate framed in glass, and as a child I regarded it with awe and hoped I might keep it to the end of my life, as a perfect proof of survival after Death. But alas, that priceless relic was lost, in our house removal very many years ago. It must have been broken or stolen.

(Mary Bruce Wallace, in 'The Messenger of Chalice Well', number 10, summer 1969)

We can see, then, from Mary's stories that TP's family was comfortably embedded in the era of Spiritualism, Theosophy and Psychical Research. Indeed, as Mary's daughter, Monica (TP's niece), writes:

Right back from Bristol days they were involved in psychic and occult matters, and had friends interested in reincarnation, and even some who remembered the 'past'. The Tudor Pole family grew up with these subjects being commonplace, and they were familiar with all the methods used by 'mediums', fraudulent and otherwise, and had various books on psychic research, etc

(Private letter from Monica Bruce Wallace to Patrick Benham, 8.9.89)

Such, then, was the family (and Victorian was the age) into which TP was born in Weston-super-Mare on St George's Day, 23rd April, 1884. His parents should have been well placed to understand a *slightly* unusual offspring. However, TP was more than slightly unusual.

At fourteen, my parents told me that when I was eleven Robert McVitie had offered to adopt me, educate me in Edinburgh and make me his heir. I knew nothing of this at the time, or I would have cleared off to Edinburgh

on my own. A millionaire foster-father should not have been discounted,
especially one who was lonely, attractive, a fine character who evidently felt
a close tie with the strange youngster I then was. My mind had matured
well beyond my years at eleven and I was already engaged on other-worldly
missions and pursuits. My affinity with Robert McV. was strong and my
attachment to my father very frail. My parents' refusal, without consulting
me, seemed unforgivable.

(Letter to Rosamond Lehmann, 10.11.66)

Father-son relationships can be very telling, especially, it seems, in
the nineteenth century, so perhaps we ought to linger. Here is what TP told
Rosamond Lehmann as follow up:

'Unforgivable' because at eleven I was more or less grown up and an
independent entity. 'I am not a chattel', was the feeling uppermost in my
mind just then. My father was of the Norman type with some Anglo-Saxon
blood. The de la Poles had been to the Crusades and my father himself
was a crusader for unpopular causes. My mother came from Owen Tudor
stock, later mixed with the Evans/Wansbrough strain, and marriage with
my father was a test for two opposing temperaments.

(Letter to Rosamond Lehmann, 15.11.66)

For anyone who enjoys the byways of history, it may be quaint to note
that in 1506 a certain Edmund de la Pole was arraigned as traitor to King
Henry VII (the first of the Tudor monarchs). Even then, to be Tudor and Pole
was to inhabit two opposing worlds.

We can gain a glimpse of TP's father in a letter full of energy and fierce
opinion he wrote in 1901, while TP was in Neûchatel, Switzerland. Queen
Victoria had just died, and apparently the local Swiss had been less than
reverent about the death. 'The insolence and animus shown in the remarks
you repeat,' blasts Thomas Pole, 'made me very angry at first until I realised
that we ought not to be angry with the ignorant and the ill-informed. The fact
is the little state of Switzerland is very much shut up to itself and the native
mind does not appear to have emerged from what we may call the small
village stage of development.' Then, having bloodied a few foreign noses, he
goes on to praise Edward VII and encourage his offspring.

You have read his speech in the Standard posted to you last night or
this morning, and Mother wishes you to have a copy of the Spectator which

I am getting for you to keep. It will be interesting when you are 50!

The Royal Proclamation was read in Bristol in four places yesterday and I gave Alex and his friend Roy a treat to come up to see it. It will be something for them to remember. Alex will probably write to you about it.

Mother is losing her cold. She will as usual reply in detail to you later and give you all news so I will not spoil hers by saying more, but Mary, who goes to Poole tomorrow, is enclosing, and I also send a good word from the dear Mother. Be brave and do well!

Your affectionate Father

(Letter from Thomas Pole to TP and KTP, 27.1.01)

This letter is just about all we have from Thomas Pole, so we must grab our chance and try to form some impressions. A man of strong opinions? Warm hearted perhaps, with a possibility of over-heating?

Heated or not, TP's family life was basically happy. His sister Katharine was always sympathetic, a close accomplice in TP's more original endeavours. Mary shared both TP's psychic gifts (hers developing later) and his active compassion for animals. His younger brother Alex was a lively contrast:

Back row: Thomas Pole (father), Mary, TP (aged about 13)
Front row: Alex, Kate Tudor Pole (mother), Katharine

energetic, keen on engineering but, in his own way, as spiritually minded as the rest. As for his mother, Kate, a glance at TP's letters to her (in chapters five and seven) will show how lively and wide ranging were their sympathies.

School Life

If family life was basically happy, however, school, was another matter. TP was sent to Blundell's in Devon, a prestigious independent school founded in 1604. Bishops and men of letters had been produced by the school, as well as scientists and scholars. Unfortunately, bullies also emerged, as TP told David Russell in a letter from in 1925:

> *If the Prefect in one's Dormitory is a decent fellow, a good worker, a sportsman, all goes well and the new boy will have little to put up with beyond a little occasional smutty talk and a few semi harmless jokes. On the other hand I have known many cases where the Prefect (usually a fellow of 17 or 18) has been a dirty minded bully who has never been taught self control of thought or action. In such cases, all depends upon the home training of the new boy and his experiences at his first school. He will be unable to avoid many terribly unpleasant and bestial sights and sounds and his innocence will receive horrible shocks.*
>
> *As a private in the Royal Marines in a huge dormitory barracks containing, as they did, some 200 of the riff raff from the streets (presided over by a foul mouthed and besotted old soldier) I have gone through many hells, but nothing in comparison with my experiences at school in a dormitory presided over by a brute and a beast and a bully.*
>
> *Strangely enough, the Prefect in question was the idol of the school and in the First Elevens, but at night he lost control of himself and two of the older boys in the room became besmirched. The consequence was that we smaller boys lived through a thousand purgatories each term and I would give ten years of my life to be able to protect my own or your sons from such experiences.*
>
> *However, Fate may be kind and such risks may never come about; also I had no real home preparation and was utterly unprepared for experiences which turned my whole school life of eight years into a hellish experience and from which shock I have never fully recovered.*
>
> (Letter from TP to David Russell, 9.5.25)

Problems are common enough at school, but 'never fully recovered' comes into a different category, as does his assertion about 'giving up ten years of my life'. Nor was the dormitory the only place where young TP encountered problems; the classroom had its challenges too.

I was christened and confirmed into the Church of England, the outlook of my parents in those days being what used to be known as 'broad Church'. My religious training was based mainly on that form of Public School Christianity which includes the thesis that the Bible (King James' Authorised English Version) is the established Word of God in every particular and therefore contains the whole Truth and nothing but the Truth. I was a thoughtful lad, and it was not long before I came to doubt very seriously the dogmatic assertion which has just been quoted. As an instance, there are certain passages in the early Books of the Old Testament which seemed to my youthful mind to border on the obscene. When on one occasion I asked the School Chaplain to explain the religious significance of such passages, he instructed me to confine my attention to the contents of the New Testament alone. In this connection I remember an occasion in my fifteenth year when I noted and wrote down a list of contradictions concerning the life and teachings of Jesus, as given in the four Gospels and in the Acts of the Apostles. This I submitted to my Form Master when called upon to write an essay on the Ten Commandments.

Needless to say I received the lowest marks in the class for this outrageous example of precocity; but no explanation was forthcoming to allay my doubts and misgivings.

It was soon after that that I gave up asking questions and began to work out a philosophy of my own, much of which has stood the test of time.

(A Man Seen Afar, 1965, ps. 18 & 19)

Remember this was the late 1800's. Spiritualism, Theosophy and Psychical Research might offer alternatives to some adults, but for most people Christianity, despite its embattled position, was the only credible way of belief. Therefore TP was showing considerable originality, although he was no rebel as the following account makes clear. Here Katharine summarises TP's early years, ending with two fascinating items:

He was the first boy after three girls and so was greatly welcomed, but he was a difficult little chap because of being so psychic and, of course, he was not understood and so had a frustrating childhood and was very unhappy as a boarder at Blundells School in Devon. The Church of England parson there who prepared him for confirmation, wrote most enthusiastically to our mother about the way Wellesley responded.

T.P. was first aware of his psychic faculties when he saw the colour of prayers rising up in churches.

When he was about eighteen he had typhoid, I think, or diphtheria, and remembered being outside his body.

(Katharine Tudor Pole, quoted in Oliver G. Villiers, 1977)

These last two items are vital for considering TP as a man of two worlds. What, after all, are prayers meant to be? — postcards to the next world — and if someone feels he is seeing them, he might feel he is seeing something of that world. If TP had any doubts, the out-of-the-body experience must have been a clincher. Such phenomena belong to the personal but incommunicable order of things: utterly convincing to the subject but a matter for polite coughing to others.

We will encounter some coughing — polite and less so — in Chapter Five, because TP was about to become a businessman, and not every business partner regards psychic faculties as ideal qualities. For now, though, TP was a reluctant businessman. He wanted to be at University, but his father had made some ill-judged decisions, so young Wellesley had to go straight into the family business, Chamberlain Pole & Co. Ltd., Flour Importers, Grain & Cereal Merchants, to try and pay off the debts. Thirty years later he was still troubled by the memory:

Whatever happens I do want my children to go out into the world better equipped than I was; for my education (so called) came to an abrupt end when I was 17 and I was in business before 18; and managing director at Bristol at 20.

(Letter from TP to David Russell, 13.12.32)

And there we can leave his early years. His 'so called' education had come to an end, though we might wonder if this was all to the good, allowing his own ideas to develop unhindered.

Whatever the answer, he was almost out of his teens, and Wellesley Tudor Pole, Bristol businessman, managing director, prayer perceiver and part time inhabitant of his own body, was about to begin his Adventures In Two Worlds.

3. The Cup: 1902-1907

The Cup: painting by TP's sister, Mary
(n.b. in size and shape it is more like a saucer)

Britain's end of century school report in 1900 might have read: 'Top of the class. Could do better.' With an empire covering one fifth of the world's land mass, Britain naturally felt itself the 'Land of Hope and Glory' depicted in A.C. Benson's 1902 lyrics. However, only a year earlier Victoria had died, leaving her son, Edward VII, to oversee a country which increasingly felt it could do better.

One reason was the Boer War which by 1902 saw Britain triumphant (top again) but internationally unpopular (could do better). This was a weighty problem at a time when Kaiser Wilhelm II was making anyone non-German feel edgy, and by 1904 Britain found it best to chum up with the old enemy, France.

Times were changing at home too with motor cars tearing along roads at all of 20 miles an hour (having graduated from a speed limit of 4 m.p.h. only in 1896). Then there was the novelty of Labour M.P's at Westminster, the worsening of poverty figures, and the dash-it-all-chaps of suffragettes demanding the vote. Meanwhile over in the West Country, a twenty three year old Wellesley Tudor Pole felt he had made a remarkable discovery.

Discussing the Discovery

To discuss what it was, we might begin with a certain Samuel Langhorne Clemens:

> *[Clemens] was at Archdeacon Wilberforce's next day, where a curious circumstance developed. When he arrived Wilberforce said to him, in an undertone:*
> *'Come into my library. I have something to show you.'*
> *In the library Clemens was presented to a Mr. Pole, a plain-looking man, suggesting in dress and appearance the English tradesman. Wilberforce said:*
> *'Mr. Pole, show to Mr. Clemens what you have brought here.'*
> *Mr. Pole unrolled a long strip of white linen and brought to view a curious, saucer-looking vessel of silver, very ancient in appearance, and cunningly overlaid with green glass. The archdeacon took it and handed it to Clemens as some precious jewel. Clemens said: 'What is it?'*
> *Wilberforce impressively answered: 'It is the Holy Grail.'*
> *Clemens naturally started with surprise.*
> *'You may well start,' said Wilberforce, 'but it's the truth. That is the Holy Grail.'*
> *Then he gave this explanation: Mr. Pole, a grain merchant of Bristol, had developed some sort of clairvoyant power, or at all events he had dreamed several times with great vividness the location of the true Grail.*

Was Samuel Clemens impressed? Did he, for that matter, believe? 'In a subsequent dictation' he offered his views on the incident:

> *I am glad I have lived to see that half-hour — that astonishing half-hour. In its way it stands alone in my life's experience. In the belief of two persons present this was the very vessel which was brought by night and secretly delivered to Nicodemus, nearly nineteen centuries ago, after*

the Creator of the universe had delivered up His life on the cross for the redemption of the human race; the very cup which the stainless Sir Galahad had sought with knightly devotion in far fields of peril and adventure in Arthur's time, fourteen hundred years ago; the same cup which princely knights of other bygone ages had laid down their lives in long and patient efforts to find, and had passed from life disappointed — and here it was at last, dug up by a grain-broker at no cost of blood or travel, and apparently no purity required of him other than the average purity of the twentieth century dealer in cereal futures; not even a stately name required — no Sir Galahad, no Sir Bors de Ganis, no Sir Lancelot of the Lake — nothing but a mere Mr Pole.

(This and the previous quotation are from: 'Mark Twain, A Biography', by Albert Bigelow Paine, 1912: pages 1387 & 1388)

It was a little harsh of Samuel Clemens not to allow our hero a more interesting pseudonym, especially as his own was Mark Twain. The Poles, you may remember, were originally called 'de la Pole', and Sir Wellesley de la Pole would make as good a francophone knight as any. As for the bit about 'no cost of blood or travel', that would come about, plentifully.

The encounter took place on 23rd June 1907, and a month later (July 20th to be precise) TP was in company with Basil Wilberforce again. This time, though, there were forty or so more present, including The Dean of Westminster, Lord Carlisle, The Duke of Newcastle, Lord Halifax, Lord and Lady Brownlow, the celebrated preacher Rev. R.J. Campbell, scientists such as Sir William Crookes and Sir Oliver Lodge, and the American Ambassador, Whitelaw Reid. They had gathered at Wilberforce's home, 20 Dean's Yard, Westminster at 12 Midday to hear more about the alleged Grail. As for Wilberforce himself, he was a cleric of some pedigree, being the son of Samuel Wilberforce ('Soapy Sam', the Bishop T.H. Huxley ate for breakfast in 1860) and the grandson of William Wilberforce (the anti slavery campaigner). The meeting opened with some words from the latest Wilberforce, Archdeacon of Westminster:

Our proceedings here are strictly private, not for publication, and the report that is being taken is for Mr. Tudor Pole's own use. For myself, I will say this, that when anything very remarkable is told me, the amount of what I believe depends not so much on the credibility of what is told me, as the credibility of the person who has told me. That is to say that suppose a few years ago, a man in the street had told me that he would give me a photograph of my bones I should have laughed, but if the same thing had been told me by Sir William Crookes, I should have waited until I got more knowledge, knowing that Sir William was a person to be depended upon. I can only say with regard to Mr. Pole that he is the soul of truthfulness. He may be deluded himself, but one thing is perfectly certain, that he is not going to attempt to delude you.

(Dean's Yard transcript, 20.7.07)

This can rank with our previous testimonials as a character-statement of TP's honesty, but in all fairness it can also rank as an indication of how strange his story was about to be. As we come to TP's opening words we must try to picture the scene: 'a plain-looking man,' as Clemens' biographer put it, 'suggesting in dress and appearance the English tradesman' and yet somehow exerting enough force of personality to hold his audience spellbound:

I became interested in Glastonbury in the spring of the year 1902. I had never been near the place before that date, and the reason I went down there in that year was because I had a very curious dream with regard to the place, which represented myself as being a monk at Glastonbury. I went there and the whole place seemed to be absolutely familiar, as if I had been down there all my life. There are different parts of it, which, from the very first, seemed more my own home than any other part of the world. I was able to gain such extraordinary light and help in my daily work in the world of commerce through these pilgrimages to Glastonbury that I became in the habit of going down there twice a year, at the beginning of the year and about August, to gain inspiration.

In the year 1904, towards the end, while I was at Glastonbury I had a very strong impression that there was a wonderful find to come to light at Glastonbury—a find that would link the founder of the Christian faith with modern leaders of Christian thought. This impression was so strong that I went to Father Field, who was a priest at the Roman Catholic College at that time at Glastonbury, and I told him that I believed that there was a wonderful find to come to light at Glastonbury, and would he keep a look-out for me, as I could only get down there about once or twice a year. He smiled at me and thought, naturally, that I was mad, and nothing further came of it.

(Dean's Yard transcript, 20.7.07)

Might any of the audience have agreed with Father Field? After all, not everyone is willing to sit piously listening to tales of another person's dreams and impressions. Who does this youngster think he is, some might wonder. Self indulgent blather, others might think. Except they didn't. And why not? Could they have felt what Rosamond Lehmann was to feel 56 years later, on meeting TP, that she was 'in the presence of someone quite formidably awake'? Might some have felt, as she felt, 'a tingling electric sense, as of being lightly showered with fiery particles—and sometimes lightly stung by them'? Whatever the answer, we must remember the strange discrepancy between the young nobody on the one hand and the assembled somebodies on the other. TP continued:

> *The same year, on my second pilgrimage, I had a very strong inspiration to find three maidens who would take up work connected with Glastonbury. I did not know where to look for these maidens, but at the end of 1904 I took my sister down for the first time to Glastonbury. She went a pilgrimage with me, and was very strongly influenced by the extraordinary magnetism of the place.*
>
> *In the following year, 1905, I found two other maidens, who came to me under rather curious circumstances, whom I immediately knew, through a very strong impression, were to be connected with this work, and I sent them down to Glastonbury together, to gain what inspiration they could. They have been in the habit of going down since then two or three times a year.*
>
> (Dean's Yard transcript, 20.7.07)

And so TP recruited his 'triad of maidens'. The sister he enlisted was Katharine, and soon he included two of her friends, Janet and Christine Allen. Christine, it would appear, was very psychic and almost got to the find before TP did:

> *The first time that Miss Allen went to Glastonbury, the first impression that she received was that of a monk who came to her and directed her to take a certain route—a certain road—and whilst she was on that pilgrimage she noticed at the Brue Stream, as she was praying, a woman's hand rising from the water holding a cup. She told us of this at the time, and we were, of course, extremely interested in the vision.*
>
> (Dean's Yard transcript, 20.7.07)

All three 'maidens' were with TP at Dean's Yard as he told the assembled dignitaries about the key moment in the narrative:

> *I was at my office in Bristol, not thinking in any way about Glastonbury, or anything connected with it — in fact, I was in the middle of a very serious business conversation — in the midst of which suddenly, without any warning whatever, I saw on the opposite wall of my office the strong impression of a place, a particular spot at Glastonbury, a spot that I had already visited and which I knew well. I had a strong impression, or very clear vision, of this particular spot where a thorn tree was growing, where there are three upright stones arranged in a particular way. At the same moment I saw buried beneath that particular spot some object that was throwing out a curious kind of white light. I could not tell what it was, but it appeared to be lying beneath a flat stone.*
>
> (Dean's Yard transcript, 20.7.07)

This is the third 'strong impression' TP has so far mentioned to his audience — the first two, remember, concerned (a) three maidens and (b) the Allen sisters. However, this third one is more than an impression: it is a 'very clear vision' and he says it involved seeing an unspecified object 'throwing out a curious kind of white light'. In the context of his life, this was pivotal. The place was later to be specified as Bride's Well, and what he saw there, or rather, couldn't quite make out, was to provide a driving force for all his future work:

> *I was unable to go down to Glastonbury that day, and my sister could not go, but the Misses Allen were on the point of going to Glastonbury that week, and I asked them definitely to go and search that spot, to look beneath the flat stone, beneath the water and the mud, which is about three-quarters of a mile from Glastonbury. We have a map here which we shall be glad to show you afterwards. I told them to dig up whatever they found and to report to me. They went down to Glastonbury and found the spot without any great difficulty. They took off their shoes and stockings and waded into the mud. They found no flat stone but a number of broken stones beneath the mud, and beneath that again, they discovered that which we are to show you today. The first impression they received was one of such great awe and sanctity that they dared not touch this relic. They seemed to be guided to wash it and leave it there. They felt that they had no right to bring it away. They came back to Bristol and reported what they had*

found. On October 1st 1906, I sent my sister down to Glastonbury.

THE CHAIRMAN: What was the date of that first visit when the ladies went down? I want to know what space of time elapsed between.

Mr. TUDOR POLE: Very nearly a month. On October 1st 1906 I sent my sister down to Glastonbury, and she found that this relic was still in the place where it had been left, and brought it home to Clifton where we placed it in a private chapel in my house, and it has remained there ever since.

(Dean's Yard transcript, 20.7.07)

Archdeacon Wilberforce interrupted proceedings from time to time to clarify details, and later on he suggested members of the audience might like to question the young ladies. What follows are the answers of 'Miss Allen', and as Janet was the older of the two she is probably the one who answers here:

THE CHAIRMAN: Miss Allen, you went to Glastonbury at the request of Mr. Pole?

MISS ALLEN: We had previously arranged our pilgrimage and then received his instructions to go to this particular spot.

(A Voice from the audience): And you got to this particular spot? Mr. Pole had accurately described it?

MISS ALLEN: We knew the spot as we had been there twice before. It was in the well, full of mud, that we actually brought the cup to light.

THE CHAIRMAN: Didn't it seem a rather hopeless task?

MISS ALLEN: Quite hopeless.

THE CHAIRMAN: But you felt that you ought to go on?

MISS ALLEN: Yes.

THE CHAIRMAN: It is a kind of fen place, is it not, and very few people go by it?

MISS ALLEN: Yes, quite away from the ordinary route.

THE CHAIRMAN: You must have got into a terrible mess?

MISS ALLEN: Yes, a great deal of mud had to be dug up.

(A Voice): What depth from the surface?

MISS ALLEN: About two feet of mud.

(A Voice): There was about four feet of water in the well, was there not?

MISS ALLEN: About three and a half feet.

(A Voice): Did your feet touch it or did you find it with your hands? Did you dig with your hands only?

MISS ALLEN: Hands and feet.

(A Voice): No spades?

MISS ALLEN: No.

THE CHAIRMAN: And it looked beautiful with the water on it? Now, you did not bring it home? That seems a rather peculiar thing. Was it something abnormal that made you feel as though you ought not to take it?

MISS ALLEN: Yes, so we simply replaced it in the well, after having washed it.

(A Voice): Could it have been seen by anyone else?

MISS ALLEN: No, it went to the bottom in the mud.

(Dean's Yard transcript, 20.7.07)

We might pause here to consider the messy job the maidens were willing to undertake: three and a half feet of water plus two feet of mud. At least they went in September, on the 3rd, when the weather might not have been too sharp, but when Katharine went a month later she had no such luck. It was a chill, rainy October day, and she had to wade into deep and peculiarly unpleasant mud. Nonetheless, she found at once the object of her search with her feet, and carried it home with her.

What Was It?

But what was the object? Who could possibly explain its nature or its origin? TP consulted various people, ranging from Annie Besant, soon to be President of the Theosophical Society, to a Swedish poet and writer on mystical themes, Princess Karadja. TP had never met this Swedish princess before but he hoped she might have some out of the way information to help him, especially as he had just drawn a blank at the British Museum and the South Kensington Museum:

> *When I came away on December 15th from the South Kensington Museum, I felt so upset at not being able to gain any light with regard to the find, that I sent up a very strong prayer that some means should be found before the day was out to gain some light. I took it back to the hotel and then visited Princess Karadja. She had no knowledge whatever of this cup and had never heard of this story, and has never seen me before or since. While I was there she said to me, 'I know a lady here who has a most marvellous power. She is in great distress. Would you be willing to*

Thomas Pole at Bride's Well near the Brue Stream,
just outside of Glastonbury, where the Cup was found

go and see her?' I rather reluctantly at the time said that I would, but I did not in any way connect this lady with the prayer I had sent up earlier in the day.

I left there at 4.30 and went to see this lady, whom I had not seen previously, and who did not even know my name. She took me into a small room and said, 'You are connected with a very holy relic' — and I said to her, 'I have a piece of glass in my possession. Can you give me any assistance?' She said, 'Bring it to me and I can help you.' This was a reply to my prayer and I promised to bring the relic for her to see the following day.

(Dean's Yard transcript, 20.7.07)

This lady, a Miss Helena Humphreys, was to remain a lifelong friend and colleague of TP's (and also, oddly, to remain in financial distress: his letters in the 1920's and 30's feature repeated attempts to bale her out). At the time, though, her part in the story was both crucial and strangely atmospheric:

I took the cup to her, and had it covered up in a silk handkerchief. I said to her, 'Do not look at this piece of glass. Put your hand underneath the silk and see what is the result. See if you can tell me whether it is ancient or modern.' It was a very dark room at the back of the house, and it was a foggy London day. She put her hand underneath the silk and the moment that she touched the glass, immediately radiated out from the point of contact, rays of luminous white which were visible to both of us.

Immediately she went into a state of semi-trance, and began to describe our Lord holding the cup in His hands, towards Peter at the Last Supper. She described very minutely certain details with regard to the table, the room, and the supper. She described the liquid that was in this cup, and said that it was either oil or white wine. She could not possibly have obtained this from my mind, because my idea was that red wine was used at the Last Supper. She went on to describe a woman who came in after the Last Supper, and took this cup and washed it and put it in her robe.

She described the Crucifixion scene and the scene at the Tomb, a certain monk or holy man who had charge of this, and she described the centre of a chapel which was adjoining a very large Church somewhere on the Continent in which this relic had been guarded in holy reverence. And finally, she went on to describe a large flat stone and water and gave a very accurate description of the ruin at Glastonbury, although she had never been near the place, and had no connection with it. After thanking her very much for what she had said, I went back to Clifton taking the relic with me.

(Dean's Yard transcript, 20.7.07)

This was one of the all-time vital moments for TP. What he does not tell the audience is that he had actually felt able (in his own uncanny way) to share Helena Humphreys' vision of the 'Church somewhere on the Continent'. Soon he had the church identified as Hagia Sophia in Constantinople, and that would set him off on his life-long Quest. However, TP was not to know this yet. What he did know was that many people were having marked experiences with the Cup, as he went on to tell the Dean's Yard meeting:

Besides myself at our little Chapel, several people independently have noticed this extraordinary radiance which seems to come out of the centre in the form of a lotus flower, and seems to be a pure, luminous, white beam of light that radiates out from the centre of the Cup. At least two people independently have seen this radiation gradually extend and increase until it became the form of a veiled woman, who took the Cup and held it out in her two hands. I have seen the vision several times, and Miss Allen and Miss Humphreys have seen it also. I might say here that the whole atmosphere of my house has entirely changed since this relic came into our possession. That is no imagination on my part because utter strangers have noticed the extraordinary feeling of holiness and peace that there is at this spot. (Dean's Yard transcript, 20.7.07)

'Our little Chapel' was an upper room, often called an Oratory, in his house at 17 Royal York Crescent, Bristol. There were white curtains draping the room, and at one end stood an altar-table on which the Cup lay in its casket with lit candles nearby.

Despite such extraordinary arrangements, we must remember that TP was a man of business, and such people cannot get by on imagination alone. Businessmen may indeed have hunches but sound businessmen will seek corroboration, and that is what TP continued to do. One source of corroboration was A.E. Waite (who, amongst other claims to fame, was the designer of a popular Tarot pack):

Perhaps I ought to tell you here that during the past week I had the pleasure of coming into contact with one of the greatest students of the Grail legends, and before I told him anything about this, he told me that one of the main legends connected with the Holy Grail is that there is an extraordinary white light seen in connection with it by those who are connected with it, and that white light is a protection to the Holy Grail, and is the cause, from a legendary standpoint, of its preservation.

THE CHAIRMAN: How many times have you yourself seen the white light?

Mr. TUDOR POLE: Six or seven times.

(to MISS ALLEN): And you several times?

MISS ALLEN: Yes.

And quite distinctly?

MISS ALLEN: Quite distinctly.

THE CHAIRMAN: What was the vision of light like? Was the place in darkness?

MISS ALLEN: No, because a lamp was always there. At one time it took the form of a dove, and at others simply the light.

THE CHAIRMAN: With regard to that, you are not under a delusion?

MISS ALLEN: Absolutely none. I saw a woman holding out her hands.

THE CHAIRMAN: A female form? How clear was it? Could you see through it? Did it appear to be objective in connection with the relic or subjective?

MISS ALLEN: It was absolutely standing beside the altar with the hands held out.

(Dean's Yard transcript, 20.7.07)

The Miss Allen replying above, by the way, was Christine, the visionary sister. Before moving on from her testimony we might take a quick backward glance at a fifteenth century Grail narrative, Le Morte d'Arthur by Sir Thomas Malory, where we can see, once again, a womanly figure and a white light:

Right so there came by the holy vessel of the Sangrail with all manner of sweetness and savour; but they could not readily see who that bare that vessel, but Sir Percival had a glimmering of the vessel and of the maiden that bare it, for she was a perfect clean maiden...

'So God me help,' said Sir Percival, 'I saw a damosel, as me thought, all in white, with a vessel in both her hands, and forthwithal I was whole.'

(Malory, 'Le Morte d'Arthur', Book XI, Chapter 14)

Nowadays some readers, in New Age mode, might interpret the 'woman in white' as the Guardian of the Cup. Back in 1907, though, at the Dean's Yard Meeting, some may well have remembered the tale of the 'perfect clean maiden' and the 'Sangrail' and wondered, like Mark Twain, if they were being 'transmigrated back into the Arthurian days'. Perhaps they even looked round to check that people like the American Ambassador and Lord Halifax and Sir Oliver Lodge were still there.

Dr. Goodchild

Matters continued in pseudo-Arthurian vein, because next to be mentioned was that most archetypal of figures, the wise old man. His name was Dr. Goodchild, and TP knew him as a student of antiquities, as did the maidens. So it was natural for TP to visit him and ask if he had any ideas about the Cup.

> When this find was described to him he started, turned pale, and immediately began to tell this story to us. I may as well say here that I have no means of proving it in any way. It has also been narrated to Sir William Crookes who will be willing, no doubt, to second anything I might say.
>
> While Dr. Goodchild was at Bordighera in 1887, he was told by a friend that there was an extraordinary piece of glass to be seen there. He went to the shop and saw it, asked where it had come from, and was told that it had been found walled up in a vineyard belonging to the man's father at Albegna many years before. Dr. Goodchild bought the cup for £6, brought it to England, and showed it to his father who said immediately, 'Do you know what this is? I think I had better take charge of it.' Dr. Goodchild handed it over to his father who locked it up in a safe place.
>
> Dr. Goodchild was in Paris in 1896 when suddenly all power of movement was taken from him while sitting in a chair, and he heard a voice saying to him, 'I come to you at very great danger to myself to tell you that the cup which you are allowed to find at Bordighera is the cup used by Our Lord, and I come to tell you that when your father dies you are to take it to Glastonbury and place it in the Women's Quarter.' Dr. Goodchild had no knowledge of the Women's Quarter and had never been to Glastonbury. In 1897 his father died and sent a special messenger to him with this piece of glass, which, on receipt, he took immediately to Glastonbury, obtained a very old map of the place, discovered the Women's Quarter, and left it at the well in which we found it.
>
> (Dean's Yard transcript, 20.7.07)

This raises more questions than it answers, the first being why Dr Goodchild's father reacted as he did. The transcript at this point is not, alas, enlightening:

> A QUESTIONER: *I should like to know whether Dr. Goodchild gives any reason as to how his father knew anything about it?*
> Mr. TUDOR POLE: *He simply said that it was a very holy thing.*
> QUESTIONER: *His father had no knowledge?*
> Mr. TUDOR POLE: *All we know is that he simply said, 'Do you know what this is?'*
> (Dean's Yard transcript, 20.7.07)

A second obvious question would be whether any collusion was involved. After all, TP was looking for something at Glastonbury precisely when Dr. Goodchild allegedly knew what was there. However, the involvement of the three maidens argues persuasively against that. If we consider their frequent to-ing and fro-ing between Glastonbury and Bristol (on pilgrimages and mud-delving sessions), we have to conclude either that the maidens were in on the collusion or that they were being deliberately misled. Both vedicts sound too unwieldy to be credible, and it seems best to accept what TP next told the audience about Dr. Goodchild:

> *He has given Sir William Crookes both in writing and verbally, his definite statement that there has been no collusion between himself and me, and that I had no previous knowledge of the story I have now told you regarding his find, until he told it to us after the relic had come to light. You have my word for that. Although I knew that Dr. Goodchild was to some extent interested in Glastonbury, interested in all kinds of antiquities, yet never at any time has any suggestion passed between us in connection with the cup.*
> (Dean's Yard transcript, 20.7.07)

What might we think to Goodchild's story now? The Cup had to arrive in Bride's Well somehow, and Goodchild's story does involve some fascinating details. Notice, for instance, where the voice says, 'I come to you at very great danger to myself.' One does not normally imagine celestial informants as being in danger, especially 'very great danger'. As a matter of fact, such strange ideas will recur frequently in later decades, as TP becomes more and more involved in the 'aerial armageddon.' For now, though, we can ask what

TP himself thought to the story.

And the answer is, he was never very enthusiastic. Even at the Dean's Yard meeting he tacked it on to the end of his narrative, rather than placing it in correct sequence. Fifty six years later, in writing to Rosamond Lehmann, (My Dear Alexias, 23.5.63), TP called Dr. Goodchild 'a clever but very eccentric medico, with a most lucrative practice at Bordighera for over thirty years' (which sounds a bit like damning with faint praise). He also sent Rosamond Lehmann a document summing up the known history of the Cup, including statements such as this:

> *Whilst none of those concerned had any adequate reason to doubt Dr. Goodchild's veracity, it should be stated that no objective evidence of the truth of his story has ever been discovered.*
>
> ('My Dear Alexias', 1979, p.38)

There seems some eloquence in the phrase 'adequate reason' (as though TP could think of a few inadequate ones). The document also mentions TP's search for the site of the Cup's emergence in Italy, which was apparently the wall of an ancient Monastery at Albegna:

> *WTP and his friend Mr. Frederick Leveaux visited Bordighera on two occasions in the 1930's but could find no trace of Monastery ruins at Albegna nor could local inhabitants throw any light on the incidents related by Dr Goodchild* above. The sole authority for his statements rests therefore on his own account of the events stated by him to have occurred.*
>
> ('My Dear Alexias', 1979, p.38)

The Prophecies

Meanwhile, back at 20 Dean's Yard, TP came to arguably the most remarkable part of a remarkable exposition, moving from role of grail questor to prophet. Prophets traditionally do two things: predict the future, and castigate the present. He was about to tell distinguished representatives of the world's top-nation how they could-do-better. Here is how he started:

> *I should like to say a few words with regard to visions I have seen at Glastonbury, and in connection with this holy relic, about things that*

---

* Footnote: For a full and sympathetic account of Dr. Goodchild, see 'The Avalonians' by Patrick Benham (1993, Gothic Image Publications).

have not yet taken place, visions that one and all can prove definitely by
the lapse of time, and I should like it to be definitely understood that I have
received instructions to say what I am about to say and you must not look
upon me as in any way the originator.

(Dean's Yard transcript, 20.7.07)

Clearly this required a bit of questioning, and that is what it got. 'What exactly do you mean by 'receiving instructions'?' asked a voice (unspecified) — to which he answered, 'A very strong intuition, much stronger than any spoken word could possibly be.' More questions came later, but for now he continued:

In the first place with regard to this relic, within a year from the present
time, definite tangible proof will be forthcoming which will go a very long
way to proving definitely that our Lord at one time was connected with
this cup.

Within a certain time — I cannot tell how long — this cup will go back to
Glastonbury. Glastonbury will become the centre of healing as at Lourdes,
a centre of healing not only of physical but also of spiritual healing.

Just as Glastonbury was the spot at which Christianity first touched
Britain, so through Glastonbury is Christianity to be renewed here in
England in the future. I have seen from the Tor Hill at Glastonbury a
vision of the leaders, both official and unofficial, of the English Churches
gathered together at Glastonbury to pray for the greater unity and the
greater union of the Christian Churches.

I have had a very strong impression — so strong that I know it to be the
truth — that within a very short period there is to be a Divine outpouring
of the Holy Spirit into the world, in a particular way, and those great
intelligences who are preparing the way and who are working towards this
end, are preparing channels through which this Divine power, this second
coming, this great outpouring of the Holy Ghost, shall be manifested.

(Dean's Yard transcript, 20.7.07)

Perhaps we should pause to examine these prophecies. The first concerns proof about the Cup emerging within a year; soon we will see that TP was hot on the trail of proof (although it was actually to elude him). The second one concerns Glastonbury becoming a healing centre (within an unspecified timespan); and we can note that it is difficult to move nowadays in Glastonbury without bumping into a healer of some sort, although their operations tend to be far more informal than those at Lourdes.

Thirdly, as regards Christian unity, it would seem incredible in those far off days that the Pope and the Archbishop of Canterbury should kneel together in prayer. However, they did exactly that at Canterbury Cathedral in 1982 (although the influence of Glastonbury in this is hard to see). Fourthly, as regards an outpouring of the Holy Spirit 'within a very short period,' TP spent his life prophesying this, and some New Agers (and social historians) might note that round about the time of his departure (1968) some very interesting developments were taking place.

How are these prophecies to be assessed? Prophecy is of necessity an inexact science, and fifty percent accuracy would be quite startling (not to say invaluable for gamblers). Does TP score fifty percent here? It is a matter of opinion, so perhaps we had better shelve the issue for now and listen to Archdeacon Wilberforce trying to clarify just what he is hearing:

THE CHAIRMAN: You are now prophesying?

Mr. TUDOR POLE: Absolutely. This is entirely visionary. It remains with the English Christian Churches as to whether they will be used as the channel through which this second coming shall be manifested... If this greater unity can be obtained, if the leaders and moulders of Christian thought at the present time can, through their strenuous activity, bring about greater harmony and make the English Christian Churches a harmonious channel for the outpouring of this Divine Power, then they will be definitely used as the instrument for the coming of the Holy Spirit.

If, on the other hand, the Christian Churches are unable, within the next few years—and it is only a question of a very few years—to come into greater harmony one with the other, then they will not be used in any way for this Divine outpouring. Other agencies will be found, and so the Christian Churches will have lost the most stupendous opportunity that they have ever had since the days of Our Lord, for carrying on the evolution of the world. If they miss this grand opportunity that is offered to them, the centre of the world will no longer remain in London or England. England will no longer remain the great nation that she is, and the centre of the world will be transferred to a very different country.

(Dean's Yard transcript, 20.7.07)

Just who did this twenty three year old prophet think he was? Let us look again at who he was talking to, this time selecting the churchmen in the audience: The Rev. R.J. Campbell (a celebrated preacher), the Dean of

Westminster, Canon Duckworth, the Archdeacon of Westminster. He is telling some top clerics (and plenty of influential lay people) that they should-do-better and arrange some harmony: quickly. Otherwise, they will blow it, not only for the churches, but for England as a whole.

We need to remember that Britain's decline from top nation status would by no means seem inevitable to the audience. World War One would be the cause, and few people were convinced that any war would happen, Kaiser Wilhelm or no Kaiser Wilhelm. Indeed, only the previous year Edward VII had visited him at Kronberg (the Kaiser being his nephew) to try and calm things down. We can provisionally notch this, therefore, as another candidate for semi-accurate prophecy. However, TP did not rest there. He went on to offer the most striking prophecy of all:

> *In the year 1911 those who have been watching and preparing the way for the second coming, will recognise a great teacher who will be here and will be recognised by a few in that year. The great teacher will be a woman and recognised by those who are, as I say, preparing the way, by a seven pointed star that will be worn on her forehead. She will not be recognised by official Christianity, and no-one will realise until her work is over that she has been the most marvellous centre and focus of Divine manifestation in this world since the time of Our Lord. I give you these particulars. I do not ask you to believe them. I ask you to wait and watch.*
> (Dean's Yard transcript, 20.7.07)

This prophecy, being the most specific, is the most interesting of all (and, as we will see in the next chapter, might be allotted an accuracy score as high as fifty percent). Now, if all this were just a matter of TP staring into tea leaves and guessing their meaning, it would be one thing, but he was quite adamant the truth was otherwise:

> *I don't want you in any way to take this from me. I am simply an instrument that has been used at the present moment in the world's affairs, a very poor instrument at that, to pass on certain information from those superior beings who are doing their utmost to prepare the way. There are plenty of signs in the world at the present time of the coming of this great force—of this second coming—and I will ask you to remember not me as having said it, but to remember that I say that it is nothing whatever to do with me, but that I have received definitely and tangibly, instructions from Higher Powers to give voice to this message today.*

THE CHAIRMAN: Do you mind questions being put to you? Does anyone wish to put questions — the most searching questions you can find. Scepticism is the mother of discovery.

QUESTIONER: These intimations of what is going to happen in the next few years have come to you 'definitely and tangibly'. May we ask you what you mean by 'tangibly'? It is a strong word.

Mr. TUDOR POLE: I do not mean to say by writing but simply that I have received a strong impression, both in connection with the relic and Glastonbury.

(A LADY): Were you awake?

Mr. TUDOR POLE: Yes, always awake.

THE CHAIRMAN: This has not come to you through a séance?

Mr. TUDOR POLE: No, I have never attended a séance.

(Dean's Yard transcript, 20.7.07)

To select a few phrases, he was passing on 'information from... superior beings', having been told to do so by 'Higher Powers'. (Years later he was to give a name to his chief source, calling him 'The Sage'.) However, for now the question was: why was TP not laughed out of Dean's Yard? Why did the assembled dignitaries tolerate his finger-wags and warnings that Britain might lose top nation status?

He must have had a remarkably compelling effect. Certainly his sister Katharine thought so, telling her diary that 'The Duke of Newcastle was particularly interested, also Campbell; and a woman who came up afterwards and simply said 'Thank you' to W. but meant a lot by it' (KTP, Contemporary Diary, 1907).

And then, after the dignitaries had examined the Cup, the meeting came to a close. Away they went thinking, 'Woman, seven pointed star?.. I'll believe that when I see it.' Or perhaps some thought, (along with Walter Lang—as per Chapter One), 'That's quite a formidable jaw he's got... most direct gaze too... for that matter, a deep and resonant voice.' Maybe some remembered Wilberforce's words: 'He may be deluded himself, but one thing is perfectly certain, that he is not going to attempt to delude you.'

But someone failed to remember some other of Wilberforce's words: 'Our proceedings here are strictly private.' The story got out, and six days later, on Friday 26th July 1907, the Daily Express carried the following:

MYSTERY OF A RELIC
FINDER BELIEVES IT TO BE THE HOLY GRAIL
TWO VISIONS
GREAT SCIENTISTS PUZZLED
DISCOVERED AT GLASTONBURY

A small circle of eminent leaders of religious thought, antiquaries and scientists are at present discussing with the deepest interest, the discovery in remarkable circumstances of a glass vessel of beautiful workmanship and supposed great antiquity, in a spot near Glastonbury Abbey.

The discovery was made by the sister of Mr Wellesley Tudor Pole, of Bristol, and two other ladies, as a result of a suggestion by Mr Tudor Pole that they should go and search in a place he had seen, either in his mind's eye or in what seems to have been a 'waking dream'.

Mr Tudor Pole has submitted the vessel to various experts, who are unable to assign a date for its origin. It may be 2,500 years old. At any rate, it has been pronounced within the last few days to be pre-Venetian.

One of the strangest features concerning it is that it was placed in a spot near Glastonbury nearly nine years ago by Dr Goodchild, of Bath, a man of much antiquarian knowledge, also as the result of what is described as a 'trance', and Dr Goodchild entertains the belief, consequent upon his strange experiences, that it is the cup which the Saviour used at the Last Supper, and which, according to the Glastonbury Legend, was brought to Britain after the Crucifixion...

While Mr Pole holds that there is not sufficient ground for believing that the object of his discovery is of the sacred nature attributed to it by Dr Goodchild, he is firmly convinced that it is a 'holy relic', and has now installed it in a room in his house, which has been set apart for it. The room is draped in white. The vessel reposes in a casket on a table, and lighted candles are kept in the room.

The Goodchild portion, by the way, is inaccurate in a vital respect, as he wrote and told the paper shortly afterwards: 'In my experience at Paris in 1897, not 1896, I was not told that this was "the Cup used at the Last Supper", but simply that it was "the cup carried by Jesus the Christ"'(typewritten document in Leveaux archives).

The Cup story placed centrally on the front page of the Daily Express

Leslie Moore's Story

The main thing to note is the date of the Daily Express article, July 26th 1907, because that is crucial to the next strange story. We can leave the protagonist to tell it for herself, because Miss Leslie Moore later published an article in The Month entitled 'Two incidents concerning Glastonbury'. The second of the incidents interests us here, the initial situation being that she was visiting South Africa, and in March 1907:

> *I was writing some home letters. It was rather late; I believe about eleven o'clock. Among the letters I was writing was one to a friend of mine, a Miss H. [Hoey]. While writing this letter I had a sudden strange and forcible impression that on July 27th of the same year I should hear of something remarkable being found. As I knew the impression I had just received would interest her, I wrote and told her about it.*
>
> *I sailed for England the following June 10th, and reached home on*

> *July 2nd. On July 13th I went to London to stay with some friends for a few days. I saw Miss H., and she reminded me of the date I had mentioned to her in my letter. She asked me to stay with her when I left my other friends, and this I agreed to do. She worked in the office of a well known magazine firm.*
>
> *On Saturday, July 27th, she came to me in great excitement. Someone at the office had happened to bring her a paper in which there was an account of an extraordinary find at Glastonbury!*
>
> (Leslie Moore, article in 'The Month', May 1920)

This, of course, is our Daily Express article, describing the Dean's Yard Meeting and published on Friday July 26th (but seen by Leslie Moore, a non-Express-reader, the following day). The coincidences concerning the Cup are mounting, but the visions are even more numerous. Leslie Moore went on to write about some of her own, but first she described TP whom she was able to meet the following day:

> *He was quite a young man, with a real business capacity, and a level head for such affairs, yet he was undoubtedly possessed of the curious faculty of second sight.*
>
> *All the while Mr. T.P. was telling us the story, and in fact since the preceding evening, I had had one of my curious impressions that papers were in existence which would give an account of the Cup. I mentioned this to Mr. T.P., but told him also that I had no idea where such papers were to be found.*
>
> *Now comes what, from the matter of personal experience, is almost the most interesting part of the whole occurrence.*
>
> (Leslie Moore, article in 'The Month', May 1920)

Indeed it is so 'interesting' that it deserves quotation at length, because here we will see the origin of 'The Quest', TP's lifelong search for documents which he hoped would regenerate world religion. Here is how Leslie Moore starts the account:

> *A few nights after my return, I had a strange experience. I was in bed at the time, but quite wide awake, having only just got into bed. It was, therefore, no dream, nor could it be called a vision in the generally accepted sense of the word. It was more as though I were remembering something, and visualising it clearly, as a person is able to recall to his mind, and*

visualise with vivid distinctness, scenes and happenings of former years.

I saw a large church, which I could, and did, describe later in much detail. Mass had just been said in the church, though I knew it was midnight, and, though I was not a Catholic at that time, the fact surprised me, for I knew it was a most unusual hour for a priest to say Mass, except on Christmas Eve. My impression is that the priest was wearing red vestments, but of that I would not be absolutely confident, though I am almost sure they were red. I was conscious of a sudden tumult without the church, and of a great banging on the doors, while the people within the church were obviously terrified.

I saw the priest show two small acolytes a way out, presumably to safety. I think he must have taken off his vestments, for I was next conscious of him standing by one of the great pillars of the church, and I think he was then dressed in a cassock or habit of some kind. The people were so terrified that the majority seemed scarcely to notice him. He seemed to me to be speaking, or thinking so clearly that I was fully conscious of the words in his mind.

'Not for my own sake, but for the sake of the treasure entrusted to me.'

The pillar by which he stood was formed of great stones. He touched a hidden spring in this pillar, and one of the great stones turned on an iron or steel bar which ran through it, disclosing a small spiral staircase within the pillar. He entered the aperture made by the turning of the stone, then let it swing into place behind him. I saw him mount the stairway till he came to the span of the arch to the right of the pillar. He passed along this span, which formed a kind of passage way, till he came to another span running at right angles to it. This span was a narrow chapel. In it, at the end in which he first found himself, was a small altar with a kind of Tabernacle on it. Yet I knew it was not a Tabernacle in which the Blessed Sacrament was reserved. He opened it, and I saw him take from it a roll of parchment, and the Cup, the photograph of which I had seen, and which had been minutely described to me.

(Leslie Moore, article in 'The Month', May 1920)

We may need to pause and get our bearings by now. We have already heard that when Helena Humphreys held the Cup she saw 'a very large Church somewhere on the continent'. Now we have a detailed account of events in a large church, possibly the same one. We find furthermore that the Cup had been kept in that church, along with a roll of parchment (which might be of considerable interest to anyone researching the Cup's history).

Leslie Moore continues with her tale of the anxious priest:

> *He then went to the other end of the span of the arch, and descended a second spiral stairway within another pillar. This pillar sank many feet into the ground, and, when he came out of it, by turning one of the stones on a pivot as he done before, he was in a kind of catacomb. I saw him go to a stone in the wall of this place, and push it aside. The stone had symbols on it, among them a five-pointed star or pentagon, and two fishes. I think he went through the opening into a sort of passage way. When I saw him again I knew he had left the roll of parchment behind him. The Cup he kept within the breast of his habit. He seemed to me to stay some time in the catacomb. At last he ascended the spiral stair, but instead of mounting to the span of the arch, he came out into the church. I then saw it was devastated and ruined.*
>
> *That was all. I returned to my surroundings, and the fact that I was in my own bed.*
>
> *The next day I wrote a full account of this to Miss H. [Miss Hoey]. She communicated it to Mr. T.P., and I received a telegram asking me to go at once to London. I went, and there I met Miss H., Mr. T.P., and the clairvoyante [Helena Humphreys] to whom he had taken the Cup. I was asked to repeat my story. On the conclusion of my recital, Mr. T.P. told me that I had described the Church of San Sophia at Constantinople, and that on a certain date, which he mentioned and which I have forgotten, Mass was said there at midnight, and before morning it was in the hands of the Turks. [note: TP later specified the attackers were an alliance of Bulgars and Arabs.] Now I can state with absolute confidence that this fact had been unknown to me. Therefore my waking vision, if it can be so called for want of a better word, had been in no way influenced by previous knowledge.*
>
> *After discussing the story fully, Mr. T.P. told me that he intended to go out to Constantinople and make investigations. I begged him not to do so, feeling it was almost absurd to put any confidence in my waking vision. He said, however, that it had only confirmed, with full detail, an impression that the clairvoyant had had, and he meant to go. He made me draw a little map of the position of the church, the catacomb and the stone I had seen.*
>
> (Leslie Moore, article in 'The Month', May 1920)

Helena Humphreys had glimpsed the location, Leslie Moore added drama and detail, but was TP really likely to rely on other people's visions? No, he relied on his own. The evidence comes in a document in his own handwriting, undated but probably from 1923, where he looks back to Quest beginnings:

> *The first intimation concerning this hiding place was received in January 1907 by Miss Helena Humphreys who described the spot and its surroundings whilst holding the Cup in her hands. Miss Humphreys was in a state of trance at this time and I was the only other person present. Immediately she began to describe her vision I found myself witnessing the scene; indeed I felt as if I had been transported to Constantinople and were in a position to make independent investigation of the conditions there. It is only right to set down the fact that it was Miss Helena Humphreys who first turned our attention towards Constantinople and that this resulted from the psychometric experience which came to her after handling the Cup for the first time.*
>
> *Subsequent to this experience my thoughts became centred upon Constantinople and I found myself transported there on many occasions both during sleep and whilst in my normal state. Several other clairvoyants were given the opportunity of psychometrising the Cup at this period, including Miss M. Hoey and Miss Leslie Moore and these ladies associated the vessel with hidden records which they felt were hidden away at Constantinople.*
>
> (Untitled manuscript, TP's handwriting, probably dating 1923, in F. Leveaux archives)

Two Further Verdicts

So there is the answer: TP shared the visions, and that is why he went hurrying off to Constantinople in their pursuit. We will see what happened there in the next chapter, but before sending him off, it is only fair to introduce a contemporary note of scepticism. A.E. Waite, the grail expert (and Tarot Card designer), had clearly had time to ruminate the nature of the Cup and by September 1907 he felt some rigour was called for. Writing in the September 1907 edition of '*The Occult Review*', he decided:

> *As a student of the archaic literature to which we owe our knowledge concerning the Holy Graal, I can say with some authority that there is no actual correspondence between the discovered object and the central Hallow of all the old legends, though it may be possible that under other aspects the Glastonbury relic may be of great interest and importance.*

Clearly for Waite (after deliberation) the womanly figure and white light were not enough. But that is all to the good: the situation would scarcely be realistic if everyone fell over themselves to agree.

However, for the Daily Express at least, the finding of the Glastonbury Cup was a story with resonance, indeed one that chimed with the times — for this was not just an age of top-nation-could-do-better; it was also an age of wonder. Let us return to that Friday, the 26th of July 1907, when the story was about to be launched onto the world. Here is part of a Daily Express commentary article:

> *This is a utilitarian age, an age of steam and commerce and speculation. But it is, at the same time, an age of almost disquieting mystery. The phonograph and the wireless telegram are things far more mysterious, actually perhaps far less explicable, than the mysteries framed and believed in past ages... A Bristol gentleman discovers a mysterious vessel at Glastonbury. Twenty years ago he would have been merely laughed out. Today, eminent men, among them divines and scientists, solemnly meet to discuss his story and to endeavour to discover what the vessel may be.*
>
> *It is good for the world to have really learned that 'there are more things in heaven and earth than dreamt of in our philosophy'. The science of the middle Victorian era was cock-sure in its materialism. It smiled loftily at the idea of miracles, it sneered at the existence of the mystic and the unseen. But wisdom did not begin and end with the disciples of Darwin and Huxley. Life can never be understood if one limits its possibilities to that which can be perceived by the senses.*

As for TP, he was determined to go beyond wonder to answers. Where had the Cup been in past centuries? What might it bring to light? The normal sequence in Grail stories is for a long search to end in discovery, but in TP's case the sequence was reversed. Discovery was about to lead to a very long search.

Constantinople in the early Twentieth Century

4. Expanding Horizons: 1907-1913

The Edwardian age was, like most ages, the best of times and the worst of times. A compassionate government brought in old age pensions, labour exchanges and National Insurance, the last two largely piloted by that energetic young Liberal at the Board of Trade, Winston Churchill (Boer War hero, ex-Tory M.P. and man with an interesting future.)

But all the while the First World War came creaking nearer like a tumbrel, with kings heads about to roll and commoners in their millions set to join them. The bright young Liberal would become First Lord of the Admiralty and, when war reached stalemate, he would seek a breakthrough in the East, sending his battleships on a quest to Constantinople. However, they only got as far as Gallipoli.

His future acquaintance (and covert accomplice), one Wellesley Tudor Pole, also had high hopes at Constantinople. He had sought his Grail in the West, he had found his Grail in the West, and, in 1907, he boarded the Orient Express, seeking spiritual breakthrough in the East. Travelling through the Balkans, he was on a Quest to Constantine's old city, the heart of the very 'Eastern Question' that was to rip Europe apart.

For TP it was a visionary adventure. If he could just find that hidden roll of parchment, if he could just find the stone under which it lay, if he could prove the Cup's history, then its influence might spread to the whole world, and then—well—perhaps the bright young Liberal need only play battleships in his bathtub.

First Quest Attempt, 1907

There is a document in TP's handwriting that must have been intended for a chapter in a book. However, the book never emerged into daylight, and the document became buried in the trunk of TP's friend, Frederick Leveaux, where it has remained till now. The tale it tells begins with TP's far vision as he 'sees' his destination:

> *When I left for Constantinople towards the end of August 1907 I carried with me no plans or papers but I possessed a clear mind picture of the places I was about to visit.*
>
> *Political conditions at that time were very chaotic in Turkey and the tragic and long drawn out regime of Abdul Hamid was drawing to a close. Every second man one met in Stamboul seemed to be a spy and it was*

impossible for foreigners to move about freely.

I had never visited Constantinople before and possessed very little knowledge concerning its historical or geographical conditions. Having put up in a hotel in Pera I allowed myself to follow my instinct and soon found myself standing near the square of Santa Sophia outside the Bab i Hümayüm. This gate was the main entrance to the Seraglio Palace and Gardens, and was closely guarded, no one being allowed through it without a pass signed by the Sultan's confidential secretary at Yildiz Kiosk.

I felt drawn to examine these gardens feeling sure that the key to my problem was to be found there, but for over a week every effort to penetrate into them failed. It must be remembered that the Seraglio was one of the Sultan's private palaces in those days and that the gardens were used by the ladies of his harem, no outsider being allowed within them.

(Untitled manuscript, 1923, TP's handwriting; in F. Leveaux archives)

Through his business contacts TP was able to obtain an English dragoman (guide and interpreter) by the name of Bryant, although TP cautiously refers to him as 'X', a necessary precaution in those far-off days when Turkey, sitting at the heart of a crumbling empire, was a place of rumour and intrigue. TP decided Bryant was a trustworthy fellow, so

I confided to him my desire to enter and examine the Seraglio Gardens. X happened to be in association with the family of one of the native gardeners on the palace staff, through whom he made discreet enquiry.

Considerable baksheesh passed and as the result of a simple if dangerous ruse I found myself at last within the Seraglio gardens. Hidden from view behind some thick bushes, I was able to spend some hours without notice. During this period I found the exact spot which I had seen so often in vision near which and concealed by vegetation was a deep hole in the ground leading down into one of the many underground passages by which Old Stamboul is honeycombed.

(Untitled manuscript, 1923, TP's handwriting; in F. Leveaux archives)

He faced a problem, however, getting into this hole because it was blocked by a marble slab, partly buried in earth and lying at the foot of a ruined Byzantine wall. Had TP been able to shift the slab he might have climbed right down, but only excavation could hope to move it, a tactic which would attract vigorous, and possibly fatal, attention. The situation was deeply frustrating for him, because he sensed that just beneath him lay the very roll of parchment which would authenticate the Cup's history.

> *Whilst standing upon a slab of stone at the entrance of this passage*
> *I suddenly felt very sure that the records for which I was searching were*
> *not far to seek. Indeed it seemed as if they were concealed in a tomb in the*
> *rock passage perhaps within 25 feet of where I was standing.*
>
> (Untitled manuscript, 1923, TP's handwriting; in F. Leveaux archives)

This tantalising proximity helped trigger an expansion of awareness. Right then, in the Seraglio gardens of Sultan Abdul Hamid II, TP first sensed something of the full scope of the Quest.

> *Perhaps my state of consciousness was not quite normal at this*
> *moment. In any case I felt a strange spiritual ecstasy as if the light of*
> *the sun had suddenly become intensified ten times and as if a brilliant*
> *illumination were ascending from the ground at my feet, an illumination*
> *which seemed to spread across the World. It was then for the first time that*
> *I realised that far more wonderful records lay buried in that neighbourhood*
> *than I had imagined hitherto and that probably the remains of Justinian's*
> *library was also to be found.*
>
> (Untitled manuscript, 1923, TP's handwriting; in F. Leveaux archives)

It was a moment that would largely determine the course of TP's life. The trail from Bride's Well and the Glastonbury Cup seemed now to be leading him to the fabulous lost library of the Emperor Justinian. Treasures of incalculable value were reputed to be part of Justinian's collection as well as many early Christian documents that had been lost over the centuries. If these documents could be found the liberating effect on world thought would be enormous. Instead of relying on the narrow, imprisoning ideas of official Christianity, people could break out into the freedom of the real thing.

Tudor Pole was not the man to shy away from a challenge. If Quest success could lead to world-wide illumination then he would pursue it whatever the cost. He tried working his way round the slab.

> *Leaving X on guard I descended into the passage but soon found*
> *progress impeded by earth and broken stones. I realised that it was*
> *impossible to descend further without the aid of excavation by dynamite.*
>
> *On returning to the surface I found X in altercation with a group of*
> *Nubian Eunuchs and the latter were amazed to see me emerge from the*

ground at their feet. The Turkish military guard were called and we were
marched out of the gardens through the Bab i Hümayüm in the direction
of the Sublime Porte.

(Untitled manuscript, 1923, TP's handwriting; in F. Leveaux archives)

In the circumstances he did well not to be shot. These were the Seraglio Gardens, after all, and the Sultan went in perpetual fear of assassination by Armenian bombers or other disaffected elements. However, it would have been risky for the Turkish authorities to execute a well-connected foreigner, and eventually TP managed to bribe his way out of trouble.

Liberal supplies of baksheesh prevented the prison doors from closing
on me and my companion, and this on more than one occasion.

(Untitled manuscript, 1923, TP's handwriting; in F. Leveaux archives)

His mission now became increasingly furtive, as he realised he 'could not move 5 yards from (his) hotel in Pera without being closely watched.' Constantinople in 1907 was a shadowy place, full of ramshackle alleys, teetering old buildings, and men with lined faces smoking hookahs and thinking their own thoughts. Every now and then, one of these men — never a woman, women were invisible — would exchange information with someone from another country, and the great game of espionage would move on another step.

TP indulged in some international meddling himself when he "heard rumours to the effect that Berlin, Rome and Athens were anxious to get permission to be allowed to excavate in the Seraglio, and round the Mosque of St Sophia" (Oratory Diary, 1.10.1907, entry in Janet Allen's handwriting, signed by Wellesley Tudor Pole). He summed it up in a letter written decades later:

The Kaiser was a keen archaeologist and did some excavating in Crete
and elsewhere, and spent some time in Turkey. When I was out there in
1907, Sir William Whittall loaned me a Dragoman [i.e. Bryant], because
the streets were not safe for foreigners and the Young Turkish revolution
was brewing. The niece of this Dragoman was one of the Sultan's
favourites and so gossip from Yildiz seeped out through her. The Kaiser's
agent, an archaeologist from Vienna was then staying at the German
Embassy, awaiting the granting of the Sultan's Firman [mandate] to allow
excavations on the sea walls and at our site.

46

> *When the Dragoman noticed my interest in this place, he told me what his niece had told him. Half in joke I said I expected the Kaiser wanted this Concession in order to erect concrete gun emplacements to close the Marmara entry to the City, and this was reported back to the Sultan and no Firman was issued.*
>
> *As to the belief that the Kaiser was acting for the Vatican in the matter, this was gossip from Yildiz [the Sultan's palace, ed.] at the time but I think it was true. Of course in August of that year the Young Turkish revolt broke out and the Sultan's days were over.*
>
> (Letter from TP to David Russell, 12.9.53)

We can get a further idea of what issues TP thought were at stake from a letter he intended sending in 1912 to a certain Sir W.F. Jackson, whose help he considered enlisting on the Quest. First of all he stressed the absolute need for secrecy:

> *The Vatican would pay a huge sum for the information contained in this confidential letter and would destroy any early Christian MSS found or bury them in the Vatican itself. They have been known to alter wording and produce a forgery on carefully preserved second and third Century parchments.*
>
> *Not long before the writer was last in Turkey, a chest full of well-preserved parchments was dug up in a certain Pasha's garden near Scutari. The find was purely accidental and was conveyed to Yildiz. On discovering that the papers were concerned with early Christian events and personages, the Sultan ordered them to be burnt, chest and all!*
>
> (Letter from TP to Sir W.F. Jackson, October 1912, not sent)

So the plot thickens now with Vatican forgers, pyromaniac Sultans and even Kaiser Wilhelm II enlisted as potential adversaries. None of this seemed to dismay TP, however. He returned to England 'in fine spirits' on September 16th, recounting tales of spies, intrigues, plans and adventures to his open-mouthed listeners. The 'powerful' help from Bryant, the discovery of the 'exact spot' in the Seraglio gardens, the frustration of Ramadan, the hopes of future excavation, all served to engage his friends in a shared warmth of purpose.

Whilst he had been away the maidens had, as Kitty noted in her diary, worked 'hard', keeping up their vigil of prayer and services in the oratory, 'taking the Cup out of the casket and putting it on the Altar' where they had kept 'a candle burning for Wellesley.' Messages had sped to them from various quarters. Leslie Moore, for instance, advised that 'the prayers in the vicinity of the Cup were sending forth an all-powerful electric flame'.

Messages did not diminish after TP's return, as enthralled visitors crowded their way to the Oratory, experiencing various impressions about the Cup. 'We still get crowds of people,' Katharine wrote on November 10th. 'Several have seen things in the Oratory lately.' One psychic lady received the words: 'This is my Cup, which was in My possession and which I give to this faithless generation which seeks for a sign.' Another lady 'felt the Cup was an auxiliary to the Grail' while a man 'felt sure that it did belong to our Lord.'

However, all was not well. The London clairvoyantes began, in their busy metropolitan way, to sense trouble and treachery in the Quest, so 'W. went up to London on Nov. 2nd. and saw Miss H.' Miss Hoey and the others had been convinced for some time that Bryant, the dragoman, could not be trusted. Their sources of information were, of course, psychic mental impressions, but Miss Hoey went further, augmenting these via psychometry (touch): 'By quite a miracle, a relation of the Englishman out there went to Miss H. and took a letter of his for her to feel.' Miss Hoey's immediate interpretation was that 'Roman Catholics and others were bribing the Englishman to deliver the documents into the R.C. hands.' Tudor Pole felt sceptical about such allegations and confident about Bryant, but when he heard Ramadan would end earlier than advised, he too began to experience some urgency.

Second Quest Attempt, 1907-8

When he set out again he was determined to make it more difficult for Turkish agents to shadow him, so he left England in disguise. However:

> *my very carefully fixed and tended beard fell into my soup when dining on the Orient Express in full view.*
> (Letter from TP to Rosamond Lehmann, 26.1.63)

Finessing the problem as best he might, he persisted in his attempted incognito till, on arrival at Constantinople, he was 'told clairaudiently' to take the beard off. The time of year was December, the weather wintry, and revolution was in the air. The Ottoman Empire was about to morph into the Turkish Empire, courtesy of the Young Turks, and for TP it was a situation demanding tact. He needed to build personal relationships, to share time and courtesies, to join in the social ceremonies of food and drink:

> *I was sitting in the walled gardens of a Stamboul inn, drinking anak*
> *with a group of young Turks. It was a cold night and we had a charcoal*
> *brazier brought out and placed near our table. Then hot black sweet Turkish*
> *coffee was served and as guest of honour I was given the first cup to drink.*
> *I put it to my lips but did not drink. One of my hosts sitting on my right*
> *then drank his cup and fell dead at our feet. Immediately the man next*
> *to him swept the tray of cups and coffee to the ground. And then they all*
> *jumped away into the darkness of the night.*
>
> *They were Ataturk's 'Young Turks' and the year was 1908... It was*
> *the Sultan's spies who had bribed the innkeeper and served the coffee*
> *themselves.*
>
> (Letter from TP to Rosamond Lehmann, 16.1.63)

Looked at from the Sultan's point of view, this is understandable. The foreigner has previously been arrested in his Seraglio Gardens, is studying particular places for obscure reasons and is now in the company of known political enemies. His removal would be a priority, although it would, of

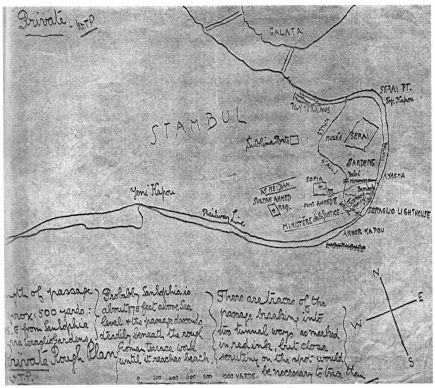

TP's sketch map of his 1907 investigations in Constantinople

course, be diplomatically unwise to execute an Englishman. However, if some deniable madman happened to murder him, that would be a matter for polite regret. Another attempt was made, but this time

> *a wild dog saved my life. Bless him. In old Stamboul, when a Turk was*
> *waiting in a doorway to jump out and knife me, I stepped by accident on a*
> *dog lying in a hole in the street. Its yelp made me lurch forward violently,*
> *and the knife missed me by several inches.*
>
> (Letter from TP to Rosamond Lehmann, 12.6.64)

This second visit was proving more difficult than the first. Nonetheless, TP persisted. If he couldn't get in through the Seraglio Gardens he could at least look for other possible entries.

> *I spent as much time as I dared in inspecting the coast line and in*
> *exploring the many caves and tunnels leading inland from the sea. Some of*
> *these explorations led me to the conclusion that it was possible to penetrate*
> *into the Stamboul catacombs from the sea and I decided to concentrate*
> *on this method of approach when the political conditions in Turkey made*
> *such a search practicable.*
>
> (Untitled manuscript, 1923, TP's handwriting; in F. Leveaux archives)

One area that particularly attracted his attention was the ruins known as the 'House of Justinian' (or 'Boukoleon') whose crumbling arches overlooked the sea from high on a cliff. A millennium and more ago, Byzantine emperors would have looked from this vantage point across the Sea of Marmara, studying the sails and oars of the vessels dotting the water. The emperors may also, Tudor Pole suspected, have descended a winding staircase to a secret chamber beneath the House. There they would have hidden any treasures they wished to keep safe.

> *(I have) examined and penetrated some 250 yards into a Roman tunnel,*
> *roof tiled, which links the Marmara Coast with the 'Crypt', or chamber,*
> *lying beneath the ruins of what is probably Justinian's palace. There*
> *are reasons for believing that a great portion of his famous manuscript*
> *library lies buried in or near this underground chamber, where valuables*
> *were stored, presumably to protect them from earthquakes. Nothing but*
> *the imminent danger of the passage roof falling in and crushing (me) to*
> *death, prevented (me) in 1907 from reaching and examining Justinian's*

library crypt.

(Letter from TP to Sir W.F. Jackson, October 1912, not sent)

He had got close but not close enough. Perhaps local fishermen, intimately acquainted with the coast and its inlets, could tell him more. Enlisting Bryant's help he asked about for information, and soon he had some informants.

Once again, he ended up in a cafe, sharing drinks and courtesies as he listened to interesting tales, although this time his companions were Greek fishermen, and their company was considerably less dangerous. The cafe was on the jetty of a small fishing cove, just north east of the House of Justinian site. Their story was told through Bryant as translator while they looked out on the shipping in the Sea of Marmara, where sails passed and oared skiffs mingled closer to the shore. The Greek fishermen

reported confidentially that ten years ago two of their number penetrated into this passage some four hundred yards and found themselves face to face with four huge bronze studded cedar doors. They feared to penetrate further and fled, but showed several Roman coins (Justinian and Cyrus' date) picked up within this most remarkable passage. Those doors are evidently the entrance to Justinian's famous subterranean library, the contents of which have never come to light.

(Letter from TP to Sir W.F. Jackson, October 1912, not sent)

TP pressed for more information, but they replied in alarm the place was haunted and nothing would induce them to go back or show its location. All in all, he thought the fishermen's story was based on fact but had become exaggerated in repetition (and possibly translation). Perhaps a single stout wooden door had become 'four huge bronze studded cedar doors.' Nonetheless, he felt the fishermen were speaking from actual experience and had no reason to tell a fairy story, as they had nothing to gain. Their information added to his feeling of certainty about the Quest.

There is more hidden 'treasure' from an historical and religious standpoint, buried beneath countless fabrics and ruins, within say a square mile of San Sophia, than anywhere else in the world. The time is coming to recover some of these ancient records.

(Letter from TP to Sir W.F. Jackson, October 1912, not sent)

When TP decided to return home he did so with the knowledge that little could change under the present regime. He would get no permission to excavate, nor would he be able to investigate with any degree of freedom. However, the present regime was on the way out, if his contacts in the Young Turks had anything to do with it, so he did not return home bereft of hope.

> *I returned to England early in 1908 feeling more than ever convinced that I was on the right track but realising the immense difficulties which stood between me and my goal.*
>
> (Untitled manuscript, 1923, TP's handwriting; in F. Leveaux archives)

The journey home was far from simple. He set out on January 1st 1908 but only arrived back on January 7th, having been delayed en route by snow. That delay had a certain appropriateness, symbolising the obstructions and delays that had already beset the Quest. Particularly, he felt reluctant to trust the inspirations of others after Miss Hoey's inaccurate warnings about Bryant, a reluctance which was supported by his own inner guidance.

The Cup too was providing problems, its fame bringing more and more visitors to the Oratory. Eventually the press of people became too much, and from January 1908 to September 1910 the Oratory was 'closed save to a very few.'

The provenance of the Cup continued to be a difficult issue. Another meeting was held at Dean's Yard on January 27th 1908 for glass experts, who considered that 'owing to its wonderful state of preservation the vessel could not be ancient' (Private document, January 1911, the Oratory). This and other opinions were eventually included in a round-robin letter sent to 450 or so interested parties in Britain and overseas:

> *As a large number of enquiries are still reaching the above address concerning the glass vessel discovered at Glastonbury, in the Autumn of 1906, it would seem wise to make a definite statement of the belief and standpoint of those who are its present guardians, in relation to its past history and present uses.*
>
> *They, themselves, have what they think to be good reasons for believing that, in some manner yet to be explained, this Glastonbury vessel was connected with the Master Jesus, and venerated as a sacred symbol by his Disciples. Research work is still going forward, and the results, if any, will be made known in due course. In the meantime, however, it is as well to state that the principal authorities on Antiquities in this country*

have given it as their final opinion that this vessel is by no means 2,000 years old. Scientific opinion as to its exact age varies considerably, some experts holding the vessel to be quite modern, others believing that it may date back many centuries.

But what in reality is of greater importance is the fact that, since this vessel came to light four years ago, it has formed a wonderful and ever-increasing focus-point for Spiritual vision, and stands as a true symbol of Love and Brotherhood between East and West.

Pilgrims from all over the world and of many Faiths, have prayed within its shrine for the dawn of Greater Joy, Peace and Understanding between the Nations of the world, and for the growth of that spirit of Unity that recognises that the fundamental Truths of Life are the joint heritage of all World Religions.

It is a remarkably significant fact that a piece of glass with a history attached to it, so entirely discredited by the outside world, should produce such a profound and cumulative effect upon all who are intimately brought into contact with it. (Round-robin letter by TP dated October 1910)

Meeting with Abdul Baha

All this uncertainty, TP felt, would be dispelled if he could succeed in the Quest and find the documents relating to the Cup. He set out for Constantinople for a third time, although he was destined not to get that far. His itinerary included Damascus, Smyrna and Vienna, where he hoped to scour the museums for any light on the Cup's origins. His first stop, though, was Alexandria.

Here he wanted to seek out a holy man he had heard of when last in the East. This man had been imprisoned for over forty years, and people revered him so much they would stand outside his prison walls in Akka hoping for a blessing. Since the Young Turkish Revolution the holy man had been released and was staying for now at Ramleh near Alexandria.

The man's name was Abdul Baha, and he was the son of Baha Ullah, the founder of the Bahai movement. It took Tudor Pole a while to find him at Ramleh, but once he succeeded he was able to verify the extraordinary power of Abdul Baha's presence, despite the difficulties of a language barrier.

I speak no Persian and my knowledge of Arabic is rudimentary, and so our conversation was carried on through Abdul Baha's grandson, acting as interpreter. At one point the latter was called away, but Abdul

Baha continued the conversation and I found myself replying! When the interpreter returned, my ability to do so ceased. To make sure that I had understood correctly, I asked for a translation of what Abdul Baha had been saying in his absence, and this confirmed the fact that I had been able to understand and to reply accurately in a language of which I was completely ignorant.

(The Silent Road, ps. 77-79)

So far the visit had been challenging but gratifying. Now a more distinct challenge arose.

In the course of conversation on my second daily visit, and much to my surprise, the Master referred to the 'fact' that I should be returning within a day or two to Marseilles on the same steamer that had brought me out, en route for Paris and London once more.

After the interview was over, I enquired of one of the secretaries as to why the Master had spoken of retracing my footsteps immediately, whereas my plans were to continue my journey in the Near East and ultimately to return home to London via Constantinople. The secretary replied to the effect that what the Master said would happen, would happen: and this reply left me in a state of considerable bewilderment and uncertainty.

('Recollection of a Healing Incident', 1950, Russell papers, ms 38515/5/11)

How could TP abandon his journey to Constantinople? How could he abandon the other places on his itinerary, particularly Vienna and its museums? On the other hand, how could he ignore the words of such a figure as Abdul Baha?

Next day I paid my third and last visit to Ramleh, and on that occasion (and very reluctantly) found myself saying that I intended returning to Marseilles by the 'S.S.Sphinx' on the following day. This decision appeared to cause no surprise, and before saying good-bye the Master handed me Ten Pounds in gold and asked me to give this sum to a certain Persian student (believed to be in Paris) whose name was Tammadun ul Molk, with the request that he should proceed at once from Paris to Ramleh. (In those days and well before the first Great War, one could travel long distances — émigré rate — for very small sums of money.)

I accepted the commission, received the Master's blessing, and went my way; somewhat chagrined at the thought that all my plans were to be upset, when seemingly the money could well have been transmitted to Paris by wire or letter. I enquired for the Paris address of the Persian student, but no one could provide this seemingly essential piece of information.

('Recollection of a Healing Incident', 1950, Russell papers, ms 38515/5/11)

It is possible that Abdul Baha was deliberately giving TP the minimum of information and in a fashion designed to raise the hackles of a less mature person. In a way, it was a typical piece of spiritual training, the sort an older figure might give a younger one in order to pass on some hard lessons of experience. Abdul Baha, of course, had had ample opportunity to learn such lessons during his forty years of captivity, and now, in somewhat less painful fashion, he was passing on the benefits of his experience. TP, naturally, struggled with the challenge, as would anyone, but he was determined to see it through.

On reaching Paris, I went to the Persian Consulate to secure the address of Tammadun ul Molk, but unsuccessfully. I then made enquiries in the Oriental Students' quarter on the South Bank of the River, also without success, and many further enquiries elsewhere drew a blank.

Having then decided to continue my journey to London, I crossed the Pont Royale en route for the Gare du Nord, and doing so, happened to notice on the opposite pavement a young Easterner, wearing an astrakhan hat, walking along slowly with a stick, as if blind. (I had been given to understand at Ramleh that the student I had to seek had poor eyesight.) I crossed the road, saluted the young man, and said to him, 'Are you Tammadun ul Molk?' Immediately he looked up at me with what appeared to be sightless eyes; and in great surprise said, in French, 'Oui; c'est moi'. Then I told him of my mission, gave him the gold together with the Master's message. Instantly his face became transformed with joy, and he told me would obey this wonderful summons as quickly as he could. He told me he had only just arrived from Vienna where he had undergone several severe eye operations, but alas that his sight was now almost gone. The surgeon had told him that there was no hope of recovery.

('Recollection of a Healing Incident', 1950, Russell papers, ms 38515/5/11)

The story has two very interesting sequels. Firstly

The upshot was that after arrival at Ramleh, the Master dropped perfumed water beneath the eyelids and gave his blessing, and that full sight was immediately restored. According to those present the student immediately set to work as one of the Master's secretaries in transcribing on tablets in fine Persian script for the Master's signature, messages to be sent out to the four corners of the world.

('Recollection of a Healing Incident', 1950, Russell papers, ms 38515/5/11)

For Tudor Pole the second 'upshot' was equally interesting.

I then went my way and returned to London and on to my home in Bristol arriving just in time (only just) to avoid what would otherwise have been a calamitous happening there in my personal and business affairs.

('Recollection of a Healing Incident', 1950, Russell papers, ms 38515/5/11)

The encounter with Abdul Baha must have been hugely significant for TP. Three years earlier he had prophesied to the Deans Yard audience about a 'great teacher' who would arrive in England in 1911. Abdul Baha, admittedly, was neither female, as specified, nor visibly wearing a seven pointed star, so TP's prophecy was not 100% correct, but Abdul Baha was about to visit England. And in the correct year—arriving in London on September 4th, 1911. A few days later, on Sunday the 10th, he gave his first ever public address, at the City Temple, Holborn. The Christian Commonwealth gave a full report, including the following:

Abdul Baha then advanced to the front of the pulpit and addressed the congregation. He spoke for eight minutes in Persian, with considerable animation, his voice rising and falling as in a rhythmic chant. Towards the close he placed the palms of his hands together as in prayer. The translation was afterwards read by Mr. W. Tudor Pole.

(The Christian Commonwealth, 13.9.11)

A fortnight later, Abdul Baha came to stay at TP's home, now open again to visitors and known as the Clifton Guest House.

Last Saturday afternoon Abdul Baha arrived from London with a few friends to spend the week-end at the Clifton Guest House. He was present at the evening meal and warmly greeted those who had gathered together to welcome him. After commenting on the peacefulness of the house he contrasted the costliness of material feasts with the pure simplicity of this meal, where the all-pervading spirit was that of love and friendship

*Abdul Baha at The Clifton Guest House; TP smiling on left; behind him
Katharine (half obscured) and Kate, his mother; behind them Alice Buckton (?);
far right Lady Blomfield; beside her Christine Allen (?); seated on ground Sir
Herbert Samuel (?)*

between East and West.

> *The same evening about eighty friends assembled to listen to the words of the great Persian teacher. Mr. Tudor Pole took the chair and introduced him by a few words on the Bahai movement. Abdul Baha then rose and spoke with impressive dignity, Tamaddon-ul-Molk translating.*
>
> (The Christian Commonwealth, 27.9.11)

Yes, this was the same Tammadun ul Molk whom Tudor Pole had sought in Paris except now, of course, he could see. Another fascinating aspect of the visit came when Abdul Baha was handed the Cup and reacted in a way both eloquent and elusive.

> *In 1911 in my Clifton home A.B. held the Cup in his hands for a very long time, saying nothing. Then he blessed it reverently and gave it back to me.*
>
> (Letter from TP to Rosamond Lehmann, 30.9.67)

Changing Times

TP had another important person on his mind at this time. He had met a certain Florence Snelling and soon they were thinking of marriage, the ceremony taking place on 17th August 1912. Their first child, Jean, arrived in February 1914, and in old age Jean wrote the following recollections for this book.

> *My mother was the eldest of the seven daughters of Henry Snelling, a surveyor and valuer, of Sidcup in Kent. Compared with the Tudor Poles they seem to have been a conventional Edwardian family, although Florence was able to go her own way and at the age of 18 she worked for the Salvation Army in the East End of London. She did some damage to her health then and was never very robust.*
>
> *I don't know where my father met her but he told me that he proposed to her while rowing on the River Severn, so she may have been visiting his guest house.*
>
> *She was not a vegetarian but she did her best to give my father what he liked and he made some concessions in her direction, i.e. he would eat fish and occasionally chicken, although he wouldn't touch red meat (how did he manage in the army?) In those days vegetarians were not catered for as they are today; it was eggs, cheese, nuts, lentils and fruit mainly...*

and I remember a cooking fat called 'Nutter'!

('Florence Tudor-Pole [née Snelling]', by Jean Carroll, short manuscript sent to the present author, 20.6.02)

Photographs show Florence as smart and attractive, and we can glimpse some of her independent spirit in the fascinating news about the non-vegetarian concessions (a fall from grace or admirable adaptability, according to whether your viewpoint is zealous or pragmatic). Florence sounds, in fact, the right partner for TP, clear enough in her mind to hold her own, but sympathetic enough to give TP the stable backing he would need.

My parents were very devoted and Florence's rather early death at 69 was a great blow to my father.

('Florence Tudor-Pole [née Snelling]', by Jean Carroll, short manuscript sent to the present author, 20.6.02)

TP wasn't the only one getting married. His older sister Mary started the trend in February 1911 by marrying the Rev. John Bruce Wallace. Then in October 1911, Christine Allen moved to Edinburgh rather suddenly and married the Scottish painter, John Duncan, on 27th April 1912. These marriages served to break up, albeit for good reasons, the group spirit which held the Triad together.

Katharine, however, remained single, and, writing for The Messenger of Chalice Well in 1969, she looked back on those times.

I have been asked to give a short account of my brother's earlier days. Wellesley ran a guest house from about 1909 to 1914. It was the Clifton Guest House, at No. 17 Royal York Crescent, Bristol. The crescent was started in 1891 and is reputed to be the longest one in the world. Several well known people lived there.

Our large sitting room could easily hold a hundred people and on Saturday evenings we often held meetings when people from London would come to speak on Theosophy, New Thought, Vegetarianism, etc. It was great fun gathering together enough chairs from all over the house.

One of our chief guests was Abdul Baha with some of his followers. I had two snapshots of them taken on the terrace. In one of them Abdul Baha (Persian seer, and son of the famous Baha 'Ullah, Founder of the Bahai Faith), is holding my father's arm. These snapshots are now with the Bahai's at Haifa.

59

Among other well known people who came and stayed were the Ranee of Sarawak and R.J. Campbell. We entertained them in the evenings with music, I playing the violin.

We turned a room at the top of the house into an Oratory (forerunner of the Upper Room!) where we kept the Glastonbury bowl. My two friends and I used to hold services there on Sundays, and in 1910 we three and Wellesley took the Cup to Iona for a week.

It was at the guest house that my brother met his wife, Florence, and their first child, Jean, was born in the room next to the Oratory in 1914.

Those were very interesting and enjoyable years. I lived in a flat next door [number 16] with my father and mother.

('The Messenger of Chalice Well', issue 9, Spring 1969, p.10)

The Approach of the Great War

'Interesting and enjoyable' the years may have been, but TP was still itching to get on with the Quest. In 1912, he prepared a detailed memorandum for Sir W.F. Jackson, an architect who had worked on repairs to Hagia Sophia.

TP's plan was to return with an archaeologically respectable ally. However, that same year the First Balkan War broke out and Turkey suffered a huge loss of territory. It was no time for maverick archaeologists to behave elusively in the Turkish capital.

1913 was no better. Bulgaria made a grab for territory it had wanted the previous year. The Second Balkan League War followed, and Turkey joined in, seizing the opportunity to take back some of the lands it had just lost. Germany and Austria looked favourably on Turkey's manoeuvre, thereby inching towards their wartime alliance. It was an even less suitable time to be English and elusive in the Turkish capital.

TP, sniffing the air, realized that more than just Balkan wars were in the offing. Abdul Baha had already forewarned him of dire events to come.

He not only predicted the outbreak of the first world war to me in 1910 but, in fact, indicated the whole course of the twentieth century. In a letter which I sent from Egypt at that time to a friend in Scotland I wrote as follows:

'The Master... anticipated a world-wide upheaval, to be preceded by a European war, probably within the next five years. This, he said, nothing can avert.

'It would appear that the seeds for this grave conflict have already been sown in the Balkans. It is evident that we are to expect in our own lifetime a lengthy period of wars and revolutions embodying what could be interpreted as becoming the Armageddon prophesied to take place at the end of this present age or dispensation.

'Whilst the Master seems entirely confident that the coming of 'The Most Great Peace', accompanied by world-wide brotherhood, is destined to come into being following this long period of Armageddon, the date of such a consummation cannot be foretold.'

(Writing On The Ground, 1968, p.156)

TP too had been able to sense what was on the way. After his return from Ramleh back in 1910, he had a powerful experience on Observatory Hill, Clifton, not far from his home at 17 Royal York Crescent.

Having just returned from the East, from places where the imminence of world war was known, the inevitability of the conflict and the apparent powerlessness of the leaders of the nations to avert it filled me with depression. In this mood I went out into the stillness of a beautiful starry night, to the solitude of a hill, when suddenly, as I was sitting in the silence, there seemed to surge up around me, as if from the four corners of the world, mighty winds. Yet, strange as it may seem, there was perfect silence. A sound of thunder followed, so indescribable and so terrible that it seemed as if the world would be rent in pieces. The thunder passed, and the hill was bathed in quiet light, and I became aware of a mighty Presence standing beside me, full of strength and illumination.

This Presence made me comprehend the significance of many events that were to transpire and gave me help and comfort with regard to those things that had to be. It was made possible for me to understand that a fresh outpouring of God's love for His creation, a new spiritual wave, was even then pouring into human consciousness.

(From The Spiritual Significance of the Hour, an Address delivered in London, 5.3.1916)

He became increasingly aware of what was coming, and on September 17th 1914 he wrote to a friend he called M.M. [Mrs Alexander Whyte, a Scottish Theosophist], giving a seer's version of the tendencies leading up to the First World War. To avoid initial confusion, it is well to bear in mind he is talking about spiritual 'air', not physical (and is hence not referring to any prototype aircraft):

> *Nearly seven years ago I was able for the first time to see and watch clearly the progress of the 'Conflict in the Air'.*
>
> *What caused the Armageddon in the air, the war between the powers of Light and Darkness? My power of vision is restricted, and I dare not look very far, because my work lies here; but I have seen (what so many Seers in East and West are seeing) the great onrushing of the Breath of God descending nearer and nearer toward the ocean of the human mind.*
>
> (From 'The Great War', W. Tudor Pole, 1915)

'Nearly seven years ago' would be some time after September 1907, in fact the time when his perceptual horizons were expanding with the Cup, his geographical horizons expanding with the Quest, and his spiritual horizons expanding with Abdul Baha. Soon he was able to see what happened to 'the great onrushing of the Breath of God':

> *In 1909 I first realised what tremendous events were about to take place, and to some extent the reason for them. In that year this great Wave appeared to me to have reached the border of our human consciousness and had begun to penetrate it. For many years, spray, as it were, from the approaching wave had been arriving to warn us of its coming. Then the tragedy began. Up rose from the human mind-ocean the powers of selfishness, carnal-mindedness, fear and the rest—a great black host. All the powers standing for cruelty, injustice, and militarism were marshalled in battle array, and the vision was an awful one! A most terrible knowledge came to me: that the powers of darkness drew their reserve forces, their ammunition, their staying power from the ocean of the mind of man. This conflict has lasted ever since.*
>
> (From 'The Great War', W. Tudor Pole, 1915)

If we read this carefully, we can see why he saw the 'Second Coming' and 'Armageddon' as consistent co-themes in future decades: because one, in his view, must cause the other. The 'Coming' stirs up a reaction, and the reaction is—put simply—'Armageddon'. The question therefore arose: could mankind handle the 'Coming' or annihilate itself in the resulting conflict? As far as TP could see, help was needed, and he also saw where it might come from:

> *Almost at the commencement of the greatest crisis of this 'War in the Air' (early in 1909) a remarkable vision came to me, and its meaning is only now becoming clear. Picture to yourself an island set in a deep blue sea, but joined to the mainland by twelve stepping-stones. On the mainland flocks of sheep are to be seen sheltering, as far as possible, from a great storm. On the island stands a great council table, oval, of carved stone, with twelve Master Shepherds sitting round it. Messengers are coming and going between the flock on the mainland and the Master Shepherds. Above and beyond the island a wonderful Light is descending.*
>
> *The Shepherds seem to resemble the great Founders of Religion, but one cannot recognise them all. They appear to be working together in harmony, while their messengers come to and fro. I believe I was intended to understand from this vision that the human race (the flocks) was approaching the greatest crisis in its history, and that Humanity's dire need had drawn toward our realm the Elder Brothers of the Race, that they might rescue us from the annihilation likely to result from a world-conflagration.* (From 'The Great War', W. Tudor Pole, 1915)

With war on its way TP had many concerns on his mind. A useful summary of the situation comes in a letter, written in 1913 to David Russell (later Sir David). Russell was a Scottish businessman, who the previous year had visited TP to find out more about the Cup, thus beginning a remarkable close friendship (and a biographer's dream, yielding letters back and forth on a more or less daily basis).

Russell along with Florence, became one of TP's twin pillars of stability over the next four decades, entirely necessary for a man who was living, with ever increasing strain, in two worlds. In his own way, Russell was as spiritually perceptive as TP, but he was far less of a signs-and-wonders man. His great strength was spiritual common sense: he simply did not accept nonsense. Over the years, he and TP bounced ideas off each other and, because each was his own man, they were able to cut through stale, dutiful or unlikely conclusions and arrive at something worthwhile.

At this stage of their relationship, in 1913, they were still somewhat formal ('Dear Mr. Russell' instead of 'Dear David' or even, in old age, 'My dear David'). The following letter includes an oblique reference to Abdul Baha's second western visit, when he again stayed at the Clifton Guest House:

Fourteen February 1913

THE CLIFTON GUEST HOUSE
16 & 17 ROYAL YORK CRESCENT
CLIFTON BRISTOL

Dear Mr. Russell,

I do not think Abdul Baha will come West again; he is 70, and 44 years of prison life and fare have left their mark upon his body although his spirit is still radiantly youthful and always will be. He is now in Paris, then goes to Stuttgart before leaving for Syria and Mt Carmel. He is due in Russia and Turkestan next Autumn and then goes to India. We of this generation cannot realise the wonderful work that is being done in Mid East and elsewhere by the Bahai's. It is almost incredible until one has lived out there and watched the Movement 'move'.

Philip Oyler [a seer friend] was here this week and spent some hours with us. He spent a while in our Silence Room and seemed too overcome by the presence of the Glastonbury vessel to say much about it. He strongly felt this vessel was used at the Last Supper, indeed all the seers who have seen it seem united upon this conviction. I am only waiting a favourable opportunity to go out East and continue research into its history.

The fate of the Guest House rather hangs in the balance just now; it is certainly becoming better known, and more appreciated by a wider circle, but my wife finds it a big concern to run even with my sister's help. As the place is not yet actually paying its way, indeed barely pays its expenses, it cannot support a housekeeper as well as a general staff of servants and I am not quite clear as to what its future will be.

Should there be any developments regarding the vessel I will let you know. Looking forward to seeing you when you are next south.

Yours v. Sincerely,
W. Tudor Pole

TP might indeed have been 'waiting a favourable opportunity to go out East and continue research' but events were about to stop any hopes.

In July 1914 I had booked my ticket intending to leave for Constantinople by the sea route on the 28th July from Liverpool. Rumours of war followed by the war itself put an end to my plan.

(Untitled manuscript, 1923, TP's handwriting; in F. Leveaux archives)

And so arrived the Worst Of Times. The Best Of Times probably peaked for TP in 1911 with the visit of Abdul Baha to England, but the conflict between the 'onrushing Breath of God' and 'the powers of selfishness' was, for him, reaching its outward phase.

Over in the East, somewhere in Orient Express territory, somewhere en route for the Quest territory of Constantinople, a Serb student (evocatively named Gavrilo Princip) was raising his revolver at Archduke Franz Ferdinand of Austria. And after the Principal assassin everyone else followed suit. Soon

David Russell as a young man

all Europeans of suitable age and gender were raising firearms and squeezing triggers.

What could a Man of Two Worlds offer in such a situation? Action in one world? Action in the other? It was to be a long war, and TP - perhaps inevitably - was to have some remarkable adventures in both.

5. War Years: 1914-1917

Archive film before World War One can seem dominated by emperors and generals strutting about in extravagantly plumed hats like so much ambitious poultry. This was a time when stiffness reached its apotheosis. Stiff backbones went with stiff thinking to produce rigid alliances, unvarying tactics, unmoving trench systems and, of course, corpses or — to put it another way, stiffs.

World War One lives on in the human imagination as a time when an entire civilisation dug holes for itself and shot anyone trying to climb out. Between those holes was an especially eloquent area, no-man's land: rats' land maybe, worms' land, but no place for humans.

How did they ever get so stuck? Various theories were speculated at the time, and some were offered by Wellesley Tudor Pole.

Some Deeper Aspects of the War

He put these forward in a public lecture at the Caxton Hall, Westminster, on Saturday 28th November 1914. The title of the lecture was Some Deeper Aspects Of The War:

> All nations that look upon brute force as worthy of worship must share the blame for what has led to the present crisis. Superficially it would appear that Germany has plunged the world into war. But if we look back into the last few centuries we shall see that nearly all the countries of Europe are responsible, among them Great Britain, and therefore they must all share the responsibility for the situation now developing.
>
> (Some Deeper Aspects of the War, 28.11.14)

This was a challenging viewpoint. After all, it was not British troops who invaded Belgium but German ones. So what was TP getting at? He suggested the audience might consider the spread of Britain's empire, which was often

> the result of aggressive warfare with peoples smaller than herself. We must remember that Germany is to a large extent only attempting to copy Great Britain — although in doing so she is not using our methods, but employing more brutal methods of her own. We cannot afford to throw stones, but as a nation should endeavour to cultivate a little humility.
>
> (Some Deeper Aspects of the War, 28.11.14)

What, his audience might think, is wrong with building an empire? TP explained, drawing on a memorable encounter back in 1910. He had been in the Egyptian desert en route to Abdul Baha when he encountered a Sheikh, a stranger, but someone with a line in political parables. Here is the one he told TP:

> *A traveller walking through the streets of a town came across a house with its windows broken and its doors askew. Inside the house everything was in turmoil. He went into the house, and finding the owner, said to him, 'Your house requires putting in order, it is full of disorder. May I call my servants and put things straight for you?' The owner of the house accepted the offer, so the traveller then called in his attendants and set the house in order. Having done this, he built a hut in the garden outside the house, and turning to the owner, said, 'This is a very nice house; now it has been spring-cleaned it is in beautiful order, and I and my servants will inhabit it; you can go into the hut and live there, but I will take possession of your house and administer it in my own way and for my own ends.'*
>
> (Some Deeper Aspects of the War, 28.11.14)

TP was challenging his audience again, using a chance-met sheikh to criticise British foreign policy. Domestic policy also came in for criticism:

> *Great Britain is learning many lessons from the War, and there is great hope for the future when we see that so much has already been taken to heart. By-and-bye we sleepy men will wake to the fact that from a social and economic standpoint it will be wiser to use the whole of our brain power rather than a part. This will be done by giving women the vote on the same terms as it is held by men.*
>
> *Within our lifetime is coming a period of illumination far greater than anything the world has seen before; it is coming through women particularly, but men also. Women and men must go forward together, working harmoniously for the common weal.*
>
> (Some Deeper Aspects of the War, 28.11.14)

All in all, the lecture offers as progressive a set of sentiments as could be wished for in 1914, but with TP the call for moral improvement always went hand in hand with augmented vision. It was partly a Two-Worlds thing: sort out this realm and you might do better in the next.

Some Visionary Accounts of the War

Certainly TP was trying to improve his next-world abilities, as he mentions in a letter sent just before the war began:

> *31st May 1914*
> *I have had a rather heavy time since Friday morning, as I received a 'call' on that day to go out and help the thousand odd poor frigid souls, a great majority of whom were drowned in their sleep, or just after waking, in the Empress of Ireland. It was rather awful, as many would not realise that they had passed on, and therefore remained full of the fear and the frost of their last moments on earth. Because of this, one could not get them either to sleep or to realise their safety in new conditions. I do want to get well-practised and 'able' at this 'salvage' work, in time for the series of unparalleled disasters that are due on this plane before long.*
> (The Great War: Some Deeper Issues, 1915)

An interesting feature of this letter is that it was written to his mother, and from the tone and content it appears they were quite used to discussing otherworldly activities. This time the news is that he is doing 'salvage' work amongst people who have recently died, especially, it seems, if they have died en masse. Furthermore, he is not the only one working hard to be ready, as he informs her in a later letter:

> *17th August 1914*
> *The most extraordinary events are transpiring just beyond our ken, far more remarkable than anything here or anything I have ever experienced before. A mighty clearing up of fear-and-sorrow-thought about 'death' has been set in motion, and a really splendid cleansing is in process. Now that the conflict in the intermediary spheres is nearly over, it is an almost unbelievable fact that the pangs and terrors of material dissolution (speaking from the mental standpoint) have considerably lessened in intensity for all mankind, and not simply for soldiers and sailors. A person who died last year was liable to a much greater strain in reaching the next level of consciousness than one who dies to-day. 'Death' is losing its worst sting as the result of the grand victory of the Forces of Light, which is already assured. It is of far-reaching importance and unique in the annals of the present Human race. One can only assume that some great edict has gone forth, and that the avenues leading to other levels of conscious*

life have become cleansed.
(The Great War: Some Deeper Issues, 1915)

There can't be many mothers who get letters like these. He went on to publish them the following year in The Great War: Some Deeper Issues. Like all his subsequent books, it is a collection of ideas and experiences, and the items so far have been quoted from Part III: Leaves from the Notebook of a Visionary, including Extracts from Private Letters, chiefly to my Mother. Something else the book included was a question and answer session from a Caxton Hall lecture. This was useful as it gave his readers a second chance to digest the otherworldly information:

Question. — Are the conditions of transition made easier for the soldiers who give their lives for their country?

Answer. — I have been watching the avenues between this stage of consciousness and the next for a number of years, and can say that, so far as my vision goes, it appears to be very much easier at the present time to pass out into the wider life than it used to be. The way is undoubtedly being made simpler and less tragic for those who are giving up their lives for a great ideal. The fact that they are holding to a principle and fighting for an ideal is a help in the turmoil called death, and the passing out is not so complex.

Question. — What is the nature of the experience by which you are aware of the improving conditions?

Answer. — I have noticed, up to a recent period, that the atmosphere, in these avenues between the worlds already referred to, has been grey and depressing. This has been caused by the thought sent out from the human world — fear of death, for instance, materialism and sensualism. But as I watched the condition in this region just before the War, I could see the light lighting up those avenues and purifying the atmosphere. This has rendered the death experience less fearful than formerly. It was the isolation that produced the feeling of desolation. When the passing souls see that they are not alone, that light is everywhere, that feeling disappears.

(The Great War: Some Deeper Issues, 1915)

TP's thesis was that rigid modes of thought, such as fear of death, materialism and sensualism actually caused the problems in the Beyond. But could his readers surrender their own rigidity and believe him? Some visionary details of the war itself might help them get the feel of things. In a

THE
GREAT WAR

SOME DEEPER ISSUES

BY

W. TUDOR-POLE

WITH FOREWORD BY STEPHEN GRAHAM

ONE SHILLING NET

TP's first published book (1915) - subsequently out of print for nearly century letter dated 14th September 1914 he tells his mother:

> *I have seen very little actual hand-to-hand fighting so far; possibly because there has been very little furious conflict between individuals — bullets and shells impelled by an invisible foe have not the same effect. I have seen gunners continuing to fight after death, whole squads of them (mainly German). They think they project shells huge distances upon imaginary foes. Evidently it is a gunner's war so far, fought over the heads of the silent and by no means excited infantry. One sees very little personal rage; some among German officers and English privates, but scarcely any in the French and German ranks. Why? It is personal anger that mainly causes a continuation of the conflict after death. The German soldiers die in such a worn-out condition that they appear only too glad to go to sleep and stay asleep. Also the arrangements on the other side for receiving those who pass over are wonderfully complete and working well. There is very little confusion, although hundreds of thousands have gone over, who, being about the same standard intellectually and morally, have congregated (naturally) at one level of consciousness. I fear that greater slaughter lies ahead than behind us, judging by the preparations made on the other side. However, these may be purely tentative.*

> (The Great War: Some Deeper Issues, 1915)

Some details, oddly enough, may seem more convincing to an audience now than to an audience then. Consider his surprise at a lack of hand-to-hand fighting. Nowadays (and used to modern warfare) we would not be amazed at this, but the idea of 'a gunner's war' would be a substantial novelty to an age whose ideas came largely from the Boer and Crimean Wars (which latter included that period piece, the Charge of the Light Brigade).

Also the 'worn-out condition' of the German soldiers is interesting. If we think about it, they probably would be tired at that stage, having marched at speed through Belgium, but who in Britain would consider their problems at the time? Enemies are traditionally to be opposed, not understood.

That much we may accept as sounding authentic, but what exactly are the 'arrangements' and 'preparations made on the other side'? So far TP has not specified, possibly because by April 1915 he was still trying 'to get well-practised and able at this salvage work'. A couple of years later, however, he had more to offer on the topic and wanted to use it in his mission to lubricate the stiff thinking of the age. His first book had been useful; now he was contemplating another. In a notebook dated March 1917 he set down various experiences he might include:

> *People still scout the idea that good and useful work can be done by the mind of man while the body lies asleep. I, for one, believe that I am constantly at work in the avenues leading to the next world, at night when my body sleeps. I bring back memories of such work and continue the same activities night after night, meeting fellow workers in that region and co-operating with them in many useful ventures.*
>
> *After prayer and meditation and a cleansing of the mind from the worries of the day, I fall asleep naturally and then find myself standing outside my physical body. Immediately I find myself (without any movement having taken place) in the 'avenues' into which we all pass at the moment of physical death. Here there is always plenty to be done. Discarnate souls are arriving, are being 'born' into this region around one all the time.*
>
> *If the unevolved man, full of sensual life, passes across into these avenues suddenly, through being artificially thrown out of his body before his time, say in battle, then he 'awakes' almost immediately, the direct result of the shock. The work of so many of us is to co-operate with the trained angelic souls in protecting these newly arrived beings from the sad effects of premature awakening, and if possible soothe them to sleep again. Premature birth into the physical world is dangerous and unnatural, and so it is on the other side... Many of the soldiers killed in battle, prematurely awakened on the other side, continue to fight in a manner automatic. They cannot control their new faculties because these are not ready for use; and premature use is very dangerous indeed.*
>
> *Immediately I 'meet' a disembodied soldier in the plight above mentioned, I construct around him a protecting arbour, shutting out the sights and scenes likely to cause him alarm. This 'construction' is purely mental; but remember, mental creations are the only 'things' that are solid and real in this region. I then 'call' for flowers, colour, music and sweet perfumes and soothe the poor fellow until he falls quietly asleep again. I have then done all I (or anyone else for that matter) is allowed to do.*
>
> (March 1917 Notebook)

What we are getting with these extracts is a view of the war from a highly unfamiliar and perhaps challenging perspective. Was there any way of making it clearer? Could TP go into the actual mind of a victim?

On Monday, 12th March 1917, I was walking by the sea when I felt the presence of someone. I looked round; no one was in sight. All that day I felt as if someone were following me, trying to reach my thoughts. Suddenly I said to myself, 'It is a soldier. He has been killed in battle and wants to communicate!'

(Private Dowding, 1917)

Private Dowding

TP never published the March 1917 Notebook, and the reason may be simple enough: he'd found something better. Private Dowding, the personal story of a soldier killed in battle, with Notes by Wellesley Tudor Pole was published in August 1917. Notice that TP claimed only to supply notes for the book. All the rest, he believed, were communications from 'Thomas Dowding, recluse, schoolmaster, soldier'. What TP did was sit at his writing table and allow his pen to move 'in an involuntary sort of way' recording thoughts and ideas which he felt were not his own. Let the reader judge as Dowding begins to speak:

My soldiering lasted just nine months, eight of which were spent training in Northumberland. I went out with my battalion to France in July 1916, and we went into the trenches almost at once. I was killed by a shell splinter one evening in August, and I believe that my body was buried the following day.

Some of my pals grieved for me. When I 'went West' they thought I was dead for good. This is what happened. I have a perfectly clear memory of the whole incident. I was waiting at the corner of a traverse to go on guard. It was a fine evening. I had no special intimation of danger, until I heard the whizz of a shell. Then followed an explosion, somewhere behind me. I crouched down involuntarily, but was too late. Something struck, hard, hard, hard, against my neck. Shall I ever lose the memory of that hardness? It is the only unpleasant incident that I can remember. I fell, and as I did so, without passing through any apparent interval of unconsciousness, I found myself outside myself!

Think of it! One moment I was alive, in the earthly sense, looking over a trench parapet, unalarmed, normal. Five seconds later I was standing outside my body, helping two of my pals to carry my body down the trench labyrinth towards a dressing station. They thought I was senseless but alive. I did not know whether I had jumped out of my body through shell shock, temporarily or for ever. I seemed in a dream. I had dreamt that someone or something had knocked me down. Now I was dreaming that I was outside my body. Soon I should wake up and find myself in the traverse waiting to go on guard. When I found that my two pals could carry my body without my help, I dropped behind; I just followed, in a curiously humble way. Humble? Yes, because I seemed so useless. We met a stretcher party. My body was hoisted on to the stretcher. I wondered when I should get back into it again.

My body went to the first dressing station, and after examination was taken to a mortuary. I stayed near it all that night, watching, but without thoughts. Then I lost consciousness and slept soundly.

When I awoke, my body had disappeared! How I hunted and hunted! It began to dawn on me that something very strange had happened. My body had been burned or buried, I never knew which. Soon I ceased hunting for it. Then the shock came! I had been killed by a German shell! I was dead! I tried to think backwards, but my memory was numb.

(Private Dowding, 1917)

Some readers may find the atmosphere of the piece authentically haunting and evocative. Consider, for instance, Dowding's helplessness as his pals carry his body down the trench labyrinth, or the way he stays near the body all night, unable to think.

If that is not sufficiently evocative, try another portion. Here we have a cinematic effect as Dowding looks down on the battlefield and hears the muffled guns — except, of course, talking pictures had not yet been invented, so the sounds cannot be based on any film TP (or indeed Dowding) had seen. There again, the part where a 'slain' soldier brings the noise and tumult over the border line shows impressive imagination (if imagination it be). Once again, judge for yourself:

I was on, or rather above, the battlefield. It seemed as if I were floating in a mist that muffled sound and blurred the vision. Through this mist slowly penetrated a dim picture and some very low sounds. It was like looking through the wrong end of a telescope. Everything was distant, minute, misty, unreal. Guns were being fired. It might all have been millions of miles away. The detonation hardly reached me; I was conscious of the shells bursting without actually seeing them. The ground seemed very empty. No soldiers were visible. It was like looking down from above the clouds, yet that doesn't exactly express it either. When a shell that took life exploded, then the sensation of it came much nearer to me. The noise and tumult came over the border line with the lives of the slain.

(Private Dowding, 1917)

Whatever the verdict, we have quite a body of evocative material from TP during the war. Many readers at the time were appreciative—Private Dowding went through three editions in 1917 alone—but how did it play amongst sceptics?

Opponents External and Internal

Happily for present day readers in search of light relief, one such sceptic resided in TP's own firm, Chamberlain Pole & Co., Ltd., by name of E. Marcuse.

Marcuse was not happy about the publication of Private Dowding under TP's name, and he certainly didn't like the press reviews that followed. He remembered previous occasions when TP had behaved in a public and controversial way—probably the furore following the Daily Express article on the discovery of the 'grail' in 1907. All in all, E. Marcuse became a very indignant business man indeed and felt the necessity of writing several letters of advice to TP. It may help the reader to gain the full flavour of these if they are read aloud in a pedantic whine:

I must refer to a matter which must I think be more irksome to me than it may be perhaps to you: that is the reference in leading papers as to your clairvoyance activities.

I am not writing this in an aggressive or unfriendly spirit: I would much rather I did not feel it necessary, especially as I was left under the impression that our last controversy would be the last, but both Mr. Gibbons and Mr. Tryon seem to be disturbed as to the manner in which customers and business friends refer to it. Up to the present I have always aimed at keeping our reputation at a very high pitch and while I have the power I must see it remains in this state. Now I ask you: why do you make my aim so very difficult? Surely, at my time of life, I deserve a little consideration! Without this I shall be brought face to face with the necessity of considering is it worth my while with such senseless countercurrents, to continue.

(Letter from E. Marcuse to 'Mr. Pole', 15.10.17)

TP should have taken note, lowered his head and promised better behaviour, but it seems the cheeky blighter tried defending himself, even citing respected names in his defence. Eminent scientists such as Sir William Crookes and Sir Oliver Lodge probably came to mind, but E. Marcuse had no intention of bowing to any heavyweight verdicts when he had mighty allies like Mr Gibbons and Mr Tryon to call upon.

> *I have had a somewhat long experience of this hard world of ours, much longer than you have had, and I imagine that my experience of men and things has not been without its value.*
>
> *You can take it from me—I am speaking in quite the most friendly manner possible—that it is impossible for a merchant if he is to conduct his affairs successfully and avoid disaster to pursue at the same time the practice of 'clairvoyance'.*
>
> *I hope you will forgive me saying so, but I can quite realise it must be a source of pleasure to you to be noticed appreciatively by men of eminence and learning: I quite envy you — I am, like you (and always have been) possessed of great ambition, but I ask you to believe me there is no such cult as 'clairvoyance'. This my view is shared by scientists and other men of equal or greater power than those you mention. Both Mr. Gibbons and Mr. Tryon share my views, as do also various Members of the Bristol Corn Exchange and others of our customers. Even the Editor of the 'Weekly Despatch' who is 'running' the so-called investigation of the subject in his paper seems to throw considerable doubt on it.*
>
> (Letter from E. Marcuse to 'Mr. Pole', 24.10.17)

That should have clinched it! How could TP persist with his clairvoyant delusions when opposed by the intellectual might of the Bristol Corn Exchange? Sadly, though, the reprobate continued distressing his older and wiser adviser, as will be seen in the next chapter.

But for now, as we bid temporary farewell to the much abused Marcuse, it must be recorded that he was not the only opponent TP faced. There was another, and it lay inside him. He explained the matter to David Russell, after speaking 'rottenly' to a 'large assembly of ultra fashionable ladies and other folk':

> *The reason I feel depressed after speaking is because I feel a mighty message welling up within me, but am so totally unable to give it adequate expression. Whenever I sit down after speaking a little devil dances before*

my vision gleefully shouting 'Failed again'! It is very curious.

(Letter from TP to David Russell, 14.3.16)

The talk in question was given in London on 5th March 1916, and called The Spiritual Significance of the Hour. Afterwards he told David Russell

I vow I will take a vow of silence until I have progressed further and am less sensitive to adverse conditions. It's a puzzling phenomenon (to me) why I should almost invariably be seized with these periods of profound depression following public addresses. Does it mean I am not ready to 'give out' and must remain silent? I fancy it must. Excuse this outburst please.

(Letter from TP to David Russell, 5.3.16)

Enlisting as a Tommy

There may have been another reason for TP's disquiet, an itchy feeling that public speaking just wasn't enough to meet the demands of the time. He felt he should do more and so, just five days later, he wrote again to David Russell:

My Board offer to release me for 'duration of war' if my services can be made of value. Is it worth while enlisting as a Tommy and one wonders what alternative there is? Salary is a secondary consideration but one longs to help at any point where 'vision' as well as commonsense would be valuable.

(Letter from TP to David Russell, 8.3.16)

He could, of course, have relied on his reserved occupation to keep him at home, because Chamberlain, Pole & Co. Ltd., Flour Importers, Grain and Cereal Merchants were vital to the war effort, particularly through their offshoot, the Nutrex Biscuit Factory at Old Bread Street, St Philips, which supplied ration biscuits to the army. However, TP was never the man to excuse himself from difficulties. He joined up.

This led to a remarkable send off, involving what he now called 'The Family Group'. His had always been an unusual family. The parents, Thomas and Kate, had long been interested in spiritual matters, Katharine was the keeper of the Glastonbury Cup, and Mary had just recently become a visionary like her brother. (The remaining member, Alex, by the way, was involved in war liaison with the Russian army; and his spiritual taste was Theosophy.) With such a dedicated cast it was only logical for the family to join spiritual forces, and several meetings of 'The Family Group' took place over the next decade. The first occasion came on November 3rd 1916, in TP's new home at Easton-in-Gordano, as the Family Group sought to give TP the right sort of send off to the war.

There are some typewritten notes of that meeting, and they begin with the words: 'Very impressive atmosphere.' It is necessary for us to imagine that atmosphere; otherwise we will miss the force of what must have been an extraordinary (and perhaps spine-tingling) experience. It would be Mary on this occasion, not Wellesley, who did the communicating. 'It is curious that when Mary is subjective and receiving visions,' wrote TP later, 'I am in an entirely objective condition and neither see nor hear! Sometimes however I can confirm what has been said or done afterwards.' (letter to David Russell, 2.8.22)

Mary transmitted the messages in normal everyday consciousness, but she was unable to guess what word would come next until it was spoken to her. So the messages emerged slowly, nugget by nugget, while an attentive family listened on. The messages on this occasion began with words addressed to TP:

> *'I have come from your Guide to tell you that certain Masters wish to speak to you. Do rest assured that you are under special protection. Make ready to take another step toward initiation. I am to let you know you are about to be consecrated... Certain servants of ours have been commanded to safeguard your wife and children. On your shoulders has been laid a special task. You must not fail.'*
>
> (Typescript, Family Group, 'Easton in Gordano', 3.11.16)

By 1916 the war had been going on for over two years and huge losses of life had already been suffered, especially on the Somme that same year. Consequently, 'special protection' would be of vital interest, as would mention of a 'special task'. Naturally, TP might wonder if this involved The Quest, although it would be hard to imagine pursuing something so exotic on the Western Front. In all there were three sessions at this time, spaced over successive evenings. On the third, and last, of these TP asked:

> *('What is my mission?')*
> *'Directly we can tell you, we will. Aim to become efficient in your*

military duties. Among us is one who will never leave you during your training. Do not question our ruling. We serve one who is also your Master. Now the Master will speak.' (Pause.)

'My son, you are to be made known to those who serve me in the world. I am going to initiate you into great mysteries. Fail not in your task, because upon you depends the successful accomplishment of a great mission.'

(Typescript, Family Group, 'Easton in Gordano', 5.11.16)

Armed with this baffling message, TP left for barracks, but life became a great deal more baffling once he arrived and encountered the horrors that passed for the military training of the time. A letter sent to a certain Walburga, Lady Paget, gives us some information.

Now that I am in the ranks I feel inclined to stick it in order to investigate the conditions under which the men are forced to live. Sleep and food are both impossible and I could make some revelations if I liked and no mistake.

Gen. Sir Neville White is the Brigadier here and it is quite impossible for a mere private to approach him, without a weighty introduction.

We are treated quite as sub-human creatures and it seems impossible to lodge complaints even were one inclined to do so. However I won't enter into details by letter and anyway you would be profoundly shocked.

(Letter from TP to Walburga, Lady Paget, 23.11.16)

One might wonder why TP was writing to a titled lady. However, she had been one of the 'large assembly of ultra fashionable ladies and other folk' to whom he had spoken 'rottenly' a few months earlier. Since then he had got to know her quite well, even going to stay at her home (Hewell Grange, Redditch). A substantial correspondence began, some of it eventually making its way to the British Museum, although most was subsequently destroyed, only six of TP's letters and one postcard to Walburga surviving [*see footnote]. It is interesting to speculate why these escaped the cull. Could they have been separated from the rest back in 1916? And if so, why? Walburga was a lady with a wide diplomatic career, who still retained government connections in her old age. So TP was not just passing on a few grumbles: he was providing information for a possible campaign.

The Authorities have become uneasy (letters are read) and come to the conclusion that I was a person with powerful friends and possibly a man of means.

It then leaked out that I was correcting the proofs of some war writings to be published in Paris [a translation of The Great War] and the fat was in the fire. Twice the General sent for me, twice the Brigade Major and thrice the Adjutant.

Who was I? Why had I thrown up my exemption? Was I a journalist? Did I know the Kings Regulations concerning privates? And so on.

They were frightened that I might reveal some of the barrack scandals, of which they are dimly aware.

Was I comfortable? Would I not come into warmer quarters and so on? They probably want to push me on to Blandford and a commission, but I shall refuse. I won't leave here until I have done some 'cleaning up' on my own.

You have no conception of what goes on, quite apart from such scandals as insufficient food, wet sleeping quarters, immoral proceedings and disgusting language. When I refused to desert my fellow sufferers and go into warmer quarters, my Barrack room (holding 30) was inspected and condemned as insanitary. Rain was dripping onto our straw palliasses. Had I not been there no inspection would have taken place. The officers know nothing. So you see there is some good reason for my remaining in the ranks, hauling coal, scrubbing floors and drilling from 5.30am to dark.

(Letter from TP to Walburga, Lady Paget, 30.11.16)

Could it really have been so bad? A future friend of TP's, Israel Sieff, offers some compelling testimony in his Memoirs. Sieff's younger brother,

---

* Footnote: TP fans may have read about the Walburga correspondence in 'My Dear Alexias' and expect that masses of letters are sitting in the British Museum. However, in 1955 TP told Russell:

I have again asked that all my letters to Lady Walburga should be destroyed, the great majority of them being of purely domestic interest, but there are two or three of them dealing with public issues and political personages (A.J. Balfour, Lord Curzon, The Earl of Plymouth, King Alfonso of Spain, and one or two others), and I see it is going to be a struggle to get these also destroyed, rather than handed over to the British Museum.

(Letter from TP to David Russell, 13.12.55)

TP would be glad to know, therefore, that, according to the Earl of Plymouth, Walburga's great grandson, in December 2001, the bulk of the correspondence was indeed destroyed. However, as TP suspected, a few were handed over to what is now the British Library, and yes, names like AJB (Balfour) and the King of Spain (Alfonso) do occur.

William, an eighteen year old recruit, said something rude to his sergeant and ended up in prolonged solitary confinement. By the time Sieff came to rescue him the boy was broken in body and mind, and he stayed that way. Writing in 1970, Sieff tells us (with the sort of simplicity that hurts):

> *He is still alive, in a nursing home in Zurich. He still recognises me,*
> *but for more than half a century he has never spoken a word.*
>
> (Israel Sieff, Memoirs, 1970, p.82, Weidenfeld and Nicolson)

So maybe TP's complaints about barrack life were justified. He gave more details a month later:

> *One is awfully driven here. Hard at it from 5.45 a.m. to after dark;*
> *coal heaving, floor scrubbing, incessant drilling and the rest of it. And I*
> *can only get bread and tea to subsist on, that is for breakfast and tea, and*
> *the only other meal at 1 p.m. meat and potatoes usually quite inedible,*
> *half cooked, cold etc.*
>
> *I can tell you that the general organisation of English barrack life is*
> *deplorably scandalous.*
>
> *Fellows here try to kill themselves even, to get out of the horrors. I*
> *have drawn up a private memorandum of a v. confidential nature and*
> *feel awfully inclined to get it put before Lord Derby. Contents are quite*
> *unprintable and deal with food scandals, venereal disease, indecency,*
> *language, corruption among NCOs, disorderly houses, utter ignorance*
> *of officers and so on. Massingham of the Nation is interested and would*
> *take it up. I know him but what could he do? I don't feel inclined to leave*
> *the ranks until my investigations are complete, but all these inoculations,*
> *damp sleeping quarters and filth will half kill me. I sometimes feel inclined*
> *to place a carefully edited statement of the facts before the Commandant*
> *here (Gen Sir Neville White) but — ? Will write again on hearing your*
> *advice.*
>
> (Letter from TP to Walburga, Lady Paget, 18.12.16)

His complaints had some validity because (a) as a businessman he had organised a workforce for many years and (b) as a manufacturer of army biscuits, he had an interest in feeding soldiers. Validity or no, he was clearly unsure how to proceed and perhaps wanted Walburga to organise a campaign. (See the next chapter for a similar tactic by which he arranged the rescue of Abdul Baha).

Eventually TP was able to leave the brutal Marine training and was transferred to an Officers' Training Course. Between May and September 1917 TP obtained his commission at No. 19 Officers' Cadet Battalion at Pirbright. From there he was posted to the 3rd Cheshire Regiment at Birkenhead on 27th September, 1917, with the rank of 2nd Lieutenant. Expecting a posting to France, he wondered what to do about '4 days draft leave before going out; I don't think I could stand another parting with F. and the babies so don't propose going south for my draft leave. Shall I come north?' (Letter from TP to David Russell, 17.9.17) By now there were two Tudor Pole babies, Jean born 1914 and Christopher born 1915. The brief reference to them and Florence is worth dwelling on for its implied heartbreak. After all, there would be a fear of permanent separation (elusive messages from Beyond or no).

Into Action

TP's survival chances improved when he found he was not going to France, after all. He sailed from Plymouth on 3rd November, 1917 in the Bellerophon en route to Cairo, a journey that was to last three weeks. The thought of his destination excited TP enormously:

> *Events of v. great interest are taking place on the Front to which I am to be attached, and this is certainly a most interesting moment at which to arrive. I feel thrilled with a sense of coming events and begin to get a glimmer as to why Fate sends me out to these parts. Am anxious as to Abdul Baha's fate should the Turks abandon that region as is probable; his life will be in imminent danger. I shall make big efforts to get out there and anyway to get funds through and provisions, for they are almost starving.*
> (Letter from TP to David Russell, 18.11.17)

Within a week TP is sending more of his distinctive thoughts as his unit marches towards the front. It is notable how he enthuses about the 'splendid fellows in (his) platoon'. After his experiences in the Marines, he possibly had a greater fellow-feeling with his charges than would the average officer.

> *We are well up now in Palestine and going further steadily; marching over endless sand whenever cool enough. Have seen no really active fighting yet but have explored several battlefields and been on duty commanding men salvaging from same. The air is wonderful, the starry nights are beyond words; even the Desert has great charms for me when the heat*

Christopher, Florence, Jean
'I don't think I could stand another parting with F. and the babies'

is not too terrific — only where the miasma of death reigns, there it is purgatory unending.

I am attached to the Devons (dismounted Yeomanry) and all the fellows are from the West so I am in my element and I have splendid fellows in my platoon.

I have had no mail of any kind yet; a goldfinch sits on my knee as I write this and lizards run round my feet!

We sleep on the ground in Bivouac sheets; dew v. heavy, nights cold; but it's a glorious life and somehow all these Old Testament places have great charm and one is taking part in history, the reclaiming of the Holy Land for real Freedom for Jews, Christians, Moslems. We shall be up toward Abdul Baha's land probably when you get this and I look forward to that beyond words.

(Letter from TP to David Russell, 24.11.17)

TP may have been a prophet occasionally, but more often he was an enthusiast ('real freedom for Jews, Christians, Moslems'). He may also have been thinking about the 'special task' and 'great mission' mentioned in the Family Group meetings. After all, in Palestine he would be fighting the Turks, and their capital was at Constantinople. So perhaps the Quest might hover again as a possibility.

Or would his 'great mission' be something entirely different? He may have begun to wonder after a conversation with a fellow officer by name of Rawson, someone he also knew as a healer and prophet. TP tells the tale, as was his occasional practice, in the third person.

During the fighting in the mountains around Jerusalem early in December 1917, two British officers of a West Country Yeomanry battalion [i.e. TP and Rawson] were discussing the war and its probable aftermath. The conversation took place in a billet on the hillside at the mouth of a cave, and on the eve of battle. One of the two, a man of unusual character and vision, [i.e. Rawson] realising intuitively that his days on earth were to be shortened, summed up his outlook in these words:- 'I shall not come through this scrap, and like millions of other men in this war, it will be my destiny to go now. You will survive and live to see a greater and more final conflict fought out in every Continent. When that time comes remember us. We shall long to play our part wherever we may be. Give us the opportunity to do so, for that war for us will be a righteous war. We shall not fight with material weapons then, but we can help you if you will

let us do so. We shall be an unseen but mighty army. Give us the chance
to pull our weight. You will still have 'time' available as your servant,-
Lend us a moment of it each day and through your Silence give us our
opportunity. The power of Silence is greater than you know. When those
tragic days arrive, do not forget us.'

The above words are quoted from memory and are not literally exact.
Next day the speaker was killed at Beit ur el Foka. His companion [i.e. TP]
was wounded and left with the enemy, but escaped to the British lines.

(Leaflet: An Appeal from the Inner Front, 1940)

It was a conversation with repercussions lasting to this day, for it resulted
in the Silent Minute, a notable feature of World War Two and a practice that
is still observed. As for the battle back in 1917, TP wrote a personal account
for his father in a letter headed 'Nasrieh Military Hospital, Cairo, 7.12.17'.
He begins:

I wired today fearing the W.O. would advertise me as wounded in
the papers before I got word through to you all and to Florence. As I am
well out of the action for many weeks and comfortable and safe, there
need be no anxiety and I think you ought to hear exactly what happened
because it confirms messages in a subtle way and gives one confidence in
the future.

(Letter from TP to Thomas Pole, 7.12.17)

Clearly he is referring here to the 'Family Group' message: 'You are
under special protection'. The letter then goes on to describe the battle in
considerable detail. It is too long to print in its entirety, but it carries such
authenticity that it demands substantial quotation:

Now you better read this letter through and censor severely any parts
that you feel would keep mother awake or worried. I must tell the whole
tale or none at all but it is strong meat and terrible. Outwardly looked at
I cannot imagine a greater number of tragic events happening in 24 hours
to a sensitive man, yet I can actually say that the whole series of events was
the most wonderful and enheartening experience I have ever had.

I posted a letter to mother on that very Sunday afternoon; such a sunny
blue day with glorious scenery everywhere. We were ordered at 8 p.m. to
start creeping up the hill in circular waves, 20 yards apart and 8 yards
between each man. It was very dark, the boulders in places were almost

insurmountable and we advanced less than half a mile an hour. The men were very cheery, good old yeoman stock, but they knew very little of what lay ahead. Only the officers knew and I for one (having had the privilege of scouting with the C.O. on the hill the day before, with powerful glasses) was quite satisfied that the enterprise was desperate beyond words. The crest was half a mile away but 450 feet or thereabouts above us in actual height. We lay down and waited for the moon, whether a good plan or not I cannot judge.

Jackals were crying out around us; otherwise there was silence. Then the moon arose across the hills, turning the country into fairyland. We could see for miles and miles across these holy crests and right down toward the orange groves, to the plains and to the sea. The hill towered above us more menacing than ever and we were seen instantly. There were Turkish snipers behind every ledge and boulder and in the trees; machine guns were hidden cleverly at the entrance to caves and ravines, and high above all were the breastworks at the hill crest, then a bare open plateau without cover, and finally the thick rough walls of the village itself.

The first 'wave' began to creep and crawl forward. The platoon I commanded was in the second wave, and we followed on, just a few yards every five minutes. I walked (bent) up and down the line to see that distance was kept and to prevent loss of touch with the flanking platoons. So far only a few stray shots had been fired; the silence was ominous. I felt anxious about the alignment of my men rather than frightened, but I had an unholy fear of showing instinctive fear later on. One never knows. It all seemed so childish, a game of hide and seek in the moonlight and I simply could not realise the deadly reality that lay behind this apparent buffoonery. I did not doubt my own safety, yet I was not at the moment conscious of any special unseen protection.

Suddenly chaos was let loose. Shrapnel burst over our heads, machine gun bullets rained down literally in thousands and how any men in the first wave escaped I cannot tell. The moon was in our eyes and we could not fire back accurately. Turkish guns, a mile away on another high ridge, began to bombard us and one could not hear one's own voice. Men began to fall; some crumpled up (mercifully) without a cry; others, sickeningly maimed, curled and uncurled and groaned and then lay still. The first wave needed reinforcements, so I took my men up into the front line, running, leaping over around the rocks, then falling flat for a few instants to recover breath. Were we not all blind and stupid fools just scrapping for two wells in an old Roman village? Water was scarce in both armies, and we were

TP in officer's uniform

fighting for it.

Bullets grazed past me, spat at my feet, whizzed through the air above. We reached the front line 150 feet from the hill crest, fixed bayonets and leapt forward onto the crouching Turks. A terrible moment and I shall not give you any details, mainly because as I jumped over the crest, stick in one hand, revolver in the other, interior guidance began and I was lifted in consciousness away from the shrieks and blood and the hell.

I gathered my men together, half were left; and we started for the village but were suddenly ordered to turn sharply to left and lie down on a flat rock ledge overhanging a valley in which the temporarily defeated Turks were gathering to counter attack. It would soon be daylight and the moon was paling. The enemy swarmed up through the trees under cover of heavy machine gun fire which simply raked the ledge on which we lay, trying vainly to fire over the ledge while we flattened ourselves out on the hard rock. Suddenly a score of shrieking Turks jumped onto the ledge, but they never went back; hundreds were behind them, skilfully led by German officers in English khaki. I had to stand up to see what was happening and where to direct my men to fire. They were all splendid but very, very scared and longing to withdraw. Orders came to hang on but not to advance(!) So we lay there to be picked off one by one while our fire went too high and did little damage. Then bombs were sent over to us and we pitched them over the ledge more or less blindly.

Someone stood by me unseen, a guardian seeming very very grave and anxious, and I knew my fate would be settled during the next few minutes. I called for reinforcements and half stood up again. There was a Turkish sniper in a fig tree just visible, but we could not move him. Awful wails from enemy wounded rose up from the woods below, but silence on the ridge; those who were struck among us were riddled and beyond pain or movement. I felt a sudden premonition that a decision had been taken as to my fate by the Presence near. The sniper in the fig-tree sniped and I fell on my knees, struck through the upper left arm and shoulder. I felt anger rather than pain; why was I not protected as promised? My sergeant came over to see where I was hit and fell dead across me pinning me flat to the ground on that bare bullet swept ledge. I was bruised and broken and bleeding freely and could not move.

The sun was rising in all its splendour across the Syrian hills, and there seemed a momentary lull. I raised my head painfully to see who was left. I remembered it was the morning of Dec. 3rd. 1917 (Rawson's last day on earth and I actually laughed). It was cold but my blood trickled warmly *down my neck and across my chest and on to the ground. What could I do? I longed for another bullet and just then firing recommenced. The sergeant's body protected me awhile. Then the 'Guide' knelt down beside me and told me to lay my head on the ground and relax. I was still curiously angry with Fate but I obeyed and lay still, and tommies in my platoon nearby thought I was dead. Then the Guide began to whisper in my ear and this was the substance of the message: 'I was needed for some special work later and was not to be allowed to die just then, however much I wanted to. The experience I was passing through was enormously valuable, especially as a test of faith in the dominion of spiritual realities. The ridge on which I was lying could not be held much longer. Had I remained unwounded my duty would have kept me upon it until I was killed. (Later I heard no one was left alive upon that ridge, piled high with the slain.) My guide, coming to a quick decision had decided how to get me away alive. I was to be wounded. (By the way the bullet took a clean, miraculous, devious course by which no bones were shattered and no arteries severed). I was to lie still a while longer and make no effort to move, while my guide arranged my escape. I must obey implicitly, faithfully'.*

That is all that comes back to me now, and at the time it satisfied me and I am so thankful now that it did satisfy me. The roar and shrieking no longer worried me and I just lay still and waited; curious, but not overpoweringly so, as to the method of my ultimate deliverance from what seemed certain death. I should think some 20 minutes passed, it may have been longer as I was probably only semi-conscious. Then I was told to stir. I raised myself and found that the sergeant's body and rifle had rolled off me and I was free. A strong hooked stick was lying by me, having arrived God knows how, for it was not there before and I only took a light cane into the battle. I hitched the stick round a rock cleft and drew myself into a crawling position and then crawled along without sense of direction. Soon I found myself in a cave, probably some 20 yards behind the Death Ridge I had just left.

(Letter from TP to Thomas Pole, 7.12.17)

It would be good to give the rest of this account because of its detailed authenticity. However, the main point has been reached and what follows is a more mundane, albeit fascinating, account of how a wounded officer gets to safety. First of all he meets some deserters, and then:

By and bye I saw Captain Fox, my Company Commander (son of Fox of Fox Roy and Co Plymouth and Bristol) about 50 yards away bravely directing operations and quite oblivious of his danger. An officer's servant passed within hailing distance and I sent him across to Captain Fox (who had rather taken a fancy to me all along). The latter sent away for his servant who came and cut away my clothes and bandaged me roughly but by no means unskilfully. With the aid of my wonderful stick and the servant's support I got up and hobbled in the direction of our second line. After a while he left me. He had to return and I wandered down a rocky path for about a mile, only under fire at certain points. Evidently I lost direction; anyway I was nearly ambushed by a Turkish outpost, having lost the path. But I was quite happy. To have descended into the chaos, to have suffered what millions are suffering today, to have experienced all the tragic futility of war at first hand; all this buoyed me up.

(Letter from TP to Thomas Pole, 7.12.17)

His empathy with ordinary soldiers is again apparent, but he was also buoyed up (as he goes on to say) by 'receiving unseen support all the time' without which 'I should have collapsed long before from the pain and loss of blood'. Next he falls in with a badly wounded Tommy (with half his face gone so it was hard to look at him), hears yells from the hill above as the Turks win it back (so he would be dead if he had stayed), meets a patrol from an Irish regiment, is directed down the track to a dressing station and then finds another friend:

A Captain Holley of our Company limped in and we palled up. A nice fellow, a big landowner from Okehampton. He was my companion for the next three days which made things easier. We set off together down a Wadi toward another and less primitive dressing station. Shrapnel burst over our heads but there were no bullets.

(Letter from TP to Thomas Pole, 7.12.17)

The next problem was how to travel in the absence of roads, and the answer was: a camel, for six and a half 'agonising jolting' hours. Eventually they reached a Casualty Clearing Station on the plain and were transferred to carts and then into a Ford car, which drove along a road full of holes and was attacked by a German Taube plane. British planes chased it off, and the car reached a railhead. They rode in a cattle truck for five more agonising hours, then an ambulance train, and finally arrived at Cairo, the Nasrieh

TP was in Nasrieh Military Hospital, Cairo, when General Allenby entered Jerusalem, respectfully on foot, on 11th December 1917 (Image courtesy Imperial War Museum, Catalogue number: Q 12616)

Military Hospital. The tale is almost over, but there is one more problem, missing kit:

> *If I do not recover my kit, I must replace at my own expense. My revolver and belt were gone. I had never fired the revolver although once tempted to, in the effort to prevent our men bayoneting the Turkish prisoners.*
>
> *It was bitterly cold and I sat on the edge of a trestle bed. The sister was curt. Where were my blankets? Officers in hospital must provide their own blankets, dressing gown, slippers, towels, sponge and so on. Where was my servant? Why had he not come to look after me? I became speechless. Then the whole thing tickled my sense of humour. I promised to send for my servant; it was rather late at night and he was in heaven (having been shot 3 days before) but I would do my best to oblige. As to blankets, I had no money, but would go out and borrow some in due course. I had reached the hysterical stage.*
>
> *One blanket was raked up, and I lay down and shivered until the morning. Then things improved. I wangled two more blankets and shared a dressing gown with two other fellows and a pair of slippers with 5 others (lavatory some way off). A John Bull breakfast was served but I sent out and got some biscuits and milk.*
>
> (Letter from TP to Thomas Pole, 7.12.17)

And there we can leave him. He is safely back, and now he is being his usual affable self, chumming up with those around him but not abandoning his principles, in this case ensuring a vegetarian breakfast. (How many would have bothered?)

So far, army life had been surprisingly uplifting. But there was plenty more uplift to come. He was in a region that fired his imagination, and he was about to embark on one of the most expansive periods of his life.

6. The Near East: 1918-1919

1917 was a year of changes. America had entered the war and become a world power. Russia had left the war and become a world pariah. America's president, Wilson, had ideas that were revolutionary. Russia's dictator, Lenin, had hijacked a revolution.

The two countries were clamped either side of Europe like a pair of gigantic headphones, each broadcasting ideas to a brain that did not want to listen. A long scar ran along the west of Europe's face, and the microscopic creatures either side felt no desire for anything fresh. They wanted nothing so much as to scratch the scar over and over again.

Lloyd George, the British P.M. despaired of his generals having a single new thought, so he mooted a Supreme War Council of Allied generals: maybe the Americans or French could do better. However, he need not entirely have despaired. There was one British general who could think differently. His name was Allenby, and he commanded the Near Eastern front, and by the next year, 1918, he would invent Blitzkriegs. Before that, though, his concern was a large amount of conquered territory, including such evocative places as Jerusalem.

He would need an administration. The administration would need bright young men. Recently wounded officers might be the sort, especially if they had previously been in charge of something like a business. One such type was a certain Lieutenant Wellesley Tudor Pole who, in keeping with the world tendency, had experienced a changeable 1917. The theme continued into 1918, and by February TP was appointed D.O.E.T.A. (Director of Occupied Enemy Territory Administration) based in Cairo. 'You have no conception of what that phrase means and what gigantic issues it involves,' he wrote to David Russell. (7.2.18)

The Rescue of Abdul Baha

Nowadays we would expect such issues to involve Moslems and Jews, but back in 1917 and 1918, TP hoped another faith, Bahai, might be the key. This hope would depend on keeping Abdul Baha alive, as TP wrote to Sir Mark Sykes (M.P. and negotiator of the famous Sykes-Picot agreement):

> *On returning from Cairo and the hills round Jerusalem, having received the close attention of a Sniper in a fig tree; I ran across my friend Mohi-el-Dine Sabri. He was anxious to send you his greeting and friendly*

remembrances and I promised to oblige. The Turkish Line will probably run through Haifa shortly. The Bahai leader and his family are in imminent danger and at the moment, of course, we are powerless. His position and prestige is not understood among the Authorities here. It is not even realised that he controls a remarkable religious movement, wholly devoid of political and military associations; which can number many millions of adherents throughout the Near and Middle East. Jews, Moslems of various sects, Christians, Parsis, Hindoos, Kurds unite under the Bahai banner of Spiritual Fellowship. May not these people contribute much, later, to the harmonising of Sectarian and Oriental Religious feuds? Is it too much to ask the Authorities at home to request the Authorities here to afford Abdul Baha every protection and consideration? Anxious enquiries reach me from America, England, France, Russia, Persia, India. A word from Whitehall works wonders.

(Letter from TP to Sir Mark Sykes M.P., 24.12.17, in File 23353/W/44: Foreign Office 371 3396)

Of course, TP would not rely solely on one line of communication. He also alerted David Russell in Scotland who duly spread the word to Mrs Alexander Whyte (M.M., the Scottish Theosophist) who wrote to her son Frederick Whyte M.P who, in turn, contacted Sir Mark Sykes on 25.1.18:

I have just received a letter from my Mother saying that she understands that Abdul Baha is living in some risk of his life at Haifa. My Mother's correspondent, as you will see from the enclosed letter, seems to think that we could do something to save him. I shall be glad to hear from you whether you think there is anything in the suggestion contained in Mr Russell's letter, which please return to me.

(Letter from Frederick Whyte to Sir Mark Sykes, 25.1.18, in File 16762/W/44: FO 371 3396)

All of this should have helped, but when TP got into his new job as D.O.E.T.A. he found that it hadn't. Part of his work involved intelligence gathering—from reconnaissance flights, captured enemy soldiers, intercepted wireless broadcasts and the like—and he did not relish the intelligence he gathered:

Early in March 1918 information reached me from our own espionage service that the Turkish Commander-in-Chief, whose headquarters was

*then between Haifa and Beirut, had stated his definite intention to take
the lives of Abdul Baha and those around him should the Turkish Army
be compelled to evacuate Haifa and retreat north.*

(Writing On The Ground, 1968, p.152)

This gave TP a problem. How could he prevent murders taking place
in a city 70 or so miles north of the British lines? His answer was to use an
unconventional weapon:

*General Allenby is always referred to in the Arabic Press as 'Al Naby'
(Prophet) this being the nearest possible Arabic translation of 'Allenby'.
Among the Moslem population in Egypt, Syria and elsewhere [such]
coincidences have aroused considerable comment, for the Eastern mind is
always on the alert to unravel any signs and symbols that seem to possess
either religious or historic significance.*

(Letter from TP to Hannen Swaffer, 31.12.17)

Could one prophet, then, be used to rescue another? Could 'Al Naby'
be prompted to make the appropriate threats on behalf of Abdul Baha?
Such threats might have the right effect, but TP would need to lobby the
right people who, in this case, were titled ladies back home. He smuggled
some blunt appeals through to the likes of Lady Paget and Lady Blomfield,
and they in turn got to work on titled men (that's how it was in 1918). The
titled men, Lords Plymouth, Balfour and Lamington, made sure the problem
was presented to Cabinet (Lloyd George, Milner, Lord Curzon and Balfour
himself) and as a result instructions were cabled direct to Allenby, who
thereupon issued orders for the protection of Abdul Baha.

Direct protection had to wait several months, though, because
Ludendorff mounted a huge offensive on the Western Front, and many
of Allenby's soldiers were diverted to France. Fresh forces arrived from
India (including, usefully for that terrain, cavalry) but Allenby wanted his
experienced soldiers back. He didn't get them.

What he did get were planes—Bristol Fighters, Martinsydes, a few
Nieuports and a single Handley Page bomber—and these were the machines
which carried out the most alarming part of Allenby's Blitzkrieg.

From the 19th to the 21st of September, two Turkish armies, the 8th
(under Mustapha Kemal) and the 7th (under Djevad Pasha) were virtually
destroyed by very low bombing and machine gun attacks—their trucks,
limbers, wagons and guns ending up as tangled masses of metal.

And thus began the dominance of air power in warfare.

The most evocative aspect of this new type of warfare is the place where it occurred: Megiddo, or, to give it the more famous variant, Armageddon. Armageddon is some way north of Jerusalem, roughly between Nazareth and Caesarea, and if there is anything in prophecies linked to its name, perhaps it is a warning about getting blasted from the sky.

A result of this particular Armageddon was that two days later British and Indian forces took Haifa, and outriders from the Mysore Lancers were immediately despatched to guard Abdul Baha's house. And thus TP's protection efforts were fulfilled.

The whole episode was summed up by the Secretary of the National Spiritual Assembly of the Baha'is of the British Isles writing years later in 1969:

> *The place of Major Tudor Pole in the annals of the Baha'i faith will rest chiefly on the part he played during 1918 as an integral part of the circumstances whereby Abdul Baha's life was spared.*

Jodhpore and Mysore Lancers enter Haifa, 23rd September 1918, thereby ensuring the safety of Abdul Baha (Image courtesy Imperial War Museum, Catalogue number: Q 12335)

At the time he was almost certainly the only British Army officer who knew the place that Abdul Baha occupied in the hearts of the Baha'is. When, therefore, he learned as an intelligence officer from reliable sources that Jamal Pasha, Commander of the Turkish Army then undergoing severe defeat in the Western Desert, had threatened to crucify Abdul Baha and his family on Mt. Carmel if the Turks were forced to withdraw from Haifa, he promptly did all in his power to bring the danger to the knowledge of influential friends in London and through them to the Foreign Office and the Cabinet. General Allenby was expressly instructed by cable to extend every protection and consideration to Abdul Baha, his family and friends when the British marched on Haifa.

(The Messenger of Chalice Well, number 10, 1969)

The Armistice

Seven weeks after this individual triumph, the larger conflict came to an end. On the Western Front, the Allies had been advancing continuously since August 8th. In the East, the Central Powers were crumbling one by one: Bulgaria on 29th September, Turkey on 31st October (they had had enough of Allenby), Austria on 3rd November. Eventually, Germany accepted armistice conditions at 11 a.m. on the 11th of the 11th, and a few hours later TP heard the news in Cairo, reacting with a mixture of gentle humour and exalted thought:

On the 11th November at 4 p.m. the news of the Armistice reached me as I was sitting in my Office at the Savoy. So far as outward demonstrations were concerned nothing happened in Cairo. Certainly a few flags were flown, windows were smashed and canteens burnt down, but there were no guns, no bells, no apparent rejoicings. I gave a dinner to my Staff, not numbering 15. I spoke for some time, partly in very light vein and partly along more serious lines.

'Many of you do not at present realise that we stand at perhaps the most remarkable point in the history of the world. One era has closed before our eyes; it closed in the midst of carnage and tumult. We are now actually witnessing the birth of a New Day—a Day during which the human race will be lighted up, transformed, regenerated. Do not let this hour pass lightly; enjoy the outward triumph of the Armistice, but let your thoughts run deep as well.

'Those of us who have looked death in the face during the past few

years and who realise something of the tragedy that War brings in its wake have determined to carry out two resolutions. We will create in the minds of the next generation such a detestation of human warfare, its horror, its uselessness, that the tradition of peace universal shall grow up firmly implanted in the human consciousness of the future and War will become inconceivable.

'Secondly, we have determined that the World of our own generation shall be lifted out of gloom and sorrow toward peace and steadfast happiness. Each one of us can do more than he realises to bring joy into the lives of those around him, and joy spreads.'

(Notes written in the German Hospice on the Mount of Olives, 16.11.18)

None of us should begrudge a war veteran his moments of optimism, no matter what hindsight may suggest.

Meeting with Abdul Baha

Nine days later TP was en route to meet Abdul Baha for the first time in a very full five and a half years. He did not find him at Haifa, so moved on to Acre, later writing a fascinating travelogue about the journey.

There is no road between Haifa and Acre and the light railway has been torn up, so one drives for 2½ hours round the bay on the hard sand close to the blue, blue sea. Half the time the carriage is in the sea because the sand is harder where the waves lap over it. From a distance the ancient walled city of the Crusades looks almost picturesque, standing right up out of the water, and reminds one a little of a miniature Stamboul. But Acre from the inside is an awful place, full of smells and slums and dirt. Its one outstanding feature of beauty is the sweet and abundant water supply brought into the city from the distant hills along a Roman aqueduct.

At last we reach the Master's house, close to the Sea Wall, but shut in on all sides by slums and courts. A long stone stairway leads up to the living rooms in this prison-house where Baha'u'llah spent the last 15 years of his life and where his son lived on and off for 40 years. The stairway is worn thin by the feet of the countless pilgrims who have passed up and down during all these years.

The Master was standing at the top waiting to greet me, with that sweet smile and cheery welcome for which he is famous. For 74 long years

Abdul Baha has lived in the midst of tragedy and hardship, yet nothing can rob him of his cheery optimism, spiritual insight and keen sense of humour. He was looking a little older than when I saw him and certainly much more vigorous than when in England after the exhausting American trip. His voice is as strong as ever, his eyes clear, his step virile; his hair and beard are (if possible) more silver white than before.

(Notes written in the Prison House of Baha'u'llah, St. Jean d'Acre, 20.11.18)

However, a 74 year old who has endured much cannot be expected to continue forever in the flesh, and three years later Abdul Baha moved on. It may be worth a quick digression here to see how TP recalled various meetings with him in a Private Memorandum written in 1921:

As I write certain memories come back to me with a strange insistence. I remember standing beside the Master in the pulpit of the City Temple, London [in 1911, ed.], watching over five thousand (5000) people breathlessly absorbed in listening to Abdul Baha's living spiritual words, and in watching his every smile and movement.

I remember walking with him through the woods at Clifton, 1911, when he spoke of the coming of a spiritual renaissance within the Christian churches; or wandering along the Banks of the Seine at sunset, 1913, when the Master spoke of the Great War that was to come, and the Most Great Peace that would ultimately follow it.

I have sat beside him at Ramleh, Alexandria, beneath the palms, and while he spoke of the essential unity of all mankind. There were Christians, Jews, Moslems, Parsis, Hindoos and Freethinkers sitting around him on that occasion, one and all united with the same faith and aspiration.

I remember walking alone with the Master on Mount Carmel's slopes, sharing his frugal meals in his Haifa house, listening to his melodious chanting within the Garden Tomb, living as one of the family within Baha-Ullah's house at Acre.

(Private Memorandum, December 1921)

TP lost close touch with the Baha'is eventually. After Abdul Baha's death they began organising as a religion, and TP felt disinclined to join, his preference being to bring religions together (and thereby reduce their numbers) rather than add any more.

The Zionist Commission

However, all this is taking us into the 1920's, and we must return to 1918 to pick up the threads of the story. The reader may remember that in February TP was appointed Director of Occupied Enemy Administration. This was followed by promotion to Captain in April, and Major in November. Such promotions mirrored the importance of his tasks, one of which concerned the destiny of the Holy Land. In old age he looked back on it all with the eye of mournful experience.

> *I was O/C Occupied Enemy Territory Administration (2nd Echelon)
> E.E.F. when the Zionist Commission arrived in Palestine early in April
> 1918. In my official and administrative capacity I was in close touch with
> most of the leading figures on the spot at that time. These included General
> Allenby, Major General Bols, Major General Sir A. Money, Colonel Ronald
> Storrs, General Clayton, Sir Wyndham Deedes and the leading lights
> within the Arab Bureau at Cairo.*
>
> *Before the arrival of its members I remember what a fluttering in the
> dovecotes had taken place, not only in British military circles, from Allenby
> downwards, but among the Moslem and Christian religious and civilian
> leaders, both in Palestine and in Egypt as well.*
>
> *At this time my office was at British Military H.Q. at the Savoy
> Hotel, Cairo, with pied-à-terres both at Ludd and in Jerusalem itself. For
> a time I was too preoccupied with organising military transport to carry
> and distribute clothing and food supplies for the civilian population to
> pay much attention to the political and religious controversies that began
> to rage following the Commission's arrival. However, I was living at that
> time on the Nile on a very comfortable Dahabieh [houseboat] with suitable
> facilities for private conferences and the provision of hospitality.*

(A Reminiscence, December 1961, Chalice Well Archives)

This Dahabieh was to provide the locus for many events—political, humanitarian and mystical—as TP continued his two-worlds type of functioning. It had a salon with a round table seating up to twelve, four cabins, bathroom and a private large state cabin in the stern, while on deck there was more space if visitors were many.

> *At one time or another I had the opportunity of entertaining most of the
> leading figures of the day, including the Allenbys, my Service colleagues,*

the Grand Mufti of Jerusalem, the Patriarchs, the Bishop in Jerusalem (Anglican) and many others including Colonel Findlay of the American Red Cross, and several members of the Zionist Commission itself.

Of the latter Dr. Weizmann was the outstanding figure, a man of immense personal magnetism, a Visionary, yet one whose political perceptions were very keen. I still remember with keen interest several private and intimate conversations I enjoyed with Dr. Weizmann. Although I am sure he realised more fully than most many of the tragic events likely to follow the creation of a Jewish State, there was a certain fierce relentlessness in his nature, that would have been capable of carrying him through the fires of hell and the throes of purgatory in pursuit of his fixed and inviolable purpose.

On one occasion whilst the Commission was still in session I remember receiving a visit from General Allenby, who had been rowed over from the Residency steps on the Nile to the mooring upstream on the opposite bank where my Dahabieh was stationed. The visit was strictly unofficial and the C. in C. was accompanied by Lady Allenby and their dogs. 'I am a soldier and I hate politics' was the keynote of his conversation on this occasion. He was deeply concerned at that time about the need to safeguard the rights and status of the Christian section of the population both in Palestine and in what has now become the separate state of Jordania.

I shall never forget Allenby's deep misgivings about the future outcome of Zionism in Palestine and his fear that the seeds for a new, perhaps global war, were likely to be sown. Since that conversation on the banks of the Nile early in June 1918, many of Allenby's prophetic forebodings have been fulfilled.

(A Reminiscence, December 1961, Chalice Well Archives)

TP had further reasons for misgivings on a later occasion when travelling by train with some interesting company, including that great defender of Arab interests, T.E. Lawrence.

There remains in my memory a night journey by train from Kantara to Ludd. The carriages were little better than cattle trucks and in the next one to mine were travelling together Ronald Storrs [Governor of Jerusalem, ed.], T.E. Lawrence, Father Waggett of Cowley and a fourth occupant whose voice I did not recognise...

The conversation veered around midnight to the personalities of those who at that time and place represented the Christian, the Jewish and the

Moslem points of view. Storrs who (officially) was regarded as being strongly pro-Zionist, launched a fierce attack on political and religious partisanship in general. Lawrence showed deep apprehension of the way in which he felt that his Arab protégés were going to be let down. Father Waggett in some distress tried to pour oil on the troubled waters, not very effectively, and I then found myself listening to some violent and no doubt scandalous accusations of grave breaches of faith as between the protagonists of Zionism and Arabism accentuated by the devious twists and turns in British foreign policy.

As I drifted into sleep in the small hours of the morning, the picture left in my mind was one which suggested the probable arrival of grim and bloody events within and around the 'Holy Land' in the times that were still to be.

(A Reminiscence, December 1961, Chalice Well Archives)

All this was of urgent interest to TP as Director of Occupied Enemy Territory Administration. He understood that British Zionists were in a strong position, because the war had pitched German Zionists and Russian Zionists onto opposite sides. Access to Palestine, via British victories against Turkey, further strengthened their position, and that same access was his responsibility as D.O.E.T.A. One member of the Zionist commission who visited TP in his dahabieh was Weizmann's secretary, Israel Sieff (later to be Chairman of Marks and Spencer), and here is how Sieff remembers this meeting:

My first impression of the Middle East was a rather weird one, and as a result of it I have never regarded 'The Mysterious East' as merely a romantic cliché. On my second day in Cairo I was told to take an official letter to a Major Tudor Pole, whose responsibility was the administration of conquered enemy territory. When I entered his office, he rose from his desk, and before I had time to utter a word, said: 'You are bringing me a letter. It instructs me to...' And in a beautifully modulated voice he summarised the letter's contents. I did not know what was in the letter, so I handed him the envelope. He opened it and read the note. 'Quite so,' he said, and handed the letter back to me to read. He had got it pat. I did not know quite what to make of this: perhaps it was a common knack in the Middle East Command. We proceeded to our business. As I was leaving he said, 'Come down to the river sometime, and see my boat'.

A few weeks later I went down to the river, where he had the kind of small launch to be seen on the Thames in summer, decked and furnished, with a couple of berths. 'Delighted you have come,' he said, with his usual courtesy. 'I hope you won't mind if I have to break off for a spell around eight-thirty. I shall be in France. If I seem distrait, do not worry; just sit there quietly, I shall soon be back.' I hardly knew whether to take him seriously, but sat down, took a drink, and behaved as if I were accustomed to being welcomed with such information. We had a pleasant and interesting conversation for an hour or so, but at eight fifteen he turned down the lamp, an oil lamp, I remember, and lay back slowly against his cushions. His face became pale, and his breathing deeper. He was obviously in, or pretending to be in, a trance. I sat there quietly and rather frightened. Fifteen minutes later he sat up, quite composed, and turned up the lamp. 'I've been to France,' he said, in a grave but otherwise normal voice. 'It's the Somme. The Germans have broken through; we're having a terrible time of it, there are frightful casualties.' His clairvoyance was beyond dispute. The Germans had blown a huge hole in the British lines and in a matter of days had pushed through many miles. We resumed our conversation and shortly after I left.

(Israel Sieff, 'Memoirs', Weidenfeld and Nicolson 1970, ps.101 & 102)

It is a rare luxury to have an observer's account of TP in uncanny mode, especially an observer whose career was built on sound commercial sense. But there is more luxury yet, because we can compare Sieff's account with TP's own. The latter is somewhat briefer, because TP had forgotten the incident for many years until Sieff revived the memory. Here is how the anecdote was passed on to Russell in October 1932.

When I saw Mr. Sieff yesterday he reminded me that in 1918 he came to the Dahabieh and during the evening the discussion ran on the possibility to see at a distance. He said it was impossible and challenged me to the contrary and we arranged a test. (I had completely forgotten this incident). Sieff named a sector of the line in France where his brother was serving and he says that after 10 minutes silence I told him about various incidents happening there. S. took notes of the time, and the time in France, and wrote to his brother whom he said confirmed the information in every particular. As Sieff told me all this yesterday, I began to remember the incident but it was not till yesterday that I knew that S. had proved the accuracy of the information given.

(Letter from TP to David Russell, 19.10.32)

There are a few small discrepancies, but if we assume Sieff's 'pleasant and interesting conversation' to be about TP's 'possibility to see at a distance', then we have a fairly consistent line. But is the case conclusive? Indeed, can any anecdote be conclusive? Here is how Sieff continues his account.

> *I saw Tudor Pole once or twice again before we left Cairo. After the war we kept our acquaintance and we met from time to time in the post-war period. One day he said to me suddenly: 'Israel, I'm sorry to have to tell you, but shortly there is to be a tragedy in your life. Somebody you know and love is going to die. I wish I could tell you who it is; I can't.' Two weeks later there was a telephone call from Algeria. It was Tudor Pole. 'Israel,' he said, 'I must tell you that your sorrow is about to fall on you.' That was all, he said, he could say. The next morning, one of my sons died in an accident. I cannot explain either Tudor Pole or his extraordinary communications. I report them exactly as my memory records them.*
>
> (Israel Sieff, 'Memoirs', Weidenfeld and Nicolson 1970, p.102)

As anecdotes go, this is as good as we are likely to get. Maybe letters in attics or unchecked biographies might turn up a few more, but for now we must give full weight to what we have, especially as TP often has remarkable tales to tell, many of them concerning the Dahabieh.

The Dahabieh

In June 1918, TP explained to Russell how special he considered the boat.

> *I have here a spiritual centre, nothing less, on the Dahabieh 'Thames' on the Nile. I could tell you of real Conferences on the Boat in the quiet evenings with some of Those who are guiding our lives. They direct me as to my outer activities; such for instance as bringing about a meeting on the Boat between the Bishop in Jerusalem, representing the Syria and Palestine Relief Funds, the Chairman and leader of the Zionists (Dr. C. Weizmann) and the Commissioner of the U.S.A. Red Cross. Outwardly this seems nothing, but out of this conference, arranged from the Unseen, great good arises for the whole of the Near East in ways I cannot even outline.*
> *Then the Boat is used by wounded officers in the afternoon and I am collecting a special library for them. Then at weekends various worn out men come down from Palestine as my guests and compare notes. Then*

TP on the steps of his Dahabieh, the Thames, with small friend

often I am alone and attend the Unseen Conferences of those working for the regeneration of the Holy Land, whose humble servant I am.

Then again high officials of the Administration up the line come down and talk frankly about their plans for the future. Things happen that could not come about in offices or camps, and the Boat has become a 'focus' and will become quite a remarkable centre as time goes on and if I can keep it on. How this has all come about I hardly know; it seems part of a big plan but I strive to keep a sense of proportion throughout.

I could tell you many things out here that would be untellable elsewhere; 'tell' is not the word, 'initiate' would be better. For the first time in my life I have been allowed to create a 'milieu' in the right surroundings, where contact with the wider world is not only possible but easy. The River flows magnetically past the Boat; the Banks are high and green with rushes and strange plants; there are wonderful flowing trees above the Banks and the clear sunlit air is everywhere. Cairo is away in the distance and the air flows straight across from the desert. Could there be a better centre, given the right conditions on the boat itself?

(Letter from TP to David Russell, 12.6.18)

Here we can see a consistent theme in TP's life, the setting up of havens hospitable and spiritual. The Guest House at 16/17 Royal York Terrace was an early such haven, and nowadays Little St Michael, the guest house at Chalice Well, is a culmination of his efforts.

As for 'contact with the wider world' one aspect of this consisted of seeking lost soldiers, as part of his unofficial, unpaid agency for the succour of the bereaved and anxious. We might picture him in his dahabieh, turning down the oil lamp of an evening, as he did when Israel Sieff visited, then lying back against the cushions and trying to pick up threads.

I am working at tracing a number of missing; sad work very. One has to live through the various episodes (whether one was there originally or not) in order to discover what became of the fellows in question.

(Letter from TP to David Russell, 7.1.18)

It sounds like his technique involved a sort of backdated telepathy, an odd and interesting concept. He may be referring to the same sort of thing a few days later:

I have quite a lot of work along my own lines to do in Cairo, among people who have seemingly lost their all in the War, sons, husbands, positions. I feel happy in that my recent experiences have given me extra power and confidence to help where I can.

(Letter from TP to David Russell, 13.1.18)

The 'recent experiences' would, of course, be his own wounding and hospitalisation. He also talks of telepathic contact with those he knows.

It is amazing to me, the number of people who seem interested in my fate; not that letters have reached me, but I am conscious of endless threads of thought me-ward from a diversity of directions.

(Letter from TP to David Russell, 9.1.18)

TP rarely discussed such activities in his letters, offering only passing references, so let us look at something which gets a fuller write-up. Here comes one of his Dahabieh stories. A version of this was printed in The Silent Road (1960) but that was not the first time he told the tale. He told it on the wireless on 24th December, 1937 and this was followed by publication in The Listener on 5th January 1938:

The Shadow Doctor
By Major W. TUDOR-POLE

Early in 1919 I was living on a dahabieh—a kind of house-boat— moored to the Nile bank above Gizeh, some miles south of Cairo. Military duties had taken me to the Jordan valley on a survey some weeks before, and I must have picked up the germ of a fever whilst camping out near the Dead Sea. The trouble was not malaria, but a wasting fever that left me listless, and unable to get on with my work. I simply appeared to be wasting away for no apparent reason, and I was getting weaker every day. It was under these conditions that the following peculiar events happened.

One evening, soon after sunset, there was a knock on my cabin door. A visitor came in. The only other people on the dahabieh at the time were my Berberin servants, and I was mildly surprised that a stranger should have been allowed to come into my cabin, where I was lying ill in bed, without being announced. I was still more surprised to see, standing before me, an Englishman dressed in a black frock-coat and carrying gloves, a bag and a top hat.

He stood beside my bunk, staring at me very straightly, and for some

*time without uttering a word. At last I said: 'You are a doctor aren't you?'
And my visitor said he was, and that he was sorry to find me in such a
low state of health. He added that my condition would rapidly become
dangerous unless the necessary steps were taken at once. This frightened
me a little, and I asked what steps he would recommend. Thereupon he
told me to send one of the servants into Cairo at once, and to tell him to
go to a herbalist shop in the Mousqué—he named the exact locality, but
not the shop—and there he was to buy a certain herb. The doctor gave its
first name in Latin and then in the Arabic equivalent. My orders were to
drink an infusion of this herb in hot water three times a day before meals,
and the doctor also gave me some instructions about diet. I was to eat no
meat, salads or fruit. As a matter of fact, I had been living entirely on fruit
and salads at the time.*

*Whilst I was trying to memorise these prescriptions, my eyes wandered
round to the dressing-table, and I was amazed to see the looking-glass
clearly reflected through the doctor's top hat. The hat seemed to have become
transparent! It was only then I realised with a shock that my visitor himself
was not substantial. But he appeared to be so real that I asked him who
he was and where he came from. He coolly told me that he was a London
specialist, and that he possessed the power to move from place to place in
this way, whilst his body remained quiescent in his London study. He
said that he was in the habit of locking himself into his study, waiting
quietly for any call that might be made upon him. He said that he did not
entirely lose consciousness on these occasions, and was only dimly aware
afterwards of the experiences through which he had passed whilst absent
from his body.*

(From The Shadow Doctor, printed in The Listener 5.1.38)

Later the doctor showed a visual image of where he lived, and TP even
noticed that

*the name on the brass plate was legible and I was able to read it. It was
a short name, and I think it began with 'Mac', and although I determined
at all costs to memorise this clue to my visitor's identity, I forgot it in my
intense anxiety to remember the name of the herb which he had prescribed
for me.*

(From The Shadow Doctor, printed in The Listener 5.1.38)

TP duly sent his servant to find the herb, and within a fortnight a complete cure was achieved. On returning to London six months later TP tried to find the house he had glimpsed, found one similar, but decided not to ring the bell, lest the five doctors named on the brass plate considered him a lunatic.

Homeward Bound

Mention of London raises the topic of home-thoughts-from-abroad. TP's time in the Near East was moving towards a close, and his focus shifted more and more to what he would find in England, though the subject had rarely been far from his mind. For instance, whilst recovering from his wound he thought of Russell and other people close to him:

> *Today I went up alone on the Mokattam Hills, overlooking Cairo and the Nile, for meditation. My arm gave me 'gip' but I forgot everything in gazing at the wonderful panorama. The air was like champagne, a poor description anyway! and I should have loved to have had you beside me. My Guardian came too. I asked him to tell me about home problems but all he would say was that all was well and they were doing everything to look after my loved ones. This applied to Bournemouth, Portstewart and Markinch, my three havens towards which thought and prayer constantly travels.*
>
> (Letter from TP to David Russell, 13.1.18)

Russell lived at Markinch in Fife, whilst Florence and the children were at Bournemouth. The rest of his family lived at Portstewart (in Ireland) and, as part of his home-thoughts, TP was keen to link Russell with them. The Family Group had been a crucial feature of his send-off back in 1916, and now he wanted Russell to mingle with that group.

> *I am so glad that you are en rapport now with my sister, Mary, and know something of her truly wonderful development. Sometime you must meet her and Bruce [her husband, ed.]. If you could only have one or two quiet evenings with our little Group, my people in Derry, I should be delighted beyond words. You would be linked up with the Unseen Presences working through the Family Group; also you would get light on your own pathway; and (because of the strong link between you and me) you would come right inside and understand what the Group is working for. I am v. keen about it.*
>
> (Letter from TP to David Russell, 9.1.18)

TP was always inclined to link people together in groups (or even triads) but in this case he had extra motivation. Reincarnation was something about which he had no doubts, and nor did he doubt the identities of some cast members from previous incarnations, such as Russell himself.

> *I want my people to understand the tie there is between us, so that there need be no misunderstandings; that's partly why I want you to run over there. Neither Florence nor Alison [Russell's wife, ed.] can quite realise the power which welds the friendship, the comradeship between you and I. It is a gift to us out of the Past, when we suffered and went through many experiences together.*
>
> (Letter from TP to David Russell, 9.1.18)

An even more pressing home-thought concerned Florence. When TP went abroad in November 1917, they both thought she was pregnant, which was cause enough for concern, but the situation gradually became more acute. He tried, in his uncanny way, to search the Beyond for any signs of an approaching child but drew a blank. Eventually he became alarmed.

> *Florence cabled on the 5th December (before hearing I was wounded) 'Distressed money'. The cable was delayed and I only got it on 20/12/17 when I at once cabled to attempt to relieve matters. I have a fund in hand for the expenses of doctor and nurse etc for the late spring. All I want to discover is what has gone wrong and how to save F. anxiety and worry. The £25 [monthly] has to cover everything, but it ought to do that and lots of officers' wives have to manage on less, far less.*
>
> *F. is not easy to understand, being v. sensitive and reserved in many ways and proud. Beyond that one cable I may get no details whatever, but I told her when leaving that you had my Power of Attorney and if anything went wrong you would advise her until I could be communicated with. Probably, however, she would be too shy to write to you about such matters.*
>
> (Letter from TP to David Russell, 25.12.17)

She did write to Russell in the end, requesting a loan of £10 to see a specialist. Something was distinctly wrong with her pregnancy, and eventually the truth of the situation became apparent.

> *Florence writes (what I have been expecting in a subconscious way)*

that there is no child coming. Rayner says things are not quite normal and I am somewhat anxious. However I feel strongly that metaphysical work should obviate the necessity for an operation.

(Letter from TP to David Russell, 9.1.18)

There is always a back-home story to every venture, and back-home stories can often involve pain. What could be more eloquent than a ghost pregnancy? The consolation for Florence was that her husband finally came home (and they duly had another child, David Wellesley, born April 1921), but for many women, ghosts were all they ended up with.

Before his return home TP had a pressing question to consider: the family business. Did he really want to return to it? The prospect appeared less and less attractive, the more he heard from Admonishing Marcuse, the Corn Exchange Sage. Here is what the Great Man posted to TP in May 1918:

Now, to come to the larger question at issue between us: your friend Mr. David Russell first got into communication with me some considerable time back, when he wrote me a letter (I do not know why or on whose instructions) defending your action in connection with the publication of a certain book. It was at the time when I was greatly incensed at your devoting yourself to those matters which I was under the impression it was definitely agreed between us should not happen again. (I still adhere very strongly to my view that the sooner interest in that particular subject is abandoned the better for you in every way, and nothing will alter this attitude).

(Letter to TP from E. Marcuse, 7.5.18)

Could anyone imagine TP ceasing spiritual activities on the Marcuse say-so? The letter then goes on to: (a) castigate Russell for trying to attend a Directors' meeting on TP's behalf ('this, of course, I refused point blank'), (b) snort about an attempted transfer of 50 shares to Russell ('such an attempt at intrusion'), then (c) whine about his own sufferings ('the willing horse generally gets the most abuse').

A thrilling aspect to the letter is that TP clearly tore it up. Its remnants in St Andrews University Library are re-assembled jigsaw fashion and held together with sticky strips from a sheet of stamps. It is no surprise, therefore, that TP wrote to Russell a year later 'I am extremely anxious to find a way of relinquishing my connection with C.P. & Co' (28.1.19). And relinquish he did, though in long-term retrospect he was less than happy about the deed.

Writing to Russell 26 years later he says:

> *Sometimes I look back with regret to the way our family business was*
> *filched away, whilst I was serving in the last War.*
>
> (Letter from TP to David Russell, 21.5.45)

Whether filched or relinquished, it was a source of income he needed to replace. What should he try instead?

> *I am tempted to accept an offer made me out here to become General*
> *Manager for a large Journalistic, Advertising and Commercial Concern*
> *with Branches throughout the Near East. It would mean much travelling*
> *across Europe and Turkey but any amount of scope and a good salary. If*
> *on investigation, I find this concern sound, it may be right to accept the*
> *post and help forward the regeneration of the Press in Egypt, Palestine,*
> *Turkey, Greece and Italy.*
>
> (Letter from TP to David Russell, 23.2.19)

Major WT Pole (formerly Second Lieutenant) mentioned in Allenby's despatch
(signed by Winston Churchill)

Regeneration was indeed what TP would desire. He would not regard journalism, advertising and commerce in the way that many of us tend to now (jaded capitalists as we are). This was 1919, the war was just over, and the map of Europe and the Near East was being re-drawn. Possibilities would seem endless at the time, with new countries about to appear (or reappear) from the old Turkish and Austrian empires, and someone like TP would not merely think of new countries but new cultures, new spirituality, in fact a New Age.

He arrived home in June and 'found Florence looking well' (which would be a considerable relief) while Jean and Chris, now aged five and four, were very fit, 'full of spirit, bathing in the sea every day.' Then it was time to sort out the projected journalistic-cum-commercial business. By November 1919 he was telling Russell about his attempt

> to carry out Allenby's suggestions when he asked me last Spring to join the Boutigny group. I have sent out two good, clean editors; Louis Avennier for La Bourse (the most important Daily in Egypt) and Philip O'Farrell for the 'Mail' and the Palestine News. We have also sent J.H. Walker to reorganise the big Printing Plants in Cairo and Alexandria.
>
> Branches or Agencies are now being formed in Brussels, Geneva, Barcelona, Naples, Athens and Constantinople.
>
> Then we have been used as intermediaries in the Egyptian question, through the Egyptian Nationalist leader now in Paris, and beyond all this we hope ultimately to launch a free International Weekly in English, French, Italian (and someday German and Russian). What a vista!
>
> (Letter from TP to David Russell, 3.11.19)

As he says, 'What a vista!' The letter suggests an expansive, optimistic phase for both the world and TP. Could anything stop them? Well, an alert reader might wonder how all this was to be funded in a world crippled by war. Would the bedrock reality match the airy ambitions?

That is for another chapter. For now TP is home, hopeful, and on the horizon a new decade is dawning. What would the twenties be like? Ah, what indeed!

7. War In The Spheres: 1920-1925

The Great War was meant to be the War To End All Wars, but what it got from the Versailles Conference (1919) was a Peace To End All Peace. President Woodrow Wilson with his Fourteen Points and high ideals came up against Clemenceau, the French 'Tiger', whose own idea of peace was a crippled Germany. Lloyd George, caught between ideals and ire, eventually settled for the latter, and the Treaty of Versailles reduced Germany to humiliating penury. This was never likely to work long term, and the Treaty became an invitation to resume the War at a later date.

Maybe a proper League of Nations would have helped. That's what President Wilson hoped when he mooted the idea, but his Senate refused to let America join the League, so another chance of stability was lost.

Matters were no better elsewhere. The Bolsheviks had mugged the Russian Revolution and were defeating the anti-Bolsheviks despite aid from the likes of Churchill (Secretary of State for War and Air by now). Then there was war in Ireland, as the Liberal Government (Churchill again) sent in the Black and Tans to fight Sinn Fein. In mainland Britain striking miners were waging a political war with the support of transport workers and railwaymen.

Homecoming

For Wellesley Tudor Pole it was a baffling situation to come home to. He had left the Near East where all seemed possible—Nile boat conferences, rescued prophets—and had returned to a London where all seemed impossible. The bold journalistic plan he had hoped to implement for the Near East crashed on financial grounds:

> *The Foreign Office offers conveyed by me to Mr Boutigny have not been accepted. I therefore hold myself free to take over the London Overseas Publicity and Service Agency and run it as my own venture.*
>
> (Letter from TP to David Russell, 30.11.19)

And that was the genesis of W. Tudor Pole, Export-Import as his headed letter paper announced from July 1920 onwards. TP took over the office at 61 St James' Street, from where he could try commercial work, selling suits to Hungary, for example, and paper to Holland.

I now have important selling agencies arranged at Amsterdam, Zurich, Cologne, Constantinople and Alexandria, and I have some useful buying agencies in London, so that the connections are made and it is a question of working them with energy.

(Letter from TP to David Russell, 8.6.20)

Yet with a post-war slump beginning, and post-war strikes under way, post-war possibilities became distinctly limited:

Somehow I seem to have been fighting harder since I left the Army than before, and with more stress and less leisure. It has been an extraordinary time and one feels that 'fighting' to pull material conditions into shape is somehow the wrong method, yet it seems difficult to find another.

(Letter from TP to David Russell, 6.9.20)

He was not the only one in trouble. His St James Street office gained a reputation for assistance and advice, and along came the casualties of peace, of whom he reported to David Russell:

I have had a somewhat sad procession of people through my office (quite apart from the usual business callers); a procession which suggests that for the majority of people post war conditions are infinitely more difficult and arduous than war conditions. Here is a summary of some of these 'cases':-

(a) A newly married couple; very charming, cultured people but of different nationalities; going through their first serious difference of opinion; the bride considering it to be a 'sin against the next generation' to bring children into the world (under existing conditions) the husband taking the other view. They asked me for a solution! Why not adopt, I say, but people hate that rejoinder.

(b) An ex officer; 45, M.A. wife and 4 children, a pension of 22/- a week, cannot get a job anywhere and almost literally starving. Offered to 'do anything' in return for food for his family.

(c) A similar case but not so desperate, as the man was younger and the family smaller.

(d) A war widow with various problems, too long to enumerate here.

(e) A very clever girl of 18 of the 'upper class', so called, in the clutches of a Secret Society, with blackmail attached. A strange but not hopeless

case.

(f) A case of obsession where the victim has (wrongly in my view) been confined to an asylum.

(g) A young business man defrauded by his partner.

(Just taken from my diary for the week).

One is inclined to wonder whether life really has become more complex or whether one becomes more clearly aware of and attracts such cases whilst travelling though difficult country oneself.

(Letter from TP to David Russell, 11.9.20)

'Inner History' of the times

There was more to the situation, though, than a queue of unhappy callers at 61 St James Street: TP could sniff something wrong in the air, which he felt was not simply the result of the aftermath of war. His sniff became a clear impression and by December 1920 he was writing to friends and family offering a startling view of what might be termed 'Inner History'. Was TP really telling the inside story of the early Twentieth Century? Judge for yourself, starting with the first letter, sent to his sister Mary in Ireland:

Everyone is in a sort of 'Purgatory' just now, and I am not surprised either, for I have discovered one of the reasons.

Certain Powers, using material from human passions and selfishness, have succeeded in drawing down a Curtain between us here in our world and our spiritual horizons. In other words the Aerial Armageddon has broken out again.

I have wondered for many weeks why the 'Avenues' were so dark, and inspiration so difficult. I find that a very grave crisis is upon us, and that our unseen friends need all the help we can send them. It appears that the present world chaos (Russia and Ireland especially) was never intended to reach such extremities, but for the time being the Forces of Light are powerless because 'on balance' their adversaries are still receiving more ammunition from the Human Mind than they are.

Russia and Ireland were to be the two special focal centres through which the new spiritual stimuli were to penetrate, and because of this very fact, when the reaction came, and the 'Curtain of dark fabric' was let down between us and our Salvation, they were the Nations to suffer the most, being more sensitive to spiritual stimuli, whether from the White or Black regions.

I was in my Office here until midnight last week, having converted it into a 'Reception Room' for unseen friends. They can only reach us now with immense difficulty, and they need all the help we can send them. They do not dwell in the spheres of omnipotence, but in the Borderland of Conflict, battling to save the Soul of the World.

(Letter from TP to Mary Bruce Wallace, 3.12.20)

His office, it would appear, had become the equivalent of his Egyptian dahabieh, a sort of staging post between the worlds, where pleas and information could be registered and forwarded. TP kept David Russell informed on the situation, telling him about 'moulds' and 'channels':

During the War, when ideals of self sacrifice raised the mental tone of many people in every nation, the guides of our Earth Race built up 'moulds' in the Racial Consciousness, attaching channels to them through which a flood of new spiritual illumination might be poured down.

This process was intended to leaven the Consciousness of man, to uplift and regenerate it, and the idealism and martyrdom caused by the war presented the opportunity. These Rivers of Light were released and their 'waters' began pouring down into the moulds so carefully prepared. The process commenced and continued intermittently during 1916, 1917, 1918 and until spring 1919; after which something went wrong.

The moulds in various centres of human Consciousness were not strong enough to carry out their task; they cracked and then broke up. Meanwhile the precious 'fluid' was escaping uncontrolled and seeing the danger the Guardians of the Reservoirs shut off the flow about the Spring of 1920.

(Letter from TP to David Russell, 13.12.20)

So far the discussion has been at an abstract level and therefore begs a few questions. For instance, what are these moulds? But TP soon becomes more specific, mentioning the people, institutions and movements that had cracked and leaked their spiritual 'fluid':

So many carefully prepared 'moulds' have been broken during 1920, even on our human plane. Woodrow Wilson was one. He was 'prepared' for the highest destiny of any living man in our generation (that is of course among the external leaders of men) and what is he now? The strain was too great, the vessel broke, and the precious fluid was dissipated.

His instrument the 'League'; like a body without a soul is the League today. Yet it was moulded for the highest, Divinest uses. They are trying to remould it from the Wider World even now. And the Peace Treaties, Bodies without souls; the shadow and the letter without the substance and the spirit. Vessels from which the right spirit has gone forth, leaked away. The Russian revolution! Another wonderful mould, starting forth with pure and noble aims. And now the spirit force has been prostituted to base ends, God is denied, and selfishness and irreligion are watchwords even among the leaders. All these and a thousand other world events are the shadowgraphs reflecting the breaking up of the moulds and channels in Borderland, that were conveying the Light into human consciousness.

(Letter from TP to Mary Bruce Wallace, Christmas 1920)

Since 1907 TP had been announcing that the 'Breath of God' was approaching human levels—that, in fact, the Second Coming was on its way. This cracking of the moulds, though, would constitute, at the very least, a hold up, a situation that few could understand, either on Earth or in 'Borderland':

Borderland, in many places, has the appearance of a field of battle, immediately after a reverse. Troops are distracted and disorganised, and Generals are hastily making plans for fresh combinations. Very few of the rank and file understand what has happened. Only the High Leaders know for certain the fact (of which we have a vague inkling now) that the Great Breath is no longer being exhaled from the 'Above', but that a period of 'Intake' has commenced, long before the allotted time, but necessary for the safety of all concerned. To 'breathe out', spiritually speaking, requires channels and vessels to receive the Breath, and if these break down the 'Breath' is withdrawn until such times as conditions make it wise to continue what we term the 'pouring down of the wave of Spiritual Illumination.'

(Letter from TP to Mary Bruce Wallace, Christmas 1920)

It is a remarkable summary, whether we regard it as poetic metaphor or in some way true. But how did TP come by these ideas — were they hearsay, or was he more intimately involved with the shaping of events?

Since 1910 I have been a member of a Group working in Borderland in preparation for the descent and control of the new spiritual currents that

119

were to leaven human thought and ideas. We each had a humble part in the creation of channels, moulds and vessels, prepared to receive illumination. Quite recently our Leader called us together and explained that we were to be disbanded and much of our handiwork was changed back into its elemental substance. We were told that the human race could not respond sufficiently to these new regenerative waves and that the project we had been working on had been postponed indefinitely.

(Letter from TP to David Russell, 19.12.20)

Business, Family and Politics

We can, of course, accept that or not as we please. However, it is fair to note that TP had experienced his own mini breaking-of-the-mould when the grand and idealistic Boutigny plan collapsed (a plan, the reader may remember, for helping regenerate the Near East via 'a large Journalistic, Advertising and Commercial Concern').

That was not his only disappointment. As a businessman he was starting out on an oddly consistent course of backing likely winners that never won. Indeed, reading his Russell correspondence over the decades, one is struck

Home again with Florence, Jean, Christopher,
David (occasionally clothed), and Sam the dog

with a sense of wonder: how could he so persistently fail to prosper? Likely proposition after likely proposition crashed on the grounds of tough luck or hidden mendacity. Was he cursed? Fated? Stringently opposed by celestial baddies?

Of course, there is a case of physician-heal-thyself here. If his unofficial psychic agency could prove so useful to others (and it did, time and again) why could it not point out a few winners for TP? Hume Pipe shares, Porta Radio, Manna Bread (the last a concoction to solve post-war hunger)—one by one they glowed with promise then dimmed to obscurity:

> *I would never have believed, had I not experienced it, how difficult it is to get a footing again since the War, unless one has Capital. Even now I don't know whether the connections I have laboriously built up these past two years are going to make it worth while hanging on or whether I had better sublet this office, square up and put in for a salaried post out East.*
> (Letter from TP to David Russell, 8.6.21)

TP needed to earn good money because by now he had three children, David Wellesley joining Jean and Chris in April 1921. T.P's letters often give bulletins of the children and their doings which come as light relief from the dramatic information so far. For instance, in September 1920, his daughter Jean, six at the time, had an accident:

> *She is mending nicely but it has entailed much pain for the dear child as the elbow was dislocated, as well as the forearm broken.**
> (Letter from TP to David Russell, 6.9.20)

A year later TP was wondering whether another fracture might be in prospect:

> *I have a Pogo Stick here in my office which I am taking down to Chris tomorrow. I am rather alarmed by it!*
> (Letter from TP to David Russell, 27.9.21)

As for David, the youngest, TP felt as proud as any father might, writing the following year:

---

* In July 2001 Jean showed me the relevant elbow, and it still looked a bit odd.

David Wellesley is the picture of health and has grown wonderfully. I have never seen a child (aged one) with such an extraordinarily wide and developed aura; it is almost uncanny to me but v. beautiful (if I am allowed to speak thus about my own child!)

(Letter from TP to David Russell, 6.5.22)

Three children were quite enough, although at one stage there might have been more:

Florence returns from the Fellowship of Reconciliation Congress imbued with the conviction that we ought to offer a home to an Austrian child this winter. I tell her we will (if and when our Ship comes home).

(Letter from TP to David Russell, 22.9.20)

It didn't. However, the incident is a reminder of Florence's humanitarian concerns, even if she had to narrow her focus most of the time on the humanity in her own house.

As for his mother, TP still liked to entertain her with long descriptive letters. In 1921 he wrote about the visit of a top Egyptian delegation to London. They were there to negotiate independence, and TP, as a man with Near East connections, helped welcome them:

It will amuse you to hear about yesterday's function. I met Sir Adby Jeghen Pasha (the Premier) and four of his Cabinet, and five of his staff, including Hassanein Bey, at the Carlton at 4.45 p.m. They would be fully satisfied if the Milner report is acted upon, but Winston Churchill is against it, and he has more power with Lloyd George than Curzon.

We got into private motors flying the Egyptian flag on their bonnets, and Rushdi Pasha plied me with questions: Who was Lady Astor? Why was she in the House of Commons?

We arrived at St. Stephen's Gate and trooped through the corridors and out on to the Terrace, where tea tables had been set out for the Delegation. No sign of Lady Astor, but a youngish man of about 40, with a cowed air, somewhat nervous, came forward and sat us down at the tables. There were a few members present: Ormsby Gore, Aubrey Herbert, Gen. Seeley and a youngish fellow called Coote, and one or two ladies whose names were not audibly disclosed. Presently Lady Astor came bustling along, dressed in a black toque and a close-fitting black and white sateen frock with pearls. (This amazing woman of astonishing vitality was almost a complete invalid before she became a Christian Scientist ten years ago. She is about 44, I imagine, and looks 36). She romped into the midst of the group and began shaking hands all round, without troubling about names or languages, and then took the head of one of the tables. I was at the other with a Lady Somebody as deputy hostess, half the Egyptian delegation and also Gore, Seeley and Coote.

The tea was execrable (as usual at the House) half cold and cakes like stones. However, it did not matter. The shy, youngish man turned out to be Lord Astor, evidently much in awe of his wife. 'Waldorf,' she cried, 'they haven't any tea down there!' He jumped up like a shot rabbit, and scurried away to play the butler, bringing back hot water and popping up and down like a schoolboy.

Meanwhile Lady Somebody at my table turned to me saying, sotto voce, 'Who are these people?' I explained who they were. 'Have they just come from Egypt? What do they want? Have they many wives each; and what do they think of us?' and so on. Here was an (apparently) intelligent woman, the wife of an English 'Lord', who had no conception of the fact that she was helping to entertain Egypt's principal statesmen, over here to negotiate for the freedom of their country.

The Egyptians enjoyed themselves immensely but what did they really think of it all? To be entertained by an American lady member of the English Parliament; wife of an American millionaire tame rabbit, a woman who seemed to have amazing influence in all political directions! What about the affairs of their own Country, now in such a sorry mess?

Comic opera, on the surface; yes, but grim Tragedy beneath, and that sums up the position everywhere today in this funny old world of ours.

(Letter from TP to 'Darling Mother', Kate Tudor Pole, 29.7.21)

The Quest revived

And that last statement returns us to our more serious theme, because the early 20's were indeed tragic in many ways. For TP the cause of it all was spiritual, and so the antidote must be spiritual also. Furthermore, he suspected he knew what an antidote might be. If he could just revive the Quest, he might yet tap into the stream of early Christianity and bring forth documents to revitalise world awareness.

The Quest had not been forgotten during the War. TP had gradually been forming a Quest Group, starting when he met Frederick Leveaux, a lawyer, in Cairo towards the end of 1918. They became firm friends, living together on TP's dahabieh and sharing ideas and ideals.

After his return to England, TP met two Russian asylum seekers, Anatole Bergengreen and Dmitry Sissoëff who claimed they could contact a discarnate spirit, BB (Boris Bavaiev). The Russians communicated with BB via a planchette—a small wooden board with wheels and a pencil attached (see photograph on page 126). They would rest their fingers on the board which would write or draw. Though by nature suspicious of 'mechanical' methods for contacting spirits, TP was impressed by the sincerity of these Russians. He asked them about the Quest, conveying the results to David Russell:

> We had a most interesting time last night here. I showed Bergengreen a photo of the rough land and terraces lying between Santa Sophia and the Sea and he got 'en rapport' at once and described the passages and chapel grotto (without of course knowing of my work out there); he 'saw' the red slab of iron stone acting as swivel door to Polycarp's tomb and described the designs upon it, several of which I could confirm (the fish and the stars and a figure of Polycarp); he 'saw' into the grotto and described the bronze wood lined chest beneath the floor containing the Polycarp* writings I am after; all in a most remarkable way. Later the planchette drew a ground plan of the approximate position of the grotto and 'B.B.' promised further aid. It could not have been telepathy, I fancy, because many things were described of which I knew nothing.
>
> (Letter from TP to David Russell, 13.5.21)

TP invited Bergengreen and Sissoëff to join the Quest Group, and they told him about a fellow mystic and exile, Michael Pojidaiev, a former Czarist officer and sculptor living in Cairo. Remembering the wonderful atmosphere aboard his Egyptian dahabieh, TP thought it would form the perfect meeting place to meet this other Russian and for the rest of the Quest Group to assemble, especially as Frederick Leveaux still lived on it. Soon Bergengreen and Sissoëff were sailing out to Egypt, and by January 1922 TP followed.

On meeting Pojidaiev he was sufficiently impressed to invite him into the Quest Group. All five members began living on the dahabieh, and as in the old days it proved an ideal location for spiritual work. On 28th January 1922, Bergengreen and Sissoëff were operating the planchette when startling information came through about the chapel grotto (now called St George's Chapel). This, they learnt, was beneath the ground near the church of Hagia Irene—just where TP had stood in 1907 when first sensing the full scope of the Quest. Now he received detailed information about what he had been standing over.

I. Objects in Armoury. (St George's Chapel.)

Tablets covered with wax brought by C. from RX. containing words of St. Polycarp.
Parchments in Greek, of III Century, containing:-
  (a) St Mark's account of the words of Jesus to those near Him in AD 32 (7th supper**)
  (b) St Peter's account of how he was saved from drowning on the lake of Gallilea
  (c) Copy of first portion of St Paul's Epistle from Rome to the Christians in Greece, Corinth and Thebes.

II. Parchment of Syrian (Greek Alphabet) Nestoria's account of the Religion of Jesus.

III. The Words of John, son of Massi, on the Testament of Jesus written down by St Polycarp.
('The Quest', p.5, private typescript by Renée Nicol, 1958)

This was only the start. In subsequent sittings inventory details followed at an amazing rate, running to seven and a half pages of valuables and manuscripts. Equally amazing were the instructions for getting access to these valuables.

Passages, wells, chambers, sliding-stones, manholes or traps, staircases, and a chapel were all eventually shown. The lengths and in many instances the heights of the passages were indicated. Numbers were given to the chambers as well as to each of the boxes containing manuscripts and objects. It took several evenings or, rather, parts of evenings to complete the drawing of this first plan which came to be named the 'Wet Way' [i.e. the entrance from the sea , ed.]
('The Quest', p.7, private typescript by Renée Nicol, 1958)

---

* TP believed that St John's own recollections of Jesus were dictated to Polycarp and constitute a lost gospel which would bring Jesus to life in the popular imagination.

** Some of this information eludes translation. The seventh supper, though, was considered to be the 'Last Supper'.

Eventually TP decided he had enough information to give the Quest another try. BB specified a wait of fourteen months—till April 27th 1923—but TP foresaw political problems with any delay.

Planchette viewed from (a) above and (b) below, showing three castors, one dismantled, and an attachable spike or pencil

> *Next year X [Constantinople, ed.] will not be under English dominance*
> *so I feel that next month when the tides suit I must make my third and I hope*
> *successful effort to bring those MSS to light for the use of the world.*
>
> (Letter to David Russell, headed 'Giza, Cairo', 25.3.22)

TP realised the post war situation was resolving itself, and Turkey, a loser in World War One, would soon gain its independence from occupying powers. Most likely, the forthcoming Lausanne conference, in 1923, would mean that Britons would lose their privileged position. Therefore, felt TP, he must go this April, this year.

> *The tides only allow of my getting into the right entrance for about a fortnight in April and even then one must swim into the tunnel entrance.*
>
> *I have now the complete plan to scale of the whole series of tunnels, chapels and chambers including full clues as to how to escape the traps and how to open certain concealed doorways; also I know exactly where to look for the various MSS etc and exactly where they are, when they were placed there and how to move them.*
>
> *Too long to go into by letter; there are over 200 documents of world import dating from 400 B.C. up to 500 A.D. There are 42 inscribed 'tables' of Polycarp of immense import; a 2nd Century psaltery; a long parchment containing John's description of the Last Supper (Polycarp); a very early Mark evangile; a 1st Century anonymous essay on Christians and Jews; a 3rd century made up book on the 'Holy Spirit' and countless other Early Christian parchments.*
>
> *There is a long document written by Sophocles himself on how to arrange the furnishings of a theatre; a love letter of Julius Caesar and some essays by Marcus Aurelius written by himself on gold sheets with a pen of iron. Don't smile when I tell you that all these actually exist and are safely deposited in two rosewood Chests in a certain Chamber and that I'm not resting until I've had a good shot at unearthing them.*
>
> *I have made plans carefully; all necessary tools are ready; rubber waterproof bags in which the MSS will be hermetically sealed, provisions for 3 days and nights underground and many other things. I feel somehow we ought to be successful this time; otherwise why has 'Fate' put the fullest clues into my hands; the handicap is the usual one, funds, for all these preparations are costly and I cannot undertake the necessary subterranean excavations without at least 2 or 3 trained workers. But I must go on; it is*

the central passion of my life. In the Royal Roman Treasure Chamber still exists the Royal Crown containing 'L'Oeil de Dieu' the biggest diamond of its day.

Please destroy.

(Letter from TP to David Russell, undated, probably February 1922)

Thankfully David Russell never did destroy any letters, although we might see TP's point: a glint of greed in the wrong person's eye could endanger what was, for the Quest Group, a spiritual enterprise.

At certain moments in life one is dominated and forced into action by some overwhelming power; usually it is the result of a great emotion inspired by love or fear or hatred or revenge; rarely the Force is Other Worldly, but when it is one's life ceases to be one's own until one has obeyed the great impulse. Such a moment faces me now and I cannot shirk it.

(Letter from TP to David Russell, 29.3.1922)

Third Quest Attempt, 1922

On the 12th April 1922 TP went alone to Constantinople. He took with him tools, bags, a camera and provisions.

All my plans are complete and I believe the days (and nights) I shall be working underground (out of touch with the world) will be either the 23rd, 24th & 25th or the 25th, 26th & 27th April. So think of me then. It will be, in any case, the greatest adventure in my life and I am hopeful as to results.

(Letter to David Russell, 6.4.1922)

His plans did not work out as expected, though. On 29th April he wrote to Russell from the Tokatlian Hotel in Constantinople:

I am delayed again. Difficult to explain in a letter; my goal seems so near and every step I take brings fresh proofs that I am on the right track. If equipment etc is ready in time I hope to make the big underground effort before 15th May. My experiences since I left London in January have been among the most extraordinary in my life.

(Letter to David Russell, 29.4.1922)

These 'extraordinary' experiences, of course, included the astonishing details received via the planchette, but they were not the only ones. There were two more intriguing occurrences around this time, and they both involve silence.

Firstly, all communication with BB stopped. Suddenly.

TP may have found the reason 'difficult to explain in a letter' but the rest of the Quest Group in Cairo realised what had happened at once.

> *On the 28th April 1922 it was learnt that BB had started a new life.*
> ('The Quest', p.18, private typescript by Renée Nicol, 1958)

Logically, if death on Earth meant arrival in the Beyond, then 'death' in the Beyond meant arrival on Earth, and this was what had happened to BB. He had been attacked by discarnate entities, forcing him to reincarnate.

As a result BB went silent at the most crucial moment for the attempt on the underground passages, and this posed a huge problem for TP. He had plenty of information and knew what equipment to take, but there were still blanks to fill in and he needed BB's guidance on the spot.

There was another silence, however, even more intriguing than BB's. TP himself went silent.

TP wrote to David Russell *almost every day* until Russell's death in 1956. Yet at the time of the third attempt on the tunnels beneath Constantinople, TP went silent. His last letter to Russell (above) was written on 29th April 1922. He did not write again until he was back in England on 26th May when he said:

> *The World nears the verge of the most wonderful series of discoveries of Greek, Roman &Christian treasure & documents (BC 300 to AD 450) that has ever been known. The direct accurate & practical guidance received has been the most extraordinary that I have ever known. An account of it must wait over until we meet.*
> (Letter to David Russell, 26.5.22)

What happened during that month of silence between the 29th of April and the 26th of May? Was an attempt made on the tunnels? Did TP find any manuscripts or treasure?

TP never did write down what happened, and Russell never gave any details of TP's promised 'account'. However, with the help of later documents, a probable course of events can be assembled.

It seems that once in Constantinople TP enlisted the help of contacts (one of them named Thompson) to hire a boat and equipment. The boat would have reached the seaward entrance to the tunnels under cover of darkness. Two large underwater stones and a blockage of sand had to be cleared out of the way before TP, carrying a waterproof bag with a lantern in it, could swim through the gap, towing the boat, to the start of the tunnel system. Here he would be faced with a narrow, low corridor, less than a metre wide and just over a metre high. Crawling through this, he would need to find a certain slit in the wall to position his lantern. Then, using long cords already tied for the purpose, he had to drag several packages (covered with tarpaulin) towards him from the boat. Lastly he had to pull a two metre long wooden plank into the tunnel.

Crawling to a certain place specified as fifty three metres from the entrance he could now use his lantern without the light being spotted from outside. Here a large stone protruded from the wall where he could rest and change into dry clothes. Crawling another sixty metres, he would stop and consult his map which showed the first of many traps directly ahead. The trap was a turning stone, which, if trodden on, would plunge him 42 metres into a well communicating with the sea. He would look for a pin whose head was concealed in a recess near the floor in the left hand wall. This pin had to be pulled out before placing the two metre plank across the turning stone. Once the plank was secure he could ferry all his equipment across before continuing another 220 metres until he reached the first bend in the corridor.

And so on. The details of the tunnel system are remarkably precise, particularly as to distances. But did TP get so far in 1922? Because of his silence, there is no firm evidence that this attempt actually took place. And what were the other members of the Quest Group doing during this crucial month?

On learning about BB's defeat the four set off to support TP in Constantinople. The next we hear of them is on 9th May 1922 when Leveaux and Bergengreen were operating the planchette in the Hotel Royal in Constantinople. With BB unavailable, they needed all the help they could get, receiving messages from a back-up group called 'All' (later known as 'Tous'). Communication with 'All' was intermittent and unclear, very unlike the messages received from BB. For instance, the following words were written in small, tangled scrawls, hard to decipher but containing clear instructions from 'All'.

[Opposite Page] The Quest: intended entry point 1922 (and 1931);
arrow shows puncture made in original photograph by planchette spike

Only way to finish the 3ST work is to start slowly. The condition sine qua non is the keeping of all documents in your own hands. The most difficult part of work is the exit and export. The present time must be used for learn the places near the lighthouse and the palace. On the sea and on the earth.

(Planchette script, Hotel Royal Constantinople, 9.5.22)

Lacking BB's detailed knowledge, 'All' needed to use the Quest group as a window to see clearly. The following evening, 10th May, the instructions were:

I think it is very necessary to see St Irene church. We all see the catacombs better when you are there.

From S.S. (Santa Sophia) walk near to the lighthouse and palace. I think the way in is 50-60 metres east north east. F.L. was on the place exact. 'All'

(Planchette script, Hotel Royal Constantinople, 10.5.22)

The next thing 'All' saw, however, was not a location but a timescale. The message came with baffling precision:

The time of the work is indicated: 1. arrive East - 17.IV.23   2. In - 19.IV.23   3. Exit - 22/23.IV.23   4. Transport - 23.IV.23

(Planchette script, Hotel Royal Constantinople, 11.5.22)

Note the date they specify for a successful attempt on the tunnels — it is April 1923, almost exactly the same date as originally specified by BB (April 27th 1923). TP had tried to ignore this, bringing his attempt a whole year forward because of the difficult political situation in Turkey, but it seems the entities in the Beyond were telling TP that he could not succeed in 1922. He must obey instructions and try again in a year's time.

Whatever he felt about this, we next hear of TP stowing a cache of tools and equipment in a bank vault before returning to England. Once home his letters to Russell resumed their normal frequency, yet he never made reference to that 'lost' month. BB also came back after his prolonged silence in August 1922

[Opposite Page] The Quest: intended exit point 1922 (and 1931); Blue Mosque to the left of the puncture mark, arches of the House of Justinian to the right

*saying he was 'released' and able to communicate again, because his
mother had suffered a miscarriage.*
(Letter from TP to David Russell, 23.11.23)

The silence was over. The third Quest attempt was over. And it was time
for TP to turn his attention to other matters.

The Sage, BB and 'The Sixth'

Since 1904 TP had been in communication with another discarnate
spirit he called 'The Sage'. The Sage differed from BB in that his concerns
were spiritual, as opposed to the material concerns of BB (inventories, tools,
routes and maps) and what The Sage now had to say concerned victims of the
Russian Revolution. TP had been working with Russian exiles, had observed
refugees in Constantinople, and now he must do something about some of
those still suffering in Russia.

*It is laid upon us to take some active steps to alleviate the lot (by clothes,
food and books) of the imprisoned Russian Patriarch, bishop and priests;
many of whom are half starved, in rags and not allowed to communicate
with the outer World... Our friend the Sage is very insistent about the
matter.*
(Letter from TP to David Russell, 25.8.22)

And so began the Appeal for the Russian Clergy. The resulting campaign
proved large and valuable, extending over a decade and bringing in much
vital aid. TP did not doubt The Sage was the origin of this Appeal. Nor did he
doubt further information from his exalted source. The Quest, it seemed, was
no longer just a question of documents, or even of Justinian's entire library;
it was a question of basic spiritual force.

*We are faced by a great Mystery, one which I vowed to solve when
the Cup first came to light at Glastonbury in 1906 and I am quite ready
to devote the rest of my life to its solution.*
*During Jesus' lifetime He was the Cosmic Centre of the earth and after
His transition 'It' remained within the circle of His immediate followers and
was referred to outwardly as the Holy Ghost. The persecution in Palestine
dispersed the first Christian groups and the 'Centre' became transferred to
the keeping, so to speak, of the Early Christian fathers at Constantinople,*

where Santa Sophia was ultimately built to form Its external Shrine.

When the Church etc was destroyed and the movement driven underground the 'Centre', occultly speaking, was in the 'Chapel' [St. George's, ed.] to which we are going and in which are still to be found MSS containing Jesus' hidden teaching and utterances as noted by John, Mark and probably Luke and mainly 'set down' by St Polycarp.

St Peters Rome became the outer centre of Christianity but this inner Centre was never moved, was sealed up and has remained intact. One cannot comprehend what the release of the Forces there focalised will mean to the World, and I believe their release is at hand.

All this comes to me through the Sage who heads a Group working with us in the unseen.

(Letter from TP to David Russell, 2.8.22)

As a result of the Sage's information, TP not only gave practical aid to the Russian Clergy, but was more determined than ever to bring the Quest to a successful conclusion by another attempt on the tunnels beneath Constantinople. However, there was a split in discarnate command. The Sage limited himself to high minded generalities, whilst the practical arrangements were consigned to BB, and BB had a very strange demand to make. The Quest Group could not proceed on another venture in Constantinople, he said, without a specific sixth member. No name was given, although later information included this description of the sixth:

He is six feet tall, agile, thin, red brown hair and moustache, wears light grey clothes usually ('even a light grey morning coat' added BB, as if in great surprise), fond of golf and racing; his ancestors were 'noble'.

(Letter from TP to David Russell, 27.8.23)

That was all anyone had to go on, and, as a final twist of difficulty, the other members of the Quest Group could not go looking for him: he had to find them. By the time the three Russians arrived in England in December 1922 to make final preparations for the next Constantinople attempt, there was still no sixth member. Hopeful bulletins kept coming ('The 6th is very close and we may contact him almost at once.') (letter to Russell, 18.12.22) However, things did not go exactly to plan:

BB says attempts are being made (from the 'Antipodes' on the Other Side) to prevent the '6th' linking up with us, and the Russian trio are

depressed and anxious. BB also said that there were 'listeners in' just now,
so that he could not give the detailed history of the Cup, because it was too
closely associated with the Trieste work.

(Letter from TP to David Russell, 4.1.23)

Whenever BB communicated there was drama, and now he was talking about espionage. Firstly, there were enemies called the 'Antipodes' (because their intentions went in opposite directions to the Quest Group). Secondly, these enemies could listen in on BB (because he operated so close to the Earth). Thirdly, the Quest work was code-named Trieste (often abbreviated to SSST or 3ST [Trieste]) to avoid giving away geographical clues. Meanwhile, the antipodal campaign of spoiling and harassment continued:

Last night BB told us that there had been a battle around the 6th but
that he was 'nearer' to us and all well. He drew a diagram to show his
relation to his own guide; the latter is in the Council [of discarnate Quest
workers] and only awaits the possibility of contact with his protégé to bring
the latter into our midst. BB thinks we may contact him next week, partly
because the 6th has just begun to wonder whether there is a special spiritual
guidance for mortals and so his guide can draw him in more closely.

(Letter from TP to David Russell, 12.1.23)

However, the Antipodes seemed more adept than BB gave them credit for. 1923 dragged on, and the March/April attempt was frustratingly postponed. The Quest for spiritual treasures was getting replaced by a quest for a single anonymous Englishman.

Reading through these bulletins regarding the 6th (of which there is no end) one becomes more and more irritated. There may indeed be more things in heaven and earth than are dreamt of in our philosophies, but they do not seem very well organised. Because of this TP could not settle to any long term plans. His instructions were to hold himself ready to go East and fulfil the Quest whenever chance arose, but who could remain that free? Not TP:

If the 6th has not turned up by the end of August and BB has nothing
definite then to say, I for one must proceed as if the Quest were to be
postponed anyway until next year. In other words I must devise means
for getting directorships or other work bringing in some regular income.
Easier said than done. I shall feel that I for one have gone to the limit that
faith and patience will allow, because it is very evident that the time factor

> *can be controlled no more easily from the unseen World than from here.*
>
> (Letter from TP to David Russell, 17.8.23)

1923 was a bad year all round. In January the French decided to revive World War One by invading the Ruhr. As a result hurricane inflation hit Germany, and exporters such as TP found trade near impossible. In November Adolf Hitler thought enough was enough and mounted the Munich Putsch. Enough wasn't enough, and he was imprisoned.

Other big names of the future were also having problems. Franklin D. Roosevelt was struggling with lower limb paralysis following a polio attack in 1921. Winston Churchill was out of office after the Liberal government fell. Stalin was happier, though, as Lenin was dying. Soon the moustachioed one would be able to weave a very tangled web indeed. Already religious persecution was intensifying in Russia, and TP responded by intensifying his appeal for aid to the Russian Clergy:

> *The Bolsheviks are making systematic war on religion in Russia. Agents of the Tcheka went round the churches seizing the treasures and vestments indiscriminately. Then the Bolsheviks arrested a large number of priests on a charge of resisting the execution of the law. Trials were instituted, and at a big public trial in Moscow in April more priests were sentenced to death. In May the Patriarch himself was arrested. The Metropolitan Benjamin of Petrograd was tried in June and sentenced to death. In all probability he has been murdered.*
>
> *In March, shortly before Easter, the Roman Catholic Archbishop of Petrograd, Monsignor Cieplak and several of his clergy were publicly tried in Moscow. The prosecution violently demanded a death sentence. Archbishop Cieplak and Father Butkevich were condemned to death; the Archbishop's sentence was commuted to one of ten years' imprisonment. Father Butkevich was executed, in spite of appeals for clemency from all parts of the civilised world.*
>
> *The Hon. Secretary, 'Appeal for the Russian Clergy,' 61, St. James' Street, London, S.W.1., will be pleased to receive subscriptions for the purpose of sending parcels of foodstuffs to imprisoned Russian Clergy and their dependants.*
>
> (Document headed 'Religious Persecution In Russia', probably dating mid 1923)

'The Hon. Secretary' was, of course, TP himself and, reviewing all this, he began to wonder if such troubles were all part of a larger problem. By October the Sage was saying yes, they were.

We are faced by grave issues. Civilisation as you know it may not be able to withstand the continued onslaughts that are being made upon it.

During the war there were moments when it seemed as if your world would enter once again the dark valley of old night. The danger was avoided and the human race was saved from terrible events. Many of us hoped the period of great darkness had passed away and that your civilisation could be purified and led forward into the light. This hope is still with us. The Powers of Illumination are available ready to pour themselves out into the hearts and minds of men.

So many doors are closed to us.

We have been faced recently with fresh attacks from the Powers of Negation whose ammunition is the greed and materialism of nations and individuals. Whether your civilisation will weather the storm or pass out to be replaced by temporary chaos is not yet clear to us. I am an optimist but it is necessary that you should know of the battles that are raging in our Spheres.

The Quest upon which you are engaged is part of the campaign launched from on high for the re-illumination and salvation of the race. Its ups and downs are a reflection of the conditions which surround us in the spheres of actual combat. It has been ordained that your Quest shall be fulfilled. We are of the opinion that the work could have been completed at this very hour. Faced by the fresh struggle to which I have referred it is deemed wise to postpone the completion of the Quest.

We are aware of the difficulties by which you are surrounded and the apparent lack of clear guidance from our Sphere. Our love and prayers have never been withdrawn and never can be. Go forward cheerfully and in good fellowship.

(Pencil message, TP handwriting, dating 10.10.23, in Russell archives)

Just in case no one has noticed: this is Armageddon. General Allenby won the earthly Armageddon in September 1918, but the aerial Armageddon was well and truly under way, with victory looking a lot less certain.

Casualties of the Aerial Armageddon

The frustration over the 6th was getting to TP, and by November 1923 his health had broken down.

> *I cannot yet move from bed. The Doctor says I need a long rest, the result of continued nervous and mental strain, and he talks of sunshine and blue sky. It is only when one is laid up that one realises what a strain normal active life is nowadays. Father is not so well and they want me down there, and things at the office are getting difficult, and I cannot yet even walk across the room. In regard to the Quest I cannot help being perturbed by the long delay in connection with the 6th's arrival, a delay which has more or less paralysed my life.*
> (Letter from TP to David Russell, 23.11.23)

A paralysing illness appears almost too symbolic to be accidental. It was diagnosed as a sort of sciatica, but it was to recur time and again in the next ten years, rendering TP more or less constantly in pain. We might wonder why someone with his gifts could not cure himself, but if we consider his financial and spiritual strains, the wonder becomes how he ever survived.

The new year, 1924, was to offer no let up. The War in the Spheres was raging as wildly as ever, and although it might offer remarkable food for thought, it did nothing for TP's health. 'This existence, as during the last 18 months, has become unbearable,' he said, 'and there must be a limit.' Soon he hit that limit:

> *Dear David*
> *Sunday, 4.5.24*
>
> *A wet Sunday afternoon and I am writing to you a selfish letter, all about my own affairs so put it away to read when you have the time as it is not urgent. I am seriously considering what to do with my business life. I am 40 and am where I was when I left the Army in 1919. If the Quest is coming off now then I must postpone decisions until it is over — if I can. But can I? The point is that I have no income of any kind that comes in regularly, that is no paid directorships and no capital invested. I am living on and by my wits and with the occasional loan. I wake up at night sometimes and hear myself shouting aloud at the memory of bills unpaid or liabilities maturing. In other words I have lost my nerve. Outgoings include such fixed items as:- Personal Insurance £110 p.a. Father's Insurance £60 p.a. Office Rent and Taxes £250 p.a. House Rent — purchase and rates £150 p.a. Miss Heyburn [TP's secretary] £250 p.a. Home Expenses £500 p.a.*

School fees £100 p.a. Office Expenses £200 p.a. Clothing for family etc £100 p.a. Help at Letchworth and Port Stewart £100 p.a. Sundries that must be met £150 p.a. In other words £1970 p.a. Say an average of £40 per week to keep going. What ought I to do? As it is I live from hand to mouth in a way that demoralises one's whole being and makes me unfit to carry on a normal life. To borrow money is no solution, rather the contrary and I am often amazed on looking back over the last 4 years to know how I've kept going at all.

I can of course hang on for another month or perhaps two but I must shape my life and not drift indefinitely. Yet what work am I trained for and what chance is there in this country? The usual cry of a million ex army unemployed. Half my time is taken up in listening to other people's business problems and trying to help them, but that work is hardly remunerative.

Well what a screed! After all I am only up against the same problem as thousands of other fellows and presumably there is a solution.

The irony is that most people think I'm prosperous and in a position to support any appeal that comes along and I'm thought mean if I don't.

Well the rain has stopped and so I'll go out for a walk and forget my perplexities for an hour.

Yours ever WTP

He was soon apologising for being 'a burden on one's greatest friend' and explaining that 'I wrote off on Sunday when feeling down at seeing Florence so aged by the constant strain of making sixpence do the work of a shilling'(letter to Russell, 8.5.24) Meanwhile, the planchette communications continued irritatingly optimistic, including, of course, more blithe promises about the 6th.

It was indicated that the time factor was now in the Council's hands and that the antipodes were defeated.

As to the 6th, he was in London, in good health and no barrier now existed between him and us. No actual date was given for his arrival but I am to be here until midday on Saturday and next week.

All this sounds hopeful and suggests that some new development is at hand, unless of course we have been deceived all the way through which is hardly credible.

(Letter from TP to David Russell, 12.8.24)

But was it hardly credible? The saga of the 6th had illustrated a disquieting trend: good and wise spirits appeared limited in power and well capable of mistakes. They seemed to (a) constantly misread the time factor, promising imminent success when it was nothing like, and (b) constantly underestimate the opposition, declaring it defeated when it was anything but. In that sense, they appeared scarcely more adept than the human race who thought World War One had been the war to end all wars. Eventually, the Sage more or less admitted as much:

> *We cannot unveil the future and very few of us here can compute the march of events in your world. No purpose is gained by dwelling upon the apparent mistakes which seem to have been made on both sides of the veil during this period of discipline and preparation.*
>
> *I doubt whether the Quest could have been completed in this generation had it not been for all the experiences that have come to the seen and unseen workers since January 1922. Rest all you can. Refuse to be dismayed. Fear nothing. Thus you will be prepared to take your part in the great drama that is unfolding step by step. Continue to obey the ruling of 'Tous' ['All', the discarnate 'Council', ed.] and B.B. so far as outer Quest events are concerned. All is well.*
>
> (Pencil message, TP's handwriting, Russell files, dated 8.8.24)

So, everyone was learning (which is an interesting concept in itself). And they had plenty more to learn. For instance, were the Antipodes really defeated? Not in TP's part of the universe (or indeed Russell's):

> *I have had a strange time since I saw you. Extraordinary 'pressure' and even curious sort of 'astral' explosions, heard even by Miss Heyburn here and Florence at the house and everything upside down.*
>
> *Early today I heard very clearly:-*
>
> *'Stand perfectly still. Take no action of any sort. You are being used as a lightning conductor. Once the adverse currents have been earthed, danger will cease and the last obstacles to the Quest removed. We did not expect this assault, but it is blind, no intelligence behind it. It is an aftermath.'*
>
> *Is this a partial explanation of our experiences throughout November?*
>
> *I am doing my best to stand still. Perhaps you were laid up just now on purpose to 'stand still' and escape some danger? Some very curious interior events have been going on and perhaps all these tremors (and the*

apparent wreckage of my outer life) are caused by adverse currents being
'earthed' for safety and through me.

(Letter from TP to David Russell, 28.11.24)

Matters were no better in the new year, 1925, with ever more bizarre information coming in. The gist was that while events on Earth might be difficult, they were even more so in 'Borderland', according to a bulletin from BB.

TELEPHONE REGENT 5655.
TELE. CYCLOMETRY.

28/11/24.

61 St. James's Street,
London. S.W 1

Dear David,

You don't say how you are? I trust you are feeling better + rested. And will not attempt work until really fit again. I have wired + written Basiaux + there is nothing to worry about in that direction. Wish I could help you more.

I wonder if the great storm did much damage in Fife? Don't trouble to read or reply to my letters, except to let me know how you are.

I have had a strange time since I saw you. Extraordinary "pressure" + even curious sort of (?Astral) explosions, heard even by Miss Beyburn here + Florence at the house + everything upside down.

Early today I heard very clearly :—

"Stand perfectly still. Take no action of any sort. You are being used as a lightning conductor. Once the adverse currents have been earthed, danger will cease + the last obstacles to the Quest removed. It is unwise for us to attempt communication yet. Let your affairs be shaken down. It will not matter. We did not expect this assault, but it is blind, no Intelligence behind it. It is an aftermath."

Is this a partial explanation of our experiences throughout November?

An example of TP's uniquely clear handwriting,
the content demonstrating his two-worlds concerns

142

> *The currents around our Group, meeting adverse currents from antipodal directions create a difficult situation both for us and for the Group on earth.*
>
> *As a result we have all passed through an unpleasant time. Our Group finds itself in the centre of a 'chaudiere buillonnante' (a bubbling boiler!) and has suffered many difficulties.*
>
> *The most difficult problem that has faced members of the Council has been to intercept attacks aimed at our terrestrial collaborators. We have succeeded to the extent that you only receive blows which cause you inconvenience and unrest but which inflict no vital damage. We are obliged to 'nous precipiter vers la terre' continually in order to deflect invisible and discordant forces from descending upon you.*
>
> *The 6th member of the Group requires our special protection as he is not able to defend himself.*
>
> *We await a lull in spherical conditions and we shall take advantage of such a moment in order to bring WTP and the 6th together. Meanwhile remain firm in faith and tranquil. We will protect you. Light and Peace, BB*

(Pencil message, TP's handwriting, 'Received 9.4.25')

Let us try to imagine how all this works. We appear to have three components in these battles. Firstly, there is the Earth—which we might picture as sending up swirls of gravity (think of searchlights in World War Two). A spirit straying into the wrong place might get tugged down to Earth by one of these swirls and, apparently, thrust into a womb for incarnation.

Secondly, we have BB and his fellows on intelligence missions, trying to get as close to Earth as possible, in order to: (a) see details on the ground (often via human minds) and (b) communicate with those minds. They dodge their way between the swirls, like World War Two pilots avoiding the searchlights.

Thirdly, we have the Antipodes, like enemy aircraft trying to shoot BB and his fellows into one of these searchlights. Presumably BB and the rest would fight back in similar style.

We can almost visualise it (computer games having trained us in the bizarre). Yet can we really accept it as the way the Next World is run (albeit only in its Borderland regions)? Someone unimpressed with the organisation was TP:

> *'Attacks' have been real enough but they have not been properly met.*

'Tous' and BB give us no spiritual weapons with which to fight and yet they expect us to be prepared at a moment's notice to undertake the dangerous Trieste task which they say has been 'Divinely allotted' to us.
(Letter from TP to David Russell, 25.2.25)

Dangerous it may have been, but not dull, although we must remember we are talking only about regions close to Earth. As TP said back in December 1920 concerning 'unseen friends':

They do not dwell in the spheres of omnipotence, but in the Borderland of Conflict, battling to save the Soul of the World.
(Letter from TP to Mary Bruce Wallace, 3.12.20)

'Spheres of omnipotence' are one thing: Borderland is another. Right now, though, TP had had enough of it all. It was time to put the whole BB thing on one side. Frederick Leveaux was thinking the same:

In July 1925, WTP and FL decided that the 'Quest' should continue under new methods, under the spiritual guidance of WTP, and more years of waiting for the accomplishment of the Quest had to take place.
('The Quest', p.23, private typescript by Renée Nicol, 1958)

Yes, it was time to get free, get out, get a life. TP liked travel. He had been invigorated by all the wartime experiences in the Near East. He had been energised by his Quest attempts of 1907, 1907/8 and 1922 in Constantinople. BB had done him no favours keeping him incarcerated in England.

Now it was time for change. After all, neither he nor the world could go on being under strain forever. The 1923 French invasion of the Ruhr had been replaced by the Dawes Plan of 1924, designed to fix Germany's reparations problem and let the European nations settle down to a few years of friendly relaxation. The 1920's could be a lot of fun if only people could stop worrying and get on with a bit of living.

Perhaps the signal was given when the Prince of Wales, that eligible, handsome young fellow, was seen dancing the Charleston in 1925. Soon everyone was doing the Foxtrot, the Tango, the Black Bottom, or all three. Churchill danced across the House of Commons and joined the Conservatives. Hitler had already danced out of Landsberg prison. Even Roosevelt was getting up and active on his crutches. TP felt like a bit of movement too. Rome seemed worth a few visits. Algeria also. It was time for fresh horizons.

8. Journeys, Sacred and Secular: 1925-1929

The mid-to-late twenties were playtime. The human race (European section) had been through some tough lessons in the last ten years—Physical Exercise in the mud followed by a harsh Economics session, so it was nice to get out in the playground and have some fun. The naughty boys who had been squabbling a few years back made up, thanks to the Locarno Pacts (1925), and that sulky little country who had lost his pocket money cheered up when the Dawes Plan (1924) eased his reparations.

Looking through the playground rails, it was obvious the kids were at the stage of adolescent rebellion. (So our mothers had waists, did they? We don't like that fashion; let's merge the waist with the hips. Our mothers had busts, did they? Flatten them. Big hair? Let's wear skull-hugger hats.)

And all the while that interesting Uncle across the Atlantic (the one with the roguish grin) kept sending across treats. He'd been ever so useful at helping break up the 1918 fight (and of course any hint of naval rivalry and potential war had been quickly diverted by the Washington Naval Conference in 1922). Now he sent over Charlestons, Black Bottoms, quaint tales of quaint gangsters shooting quaint holes in each other, pyramid selling, stratospheric share prices and—finally—just to prove you should never trust an Uncle with a roguish grin—the Great Depression.

That was it. Playtime over. Back in the classroom, and if you thought the previous syllabus was tough, just wait for the next one.

The mid-to-late twenties had their uses, though. They provided a break from anything too deep or demanding, and nobody needed it more than Wellesley Tudor Pole. The Saga Of The Sixth had kept him penned and ineffective in London, but now he set off to places like Italy and Algiers where he could be less penned and a lot more effective.

Italian Ventures

The initial reason for his Rome trip was to see about investing capital on behalf of the financier, George Leavey. The scheme was for land reclamation in the Gargano peninsula (which, if you regard Italy as a boot, is the spur on the heel of that boot). The prospect didn't look too good at first, but persistence made it look better, and by July 1925 he was able to tell David Russell

> *My trip to Gargano and Lesina was successful and it looks as if this business would go through well. Wish I had time to describe all my*

experiences. Lake Lesina is a large sinister stagnant spectral stretch of shallow water, surrounded by many miles of malarial swamps and marshes. A regular plague spot, where 80% of the population are infected. It is also a focus for evil Astral forces, and I realised for the first time that Malaria is primarily an Astral disease. I am delighted to be connected with this undertaking which will turn a hundred square kilometres into a happy healthy fruitful region.

(Letter from TP to David Russell, 2.7.25)

He was accompanied by, amongst others, Count Pecorini, a Venetian businessman, who dictated his own account of the trip, offering some fascinating flavour-of-the-age as he describes Southern Italy in the 1920's.

The inhabitants all yellow from malaria, the children naked on the roads, showing their swollen bodies, make us think our drainage work as a blessed work of redemption. Lesina, like all the other towns of the Gargano, does not know what modern comfort is. The towns are without sewers, aqueducts, electricity, tramways, and the greater part of the inhabitants are illiterate. Afflicted by malaria, they live a life of superstition, which seems to be the only thing which distinguishes them from the animals surrounding them. We do not want only to bring material comfort to these people, but with the drainage work, we desire to provide for their moral improvement. We hope to establish schools and teach the young generations that life can be lived in a different way.

('Journey To The Gargano, dictated by Count Daniele Pecorini', July 1925, Russell archives)

On the same trip TP and Count Pecorini visited Monte Gargano with its famous sanctuary of St Michael. Then they called in on a famous holy man living nearby, one still venerated by Roman Catholics today, Padre Pio.

Soon after noon Padre Pio emerged, after seven hours in the Confessional Box, and we followed him into the Sacristy. He is a man of medium height, dressed in the simple garb of the Franciscan Order. His hair and beard are brown and his brown eyes seem aflame with an inner fire.

We asked his blessing upon the work of freeing the district of Foggia in Southern Italy from the age-long curse of malaria. We were rewarded by a wonderful smile and the promise of prayers and help. I noticed that Padre Pio wore mittens to cover the marks of the stigmata on his hands, and that he walked with difficulty, owing to the wounds on his feet.

He gave me the impression of being a simple-minded, child-like soul, filled with an other-worldly spiritual ardour. I can well understand how pilgrims from many nations and of diverse faiths have been drawn to San Giovanni by the influence of this holy soul.

Locally Padre Pio is looked upon as a reincarnation of St Francis, and the people speak of him with reverence and the light of loving adoration in their eyes.

('Padre Pio of Pietrelcina', typescript by TP, 20.7.25)

There was a practical two-worlds aspect to the visit because TP and his partners needed help 'to induce the sturdy peasants from the Gargano hills above to come down to this disease-infested valley to work as labourers and artisans.' Padre Pio was that help.

He showed keen interest in our undertaking and told me to let it be known throughout the district that he had blessed our work and all who were engaged upon it. This I did. Within a week over two hundred of the hill folk—men, women and children—had come down from the hills to offer their services. The only accommodation we could provide at the time was a tin shack where meals could be served, and the bell tents for sleeping quarters. The deadly mosquito was soon at work, as the necessary netting for protection was in short supply. During a period of over eighteen months not a single case of malaria was reported among them, and our workers finally returned to their hillside and forest homes cheerful, and in the best of health.

('The Silent Road', 1960 ps.81-82)

Backed by such formidable resources the project duly prospered under the acronym SACI (Sindicato Agricolo Cooperativo Italiano), and by November TP was able to report that

Our vast and interesting undertaking moves forward, slowly but surely, and I feel that the foundations are secure. SACI now has control of the Government reclamation and irrigation works in the Gargano; some 8000 acres of land (good soil and on the proposed railway route); control of the Railway contract and of its operation, and a considerable interest in the valuable Lesina fishing rights. If we could now secure a controlling interest in the Banca di Pughlia, then with the Land, Reclamation work,

Railway and Bank, we should have the whole of the Gargano region in our hands, and be able to develop industries and agriculture on sound paying lines. In fact we should be Kings of a large section of a fruitful province, containing 500,000 people, and our potency for good could be immense.

(Letter from TP to David Russell, 18.11.25)

La ferrovia del Gargano
Una relazione dell'on. Canelli al Capo del Governo

L'onorevole Canelli ha redatto per il Capo del Governo, un breve memoriale sulla Garganica. Il memoriale contiene alcune date, che segnano le fasi attraverso le quali la pratica è passata negli ultimi anni, cioè in regime fascista. Le date sono queste:

15 *Dicembre* 1923. — Il Consiglio Provinciale Fascista di Capitanata delibera un sussidio chilometrico di 1000 lire-oro.

11 *Settembre* 1924. — L'on. Mussolini riceve una rappresentanza della Regione, alla

Tramvie del Mezzogiorno » concessionaria della Garganica, in luogo del « Sindacato » al quale deve ritenersi subentrata.

30 *Aprile* 1927. — È redatto il progetto esecutivo, che trasforma per tutta la linea lo scartamento in *normale*, la trazione in *elettrica*, con *stazione unica* a S. Severo e *variante* per S. Marco in Lamis.

30 *Luglio* 1927. — Il Consiglio Superiore dei LL. PP. esprime voto favorevole su tale progetto.

27 *Agosto* 1927 — Interrogazione dell'o-

Italian newspaper report from the 1920s on TP's Gargano project

Part of the good he planned was for 'a Riviera on model lines, without Casino but with tennis, golf, bathing, fishing and sailing' *(letter to David Russell, 5.10.28)*. As history and humanity would have it, they did not get that far, although the main work of drainage and infrastructure prospered, and nowadays Gargano is described in the brochures as an unspoilt region with breathtaking scenery and picturesque fishing villages. Meanwhile, news of such transformative efforts spread, and more offers were coming in:

> *Whilst in Rome and since returning from Italy I have been approached indirectly both through Mussolini and H. H. Cremonesi, Lord Mayor of Rome, in connection with the important building and re-building operations that have been decided upon by the Government for the improvement of the Capital, and the development of its resources — to include of course the full protection of its antiquities. The possibilities in connection with these projects are very great.*
>
> (Letter from TP to David Russell, 7.7.26)

And so another land development company was born, usually referred to as 'Aureliana' after the section of Rome they worked on. TP's impression of Mussolini is worth mentioning:

> *I saw Mussolini speaking from a Balcony. He looked like an ardent spirit, quite ruthless, a flame that was wearing out the body very rapidly.*
>
> (Letter from TP to David Russell from Rome, 24.6.25)

This deserves thought. We are used to considering Mussolini as a strutting fool who followed chicken-like after Hitler and led Italy into misery. But that was Mussolini mark two. Mussolini mark one (the 1920's version) was admired by many (including that noted anti-totalitarian, Winston Churchill). So what brought about the change? Maybe he did indeed burn himself out as TP foresaw, except not the body but the soul. However, before that burn-out he achieved much, as TP insisted on telling a sceptical press:

> *Though we may not agree with the Fascisti regime, yet any unbiased traveller touring Italy cannot help being struck by the happiness of the people in town and country, and the wonderful way in which the whole country is at work.*
>
> (Correspondence column, 'Daily Express', 27.10.26)

Three years later TP still felt positive, although once again he feared burn-out:

> *The work Mussolini has done and is doing for babies, children and youth is perhaps his most remarkable achievement and more ought to be known about it abroad. But can he safely cram into one generation the energy and work normally needing at least a century to unfold?*
> (Letter from TP to David Russell, 9.5.29)

Within a few years, alas, such questions would be answered, but for now Italy seemed a good place to do some planetary uplift, and TP's two schemes, Gargano and Aureliana, seemed highly promising. So long as the country and its leader remained un-burnt-out (Mussolini mark one, in effect), the monetary investments would be safe.

TP and Ivan Basiaux high in the
Atlas Mountains with an esparto grass milling machine

North African Ventures

TP's other area of foreign activity was North Africa. Once again, the reason was business, but this time the business involved his good friend, David Russell. The Tullis-Russell mills needed esparto grass to turn into paper, and Algeria supplied the right sort. So far so good. However, Russell's accountant, John Black, thought a bit of swindling might be going on at the Algerian end, whereas TP thought it was a bit of misunderstanding. So off went TP to Algiers in October 1924 to find out. He duly met one of the Basiaux brothers, who ran the agency out there:

> *The younger Basiaux seems quite straight, but impulsive, and he was only too ready to show me everything. There is no sign of double dealing and no cause for anxiety on that score. He confesses their error in buying Tunisian grass for your account so heavily last year and that of course is stopped entirely.*
>
> *These concession contracts require closer scrutiny and control from your end; Basiaux Frères have had too free a hand and it is fortunate that they are honest and on the whole very businesslike in their methods of bookkeeping and checking stocks.*
>
> (Letter from TP to David Russell, 5.10.24)

TP might be happy, but John Black remained unconvinced. The solution was as follows:

> *Owing to the very evident feud between Basiaux and Black (for which there may be some justification on both sides) we must lift the grass business out into an independent company in which you hold the bulk of the 8% Preference Shares and 51% of the Ordinary Shares with a Board consisting of yourself Chairman, possibly myself, the two Basiaux and another representative of the Scotch side.*
>
> (Letter from TP to David Russell, 11.7.25)

And there we are. By a dose of diplomacy and a bit of business acumen, TP had turned a divisive situation into a useful one, forming a new company, known by its acronym EAAN (Exploitation Alfatieres de L'Afrique Du Nord). Not only that, he acquired some more friends, taking his daughter Jean, now 13, out to stay with the Basiaux family in April 1927, then bringing their daughter, Yvonne, back to stay in England. ('Jean and Yvonne were enormously affected by seeing the Eclipse at Southport'—letter to Russell, 8.7.27)

At this period TP was visiting both Italy and North Africa once or twice a year. If we want a flavour of the North African business, we can accompany him on the trip of November 1929. On this occasion he had no less a companion than John Black, the suspicious accountant, and he was determined that Black should enjoy the visit but also develop a sympathetic attitude towards their business partners. The venture did not begin well, as

TP wrote from Algiers:

> *The poor man arrived a perfect wreck. Had been violently sick and*
> *had jammed a finger in the door, result a nasty bruise and a lost nail. I*
> *drove him to the hotel, gave him a bath and some tea and put him to bed*
> *where he remains. He wanted his door and window locked for fear 'an*
> *Arab with a knife might try to get in'!? How he will manage in the desert*
> *I cannot think.*
>
> (Letter from TP to David Russell, 10.11.29)

We might recall TP devoted much time and energy to his unofficial
unpaid agency for the assistance of the anxious and distressed, and here
we can see him exporting the practice. The measures seemed to work, and
a week later Black was in better spirits, ready to appreciate a tour of several
thousand kilometres through Algeria and Tunisia.

> *Mr Black has recovered and is enjoying the journey in his own way*
> *and gathering impressions faster than he can absorb them. He finds the*
> *pace a little trying. Weather is now glorious but somewhat cold. We reach*
> *Tebessa tonight. From Tebessa we go into Tunisie next Wednesday. I have*
> *shown Black the wonderful Constantine gorge, one of the greatest sights*
> *in the world; a stupendous natural phenomenon; but he has no eye for*
> *natural wonders and it is not easy to rouse his enthusiasm or even interest.*
> *However he gets on quite well with Yvan (Basiaux) and begins to realise*
> *some of the problems that face the grass producer.*
>
> (Letter from TP to David Russell, 17.11.29)

There were a few other comments—about such matters as gracious
behaviour and developing 'savoir faire'—which tell us quite a bit about TP's
own modus operandi. Indeed, bearing in mind his careful, affable approach,
the question once again arises as to why he never got rich, or even, for that
matter, reliably comfortable.

As for the North African trip, its interest did not let up, but Black's
reservations gradually did, as TP wrote from Tebessa:

> *Here at 3500 feet it is bitterly cold with heavy winds. Mr Black is now*
> *much better and is enjoying the journey in his own way. It will do him a*
> *great deal of good and I am very glad he came. We leave for the frontier and*
> *Sfax tomorrow and have made a comprehensive inspection of the Tebessan*

concessions which are 100 miles across country both mountainous and wild, where bandits still abound and where vipers and cobras (actually!) are still found. The French Governor of the area has most kindly housed both Mr Black and myself as the local hotel is impossible. Black begins to realise the problems of such a concession as this and will I hope give you a full report in his own way.

(Letter from TP to David Russell, 19.11.29)

Note how TP has three times used the phrase, 'in his own way.' Note too his concern in both letters that Black should 'realise the problems' faced by business partners. Such stress on empathy underlines his approach, and it worked well. John Black may have been reserved during the trip itself, but afterwards he called it the most wonderful experience of his life and wrote the whole thing up for the Rothmill Magazine in Fife (so he really had been taking it all in).

Revival of Spiritual Centres

As for TP, productive journeys in the outer world could not entirely satisfy him. He needed progress in the inner worlds, for which Constantinople was a key interface. Since progress there continued to be strangely blocked, his attention became focused on somewhere nearer home. A typescript by Frederick Leveaux recounts some remarkable events at Tintern Abbey in May 1925. These may be taken as introducing a new phase in TP's life, so we must pay them proper attention. In the following account Leveaux refers to himself as FL.

FL was staying at the Hotel opposite the Abbey, and having work to do had a sitting room. TP paid him visits on one or two occasions, and after dinner they went to FL's private room and sat before the fire. TP saw in the room that evening a discarnate being who had been a monk at Tintern, and he called himself Brother Brighill. This may not have been the monk's first appearance to WTP. There appeared beside the Monk the beings known to TP and FL as Jack and the Sage.

('Visit to Tintern Abbey in May and June 1925', typescript by F. Leveaux; Leveaux archives)

The Sage we have already met. Jack, another discarnate being, had previously been a friend in this world. His full name was John de Carrich

Cheape, and before the war family problems had resulted in his being a ward of TP's. He was killed on the Somme on 3rd September 1916, since when he had, TP felt, been frequently and usefully in touch. One area of usefulness was that he 'spoke the language' and in the hotel at Tintern he did so in more ways than one, translating Brother Brighill's Latin into contemporary thought, which TP approximately relayed to the rapidly scribing Leveaux. Here is part of the result. It includes many names, but they are fascinating ones, so perhaps the reader will tolerate substantial quotation.

> *Brother Brighill put his finger on a 'map' and where he did so there was a light (almost a blaze). He touched Chapel Hill, Tintern (which we are told was formerly known as the Hill of the Brig, the name of a stream) and then touched Weary-all Hill and the Tor, Glastonbury, the Hill of Mount Avala in Jugo-slavia, Mount Scopus in Jerusalem, near certain stones where TP and FL had once lingered, and then the Seraglio Hill at Istanbul; his hand then went back as if linking-up these places. He then put his finger on Iona, Holy Island, St Margaret's Chapel Edinburgh, and St Albans Cathedral. Later on he went to the former Oratory of the TP family at Clifton, as if working something out. He then touched a spot in Provence (possibly Avignon or St Michel de Frigolet).*
>
> *After some conversation Jack and Brother Brighill compared the Map with another, and TP saw places lighted up in Tibet, Persia, Abyssinia, the Black Forest, and a spot in mid Atlantic; and a blaze of light came from the place known to us as 'SSSt.'*
>
> ('Visit to Tintern Abbey in May and June 1925', typescript by F. Leveaux; Leveaux archives)

'SSSt', their code name for Trieste, reminds us that they would be listening carefully for clues about the Quest, although the time for its resumption had not yet come. Other activities were on the way. It has become almost a commonplace of New Age endeavour to work on reviving 'spiritual centres', but back in the Twenties it was a rarity. TP had already, in pre-war years, quested around Glastonbury and Iona with his 'triad of maidens', as well as initiating a search in Ireland for the 'Holy Isle of the West' (see next chapter). Now, in the mid-to-late 1920's, he was about to set new projects in motion. A visit to Cornwall, once again with Leveaux as companion, provided the impetus as he discovered more about the kinds of places specified by Brother Brighill.

I was given extraordinary light and information on St Michael's Mount. A spiritual renaissance is coming gradually. St Michael and his Angels are directing this spiritual flow as they have done in past ages, and the two St Michaels (Cornwall and Normandy) are psychic Centres where invisible groups of Workers under his Banner have their focal points (among other places) in contacting this planet and especially the British Isles.

The psychic centres stretch from St Michaels Mount through a 'lost' centre on Dartmoor on to Avalon, then to Tintern, Holy Isle Anglesey and across to Holy Isle Northumberland, then across to Iona where the living psychic strand linking these 'spiritual lungs' of our Nation branches, one branch going to Tara and a hidden centre in Western Island, and from there back to St Michael's Mount; the other going North East to a spot in the far Highlands.

From there a strand goes South to link up the secondary centres which include St Margaret's Chapel Edinburgh, a place in the hills near Malvern, the St Albans Letchworth centre; on to the 'Coronation' stone Westminster and from there back to St Michael's Mount.

Contact with European and Near Eastern centres is through the 'chain' linking St Michael's Mount with Mont St Michel; these are two spiritual wireless receiving and transmitting stations.

When the Beacon lights at the psychic focal points dim or go out, the spiritual life of the Nation declines and the civilisation goes. When such centres in China, Persia, Egypt, Greece, Rome lost their power these civilisations went and it would be the same with British and Western civilisation.

All this was 'told' me by one of the guardians of the Mount, who is of the Order of St Michael; and as I stood beneath that wonderful Cross there, I found myself in the air at night looking down on the British Isles and could watch the light radiation from the various centres and the pulsating chains of 'fire' that linked them together.

(Letter from TP to David Russell, 27.1.28)

Perhaps predictably, TP found himself enlisted in another spiritual campaign.

I was asked to form a group of people, ultimately to become an Order, to think and work for these sacred centres, to make pilgrimage to them and to carry out other activities.

(Letter from TP to David Russell, 27.1.28)

At this TP paused for a while, deciding what to do next. A round-robin invitation to likely participants seemed the best plan, so the following March he sent out his invitations:

> *Those who take a real interest in these centres should form themselves into groups, each group to be associated with a particular shrine or holy spot. Later, such groups might be linked together to form an Order with St Michael as its patron, an effort being made to work in association with the unseen Guardians whose duty it is to watch over and protect these sacred places.*
>
> *Those who desire to form or join such groups are asked to communicate confidentially with Mr. W. Tudor Pole, 61, St. James's Street, London, S.W.1*
>
> (Chalice Well Archives, Box file 10: document dated 5.3.28)

One shrine that TP himself was to focus on was Chalice Well in Glastonbury, which he effectively bought for the nation in 1959, and which since then has become a powerful and joyful place for pilgrimage or visits. Back in 1928, though, TP was busy researching St Michael, and that autumn he published an article about where and when Michael sanctuaries came into recognition. Here come some more of those names fascinating to trace on a map.

> *The legendary record of the Archangel's footsteps in the Christian era takes us from Bethlehem and Mount Tabor, Palestine, to Colossae (Phrygia) in the first century A.D., then to Constantinople and the shores of the Bosphorus in the fourth Century, and from there via Mt Avala, in Serbia, to the Gargano [TP's area of land reclamation, ed.] in Southern Italy, in A.D. 391, Rome A.D. 590, and then across Europe to the two St Michael Mounts which became Sanctuaries to St Michael from about A.D. 708 and onwards to this day.*
>
> (From 'St Silas-the-Martyr, Kentish Town, 21st Anniversary Number, September-October 1928)

As we read all this, we might imagine that TP was having a splendid time spiritually in the mid-to-late twenties. Yet the opposite was true. His Tintern and St Michael's experiences were exceptions to an otherwise frustrating rule. He just could not make contact with the other world like before. Nor did he consider others were doing better. Eventually, he emerged from the isolation inflicted on him by BB and set about correcting a few misapprehensions. He had not published a book since Private Dowding in 1917, but he did not mind having a go at someone who had.

Writings Published and Unpublished

Sir Arthur Conan Doyle, creator of Sherlock Holmes, had been playing spiritual detectives and felt he knew what was coming up, letting the public know about a few tasty disasters on the way. TP was not happy about this, telling Sir Arthur that people had quite enough to worry about.

> *Conan Doyle is highly diverting. His guide 'Phineas' (whose predictions so far have been fulfilled he says) tells CD that the world is on the eve of a gigantic Cataclysm, a greater upheaval even that the Atlantean Deluge. Hundreds of millions of people are to disappear (mainly the wicked ones apparently) and we shall have several years of earthquakes, tidal waves and volcanic eruptions. The genesis of it all is to be found around the North Pole. He talks as calmly and confidently about all this as Rawson [TP's 'Silent Minute' soldier friend of 1917] used to talk about the end of the World. He seemed rather taken aback by my friendly comments and showed that he has not even a groundwork knowledge of Occultism or Metaphysics. 'The same sort of things on a smaller scale have happened before,' he said, 'and why not again? The world needs a great awakening.' I enquired whether this meant that natural human evolution had broken down and was it a confession of failure on the part of the Divine and he said, 'No, it was all part of the Plan.'*
>
> *And this from the acknowledged leader of the Spiritualist Movement!*
>
> *Probably the time has come for some of us to come out into the arena again. I can't sit silent indefinitely whilst so much rubbish is being sown right and left.*
>
> (Letter from TP to David Russell, 21.5.25)

Conan Doyle, of course, was not a man to retreat under fire, and he attempted to defend his position, informing TP about his guide's prowess:

> *He has foretold with accuracy so many things which have actually happened—some of them quite improbable ones—that I am bound to take him very seriously. Then there are the sixty independent corroborations*

from all parts of the Globe. I have them all—or nearly all—typed and could show you them. They would take a lot of explaining away. Some deal with one aspect and some with another, but they all fit with the connected scheme as given to me.

(Letter from Conan Doyle to TP, 25.9.25)

TP was unimpressed, suggesting to Conan Doyle that intelligences in the Beyond might actually get things wrong:

You are probably aware that in the sphere immediately around this world, events likely to project themselves upon the earth often appear either in magnified or distorted form, making it extremely difficult for onlookers on that side to gauge either time-factors or the exact manner in which events will manifest in the world. The difficulty is to know whether our friends on the other side can read astral distortion and magnification in the correct manner.

(Letter from TP to Conan Doyle, 27.9.26)

We know well enough where TP's reservations came from after his experiences with the Quest attempt of 1922 (not to say the lady psychics of 1907). He might trust informants of the stature of Abdul Baha, but not any Tom, Dick or Spook. As for his own abilities, he was in the middle of a spiritual drought. So what does a man of two worlds do in such circumstances? How about a book?

The book that TP wrote was called The Cosmic Touch, and no one seems to know a thing about it. He wrote it in 1926 for his and Russell's Deeper Issues Series, but J.W. Watkins, the publisher, said No, and TP was not the man to go barging insensitively on. Therefore, all that remains of The Cosmic Touch is a set of disorganised carbon copies in the Russell papers at St Andrews.

The best place to begin on it would be TP's draft introduction, because it helps give the feel of the age, and one way it felt, beneath all the jolly frivolity, was tense.

The great European War of 1914-1918 has left much misery behind it and has proved to the World once more that material force can solve none of the great problems by which mankind is faced. Out of this war was born, among much else, the Russian Revolution. Many thinkers believe this latter event is likely to produce greater changes and upheavals than the Great War which preceded it. Meanwhile the consciousness of man has become leavened with new forces and fresh ideas. So far as the Western World is concerned the mental stagnation and the materialistic outlook of the 19th Century have given place to a period of great restlessness. The reactions from the War and the Revolution have created mental and spiritual tension, making it difficult for the individual to retain inner serenity and poise.

(TP: 'The Cosmic Touch', draft introduction, 1926)

That, perhaps, is the picture we retain of the twenties: people frantically dancing to 'Tiger Rag' or 'Yes, Sir, That's My Baby', as though to distract themselves from some unspeakable malaise. T.S. Eliot spoke something of it in The Waste Land, the unions mimed some of it in the General Strike. Churchill, always on the look-out for a dragon to slay, and now a Conservative, attacked the very workers he had supported as a Liberal. Even the Church of England was at war over the revised Book of Common Prayer. Meanwhile King George V fell dangerously ill with a chest infection, and while the surgeons operated, there were 'flappers' in the streets nearby, shocking their elders by smoking in public or applying lipstick in full view, before stepping into smart hotels to drink cocktails. As TP said in continuation:

Restlessness is in the air; indeed to such an extent is this the case that there are many who predict the coming of world-shaking cataclysms and catastrophes.

(TP: 'The Cosmic Touch', draft introduction, 1926)

And they were coming alright, not the Conan Doyle ones, but events sufficient to shake people thoroughly. The book, having shown us one picture, went on to discuss another:

Throughout history mystics and seers have become aware during moments of ecstasy of the One Life Principle upon which our whole Universe is based, but we are never told in any detail how it is possible to bring about this relation, or how to become conscious of what may be termed the Cosmic Touch in our own lives.

(TP: 'The Cosmic Touch', draft introduction, 1926)

This is a highly promising opening. Is TP about to tell us how to do it? Not totally, but he does quote many encouraging examples from, for instance, Jacob Boehme, Abu Saad, St Teresa and Edward Carpenter. As for his own experiences, he does, with due hesitation, log some, and these might be worth a look, as offering precise data in an area where precision is hard to come by.

> *Some years before the war I was sitting alone in my study on a peaceful summer evening with the windows open to the setting sun. Without warning the room became filled with the tumult of rushing wind, yet the evening was a quiet one and I noticed with surprise that the curtains were still. The wind ceased as suddenly as it had begun and was followed by a strange and complete silence. Then the four walls and the objects in the room seemed to dissolve so that they became transparent. Values changed. The material objects around me became unreal and illusory. I passed into a new dimension of consciousness and in a flash the spiritual realities underlying the external world became a part of me, or I a part of them. A sense of exaltation took possession of me until my mind lost itself in a feeling of inexpressible joy.*
>
> *I felt as if I knew God, understood Creation and the goal toward which mankind is striving. I was lifted into the heavenly heights and the light within and around me became unbearable. It seemed as if the true purpose of life had become revealed in a blinding flash and I could hear myself repeating over and over again — Thank God! Thank God! Thank God!*
>
> *I remember that I was struck by the fact that I could hear the clock ticking, although the clock and the mantelpiece on which it stood had become invisible. Centuries seemed to pass and then the room came back into view, the silence left me and I found that the whole experience had occupied less than five minutes.*
>
> (TP; 'The Cosmic Touch', typescript pages 19 & 20)

The still curtains and ticking clock seem particularly eloquent details — emphasising, by contrast, the rushing then the silence. It is somewhat characteristic of TP that while he is zooming into one world, he still retains a noticing toehold in the other. He goes on to say that this was one of a number of such events.

> *Experiences somewhat similar to the one just described have come to me since and at the most unexpected times and places. During sleep, in the Desert, in the King's Chamber within the Great Pyramid of Gizeh, on the battlefield in Palestine, on a Scotch hilltop, in Factories and in the Street. Suddenly time ceases to exist, a great silence descends usually following the rushing of a mighty wind, material objects dissolve and then comes the*

sense of AT-ONEMENT with the Centre and Circumference of all Life.

I suppose it is impossible to convey to others the depth and significance of such experiences as these. One's angle of vision changes to such an extent that the so-called tangible realities of everyday life become illusory to the point of non-existence and the intangible spiritual forces which invisibly surround us always, become actual and even visible. This awareness of Cosmic realities must be a spiritual and mental process, a faculty lying dormant within us all. Our task is to awaken this faculty so that it may serve our purposes and enrich our lives.

(TP: 'The Cosmic Touch', typescript pages 21& 22)

Nowadays an anthology of such experiences might easily squeeze its way onto the heaving shelves of New Age uplift. Not so in 1926. TP was convinced it filled a gap, and in 1931 a German translator thought similarly, but in England, Watkins, the publisher, begged to differ:

Herbert von Krumhaar wants to know if there is any objection to an authorised German translation being prepared? I don't agree with Watkins that there is no room for a small book on Cosmic experiences and am sorry he put us off.

(Letter from TP to David Russell, 5.1.31)

And that is the last we hear of The Cosmic Touch*. If Herbert von Krumhaar did translate and publish it, TP never mentioned the fact, so— barring unexpected updates from Germany—that is where the matter rests.

Family and Health

This was a time, however, when TP faced deeper distress than lost publishing opportunities. His father, Thomas Pole, died on 11th June 1926 (although, of course, TP would insist that no death takes place, only a transition). His mother followed soon after, somewhat unexpectedly, on 19th September 1926. TP reported that his sister Katharine 'was very brave,' but his other sister struggled, as did his brother.

---

* During this period TP and David Russell put a great deal of time and effort into helping publish The Scripts of Cleophas by Geraldine Cummins, alleged discarnate communications giving details of early Christianity in extraordinary detail. They were first published in 1928 and drew approving reviews from prestigious contemporary academics, including Professors at the Universities of London, Edinburgh and St Andrews.

I found Mary much broken up and looking older, but she has regained self control and fortunately has her husband and child to fill her life with interest. Alex feels the loss very severely; he has been anxious to marry for a long time, but he meets so few nice girls in his wanderings.

Frederick Leveaux has been very nice and sympathetic but he is somewhat importunate:— 'Why don't I go away for a change? Why do I work so long at the office? Why do I publish a book [well, try] when my psychic faculties are under a cloud? Why don't I take some steps to get them back?' And so on, when I would far prefer to be allowed to go my own way quietly, and allow the psychic side to return in its own good time.

(Letter from TP to David Russell, 1.10.26)

'Its own good time' occurred, briefly, the following April while TP was in Rome, and he hurried to tell Mary and Katharine about it.

Darling M & K,

This morning at 9 a.m. Mother came through quite surely and clearly. I was just going to have my coffee at the Regina Hotel and was not thinking about her, so it came as a great and pleasant surprise. I wired you at once. She was so overflowing that I could hardly keep pace, but I think she will find it easier now to get through fairly regularly. Everything is going well with Father and herself and she is now able to use her faculties and her new body, move about easily, understand what she sees and hears. Says she cannot yet get information easily about earth affairs, except those affecting our immediate home selves, the little ups and downs of our daily lives that can be sensed by the way our thoughts run. Apparently conditions round our planet are pretty awful and so all psychic contacts difficult.

(Letter from TP to Mary and Katharine, 6.4.27)

And difficult they remained. Indeed, looking back on it all, he realised that

Sometime in 1927 there were further 'spherical upheavals' and in some way not yet clear to me, my clairvoyant power received a shock during this so-called 'attack' and has never fully recovered.

(Letter from TP to David Russell, 31.3.30)

Part of the problem may have been physical. He did not like to pay a lot of attention to this side of things, but ever since 1923 he had been liable to attacks of 'sciatica', and Florence was paying attention even if he wasn't. Finally she thought she had better tell Russell about a recent trip to Algeria:

> *I thought he would be likely to die out there as he was really so very ill. I think he has come through a serious crisis, and might easily have had heart failure, or brain fever. He is still most unfit, and says himself he feels such brain lassitude that he doesn't know how to set to work again tomorrow.*
>
> *I have woken up to the fact that he is gradually taking on the habits of chronic semi-invalidism, always having meals in bed, never any visitors at home because he is too tired, never going out to a theatre or to see friends as he sometimes used, but he just lies in an armchair with his feet up and has Bengers food brought to him. (This is perhaps an exaggeration, but not altogether.)*
>
> *I am telling you this because I am getting so used to his always lying about and requiring waiting on that I take it as a matter of course. No one else knows, because in front of other people he is always bright and lively. I want him to have at least a month's real rest.*
>
> (Letter from Florence Tudor Pole to David Russell, 15.7.28)

His problem was a mystery which would not be solved till 1934. In the meantime, sciatica alone could not account for every symptom, but it did seem a factor, as he finally admitted to Russell.

> *I have had a return of acute sciatica and can neither move nor sit still without violent pain. I hope this will prove only a brief aftermath and fortunately this is a slack week.*
>
> (Letter from TP to David Russell, 7.8.28)

And that was the trouble: he had to rely on slack weeks to get any sort of rest. Some businessmen prospered in the twenties, but TP was not one of them, and it was only through his trips to Italy and Algeria that he earned enough commission to keep going. Indeed, he and Florence had to sell their house to afford the children's school fees, but, typically for TP, the situation acquired a positive side. They could live on a houseboat. The one in Cairo had been named 'Thames', so what should they call its English cousin?

Our home address for the next few weeks will be:
THE NILE HOUSEBOAT, Palace Reach, East Molesey, Surrey
(Letter from TP to Miss Bell, Russell's secretary, 14.12.28)

It sounds like the family had great fun in winter.

The weather here has changed and we had a tremendous downpour last night so that the River is running very full. One takes a lively interest in the vagaries of nature when one is living as close as we are to nature, but the boat is very warm and comfortable, and the children are much enjoying the novelty of the situation and so far have been able to get in rowing exercise each day. We also have a fairly large barn near the garden where they can play Ping Pong and other Games for which there is no room on the boat.
(Letter from TP to David Russell, 28.12.29)

Summer was good too, especially with the addition of a motor boat.

We went up to Sunbury and then down to Richmond in our little motor boat, much to the children's enjoyment, for the River is now perfect. The boat is the underpart of a Government hydroplane, a sort of light punt with room for 5 or 6 and it has an Evinrude outboard engine; the whole cost £15 which I expect to get back on resale as the engine is virtually new! If the weather holds and I can get away we hope to go up to Windsor and Marlow next weekend and possibly camp out.
(Letter from TP to David Russell, 26.8.29)

The weather did hold, and

We had a most excellent up-the-river trip, going about 90 miles in our little motor-boat, with splendid weather all the time.
(Letter from TP to David Russell, 2.9.29)

Trips on the river might be all very well, but what did Florence think to giving up a house on dry land? What, for that matter, did she think to her husband's more substantial journeys abroad? Their daughter, Jean, had this to report in old age.

She put up with my father's frequent absences with equanimity and also the ups and downs of his business fortunes. We moved frequently, according to our circumstances, from house, to flat, to houseboat ('The Nile') and back to house. It must have been hard for my mother! How often did I hear the words 'When Daddy's ship comes in' when I asked for this or that which could not be afforded.

My mother supported WTP in everything he did and frequently had psychic experiences herself. They entertained a lot and there seemed to be a constant stream of visitors, either people down on their luck, refugees from Russia, struggling pianists and so on, as well as people interested in spiritual matters. All this made for a lot of work for Florence, but she enjoyed it and her parties were famous.

('Florence Tudor-Pole [nee Snelling]', by Jean Carroll, short manuscript sent to the present author, 20.6.02)

Jean contributed further details on parties and hospitality in a short booklet, Wellesley Tudor Pole, Appreciation and Valuation, put together by Oliver G. Villiers in 1977:

My parents loved to entertain and the house was often full of interesting people, both from the world of business and the arts and with those who had the same interests as themselves. My father was a very good host and to use a commonplace phrase, was the life and soul of the party.

(From 'Wellesley Tudor Pole, Appreciation and Valuation', by Oliver G. Villiers, 1977)

One of the 'interesting people' was Michael Pojidaiev from the Quest group.

The Russian I remember most clearly is Podgy, when he lived with us in Hampstead, sculpting away in the attic. He did a most impressive bust of Zoroaster which William [TP's grandson] has still got. Most people find it rather 'sinister'. Podgy was an attractive person but his appearance was slightly bizarre as he had silver teeth. What they were made of I am not sure.

(Letter to the present author from Jean Carroll, 11.6.02)

The Wall Street Crash

River trips, famous parties and Podgy's silver teeth could not alter the

Michael Pojidaiev (Podgy) pictured in later years (1938)

fact that this was the late 1920's, and the fun was about to stop, suddenly and emphatically. TP perhaps saw the trouble coming. Every New Year he received impressions of the year to come, and sometimes they were clear enough to write down. Here is part of what he wrote for the end of the decade:

> *London Jan first 1929*
>
> *In historical events 1929 will prove to be the most important year since 1914.*
>
> *Continuation of tension between the nations very marked.*
>
> *Also tension between leaders of thought holding opposite or conflicting points of view.*
>
> *No war on a large scale is indicated, but continuing small conflicts and revolutionary outbreaks.*
>
> *Not a good year for the League of Nations.*
>
> *A change of Ruler and a modification of government possible in Britain during the year.*
>
> *An economic crisis in USA, late in 1929, is probable.*
>
> *Improvement in British economic conditions is marked, but not strongly so, and not until later in the year.*
>
> (Hand-written document by TP, in the Russell files, St Andrews University Library)

He spots the Wall Street Crash and even gets the time of year right (late October), but he does not put it very high on the list; and his assessment of the British economy is off target. However, he gets the change of government right, Ramsay MacDonald being re-elected Prime Minister in June. (In case the reader is unaware, MacDonald played tag with Stanley Baldwin for over a decade, and this time MacDonald was 'on'.) Much of the other material is hard to assess (e.g. 'Not a good year for the League of Nations': well yes, but you didn't need to be Nostradamus to see that.) However, the top item was exactly right: 'In historical events 1929 will prove the most important year since 1914.'

That was true. You could make a strong case for saying the Wall Street Crash caused World War Two. (Take money out of people's pockets and they feel like taking it out of someone else's.)

The Crash did not cause too much trouble for Britain, or indeed TP, at first. He was in Rome with George Leavey, the financier, overseeing their Italian operations, when the Crash came. Then he was in North Africa (on the John Black trip). However, by the time he got back (December) the dominoes were beginning to topple. Two companies recommended by George Leavey proved dubious, 'Combined Pulp & Paper' (CPP Ltd) and 'Symphonies'. CPP particularly rankled. Many people, including TP and David Russell, had invested in this, trusting Leavey's say-so, and all the while the company was being run by a crook. There was no suggestion of Leavey being equally crooked, but there was much frustration that he had recommended without checking.

> *CPP Ltd I don't know what to say. One feels that we don't yet know the whole story. I am surprised that Leavey should have been fathering the shares for so long, without full knowledge of the Company's management or mismanagement.*
>
> (Letter from TP to David Russell, 20.12.29)

He suffered sleepless nights over CPP, and the situation dragged on for over a year, with TP taking a seat on the board, organising legal action, pursuing miscreants through the courts and eventually ending up with such a measly dividend (for the 'many who cannot afford the losses') that it was scarcely worth the effort. In the process he and Leavey became estranged, Leavey pulled the plug on his Italian ventures, TP missed lots of commission, and, in summary, the knock-on effects of a financial slump caused inevitable knock-downs.

More was to follow for the nation, with three million unemployed, unpopular pay cuts, detested means testing, clashes with the police, even a naval mutiny, and eventually the Jarrow March. That was for the future, though. Back in 1929 TP was feeling 'shaken down to the bedrock' and he did not feel any better the following February.

> *The fact is I don't quite know what to make of life just now (my own anyway!) and am wondering in what way my mental or other attitudes and activities are wrong, in that I cannot come through into smooth water and have to devote almost every waking hour to meeting problems and carrying on. If external circumstances are a direct reflection of one's mind's activities, or a result thereof, how wrongly directed my own thinking must often be to land me in so many messes.*
>
> (Letter from TP to David Russell, 19.2.30)

He was quite right to wonder. How, after all, could such an affable, hard working fellow, gifted with insight and instinct, so consistently come off worse? It really is uncanny, almost like those cases of people who score significantly below average on ESP tests such as Zener cards (which, by the way, were just coming into use with Dr J.B. Rhine at Duke University in North Carolina). Is there a law of nature at work, which reverses normal expectations?—such as 'it is easier for a camel to pass through the eye of a needle than for a spiritual man to get rich.'

Whatever the explanation, TP was in a considerably battered condition by the time he arrived at two of the most remarkable years of his life, so remarkable that they demand a separate chapter all to themselves.

9. Dispatches from a Spiritual War Zone: 1930-1931

1930 was a point of balance. Like carriages on an old wooden roller coaster, the 1920's had ratcheted their way to the top of their climb. Now came the moment of vertigo. The Economics carriage was already plummeting away on its mad descent, and it was entirely likely the Political carriage would follow.

In the German elections of September 1930 the Nazi party suddenly polled 6 million votes and won 107 seats: Hitler was creeping ever closer to power. In Russia, Stalin had disposed of Trotsky and was eliminating 'kulaks': his power was becoming increasingly unassailable. In Japan, the army was angered at losing overseas trade: an invasion of mainland Asia became ever more likely.

In the West matters seemed a lot less certain. Franklin D. Roosevelt, paralysed legs and all, was re-elected Governor of New York but was still a long way from the White House. In Britain, Churchill, always on the look out for a dragon to slay, took a thrust at Gandhi and had to resign from the Opposition Front Bench. It looked for the time as though he was finished. Then there was a certain Wellesley Tudor Pole who, by the end of the year, thought he had helped bring in a New Spiritual Dispensation...

The Holy Isle of the West

TP's story chimes with the age, balanced as it is between ratcheting hopes and plummeting uncertainties. It involves a remarkable character, one Gertrude Mellor*, and a remarkable place, 'The Holy Isle in the West'. For over 25 years TP had been speculating about the existence of such an island but research had proved futile—till she arrived:

> *Certainly Miss Mellor is a very remarkable person. She came to see me today to arrange the rendezvous for St Michael's Day. She is about 50 I should say and of immense physical proportions, and with a sense of power and dignity that must rest on mental and spiritual foundations. Has been closely associated with cosmic centres all her life and seems to act under very distinct 'commands' in all she does and says. Knows Glastonbury and the West Country centres inside out, and Tintern, often visits Iona*

---

* It was Geraldine Cummins who pointed TP towards Gertrude Mellor and the Holy Isle of the West, the information coming to Cummins via her 'Cleophas' contacts. (See footnote on page 161.)

and many other shrines.

She has been working at the Irish centre for some three years; it is reached by motor launch from Lough Erne Hotel near Enniskillen, being about one hour from there. All she tells me about this island is of intense interest and confirms and amplifies my own instinctive feelings. It is arranged that we start the pilgrimage on St Michael's Day itself.

Apparently she was 'told' to expect me to cross her path, about a year ago and has been preparing for it. Has worked on the St Michael traditions and centres all her life. Well well, life sometimes contains strange events and this one is of thrilling interest.

(Letter from TP to David Russell, 18.8.30)

So thrilling was the interest that he needed to add a postscript:

For the first time since I began to take an interest in these Centres over 25 years ago, I have independent and what I consider to be authoritative confirmation of the main ideas and principles upon which our thought on these lines has been built up.

(Letter from TP to David Russell, 18.8.30)

This thought concerned Avalon, Iona and the Holy Isle of the West, the three great centres of Britain and Ireland which, so TP felt, needed reviving through pilgrimage and prayer.

You are asked to remember in your prayers during St Michael's Day, September 29th, and on Tuesday, September 30th, 1930, the sacred shrines of Avalon (Glastonbury), Iona and the Holy Isle of the West in Ireland, that the light of these centres may be rekindled and their spiritual powers released once more.

On these days (probably for the first time for many centuries) a special pilgrimage will take place to the Irish Shrine, the Holy Isle of the West, during which the three great centres (Avalon, Iona and the Holy Isle of the West) will be re-linked in prayer and thought, that they may regain their place in the national life as sources of joy and inspiration.

(Manuscript ms 38515/6/39, Russell archives, St Andrews)

Now at last seemed the moment for TP's ideas to come to fruition. However, it was also a time when he was in ever increasing distress. The surrounding economic disasters caused much anxiety, but to these could be added his ongoing mystery condition (of sciatica-like discomfort). 'On Thursday night I had a return of very acute pain and had to take morphia,' he told Russell (19.7.30). 'I have never had such acute and lasting pain in my life.' In addition to this he was 'suffering from a sort of shock', probably of a psychic nature, although he couldn't be sure if this was just 'the result of an accumulation of problems and events' (letter to Russell, 9.8.30).

This, then, was his general state of health when he set out on the pilgrimage at the end of September, and a glance at the letters he wrote at this time show him still writing the date as August (though St Michael's Day stubbornly and immovably falls in September). This symptom of disorientation is an interesting, nay poignant, one as he was especially scrupulous about times of day in the account he wrote afterwards. It is a long account, and we can see how important TP considered every detail by these repeated time-checks:

> On St Michael's Day 1930 WTP reached Lough Erne Hotel at noon (Irish time), and there met Miss Gertrude Mellor (known in some circles as the Woman of Power or the Woman of the Ark). At 12.45 pm (Irish time) Miss M and WTP set out in a motor launch for Eron. The day was calm and although there was little sunshine yet the waters of the Lough reflected a silver light and the surrounding hills looked very beautiful.
>
> The journey took 50 minutes. WTP was very conscious of a spirit of peace and happiness. He seemed aware of a great invisible choir of angelic beings singing anthems of praise and thanksgiving and this seemed to continue, almost without a break, throughout the rest of the day, and throughout the following day.
>
> Eron came into view, the Abbey ruins and the Watch Tower standing up against the sky, and a landing was made just before 1.45 p.m. (Irish time).
>
> Leaving the launch in charge of a mechanic (a fine young fellow from Killadeas, who holds Eron in great awe, as is the case with most of the local people), Miss M and WTP mounted to the top of the green hill at the southern end, which overlooks the tower and ruins and gives a clear view of the whole island. It was here that the ceremony was to take place. The hour was 2 p.m. (Irish time) or 12.30 pm Greenwich sun time.
>
> (From a 17 page document hand-written by TP, enclosed with a letter to David Russell on 6.10.30)

The name they used for the island was Eron, although a more common name now is Devenish. It lies at the southern end of Lower Loch Erne, just by Enniskillen, and significantly close to the border between north and south. It was in this dramatic situation that the two set about the main business:

The singing seemed to have ceased and there was a great stillness. Both became aware of a great concourse of invisible beings who circled the hill rising tier above tier until lost in the clouds. A prayer was said for all those who were watching and praying at various shrines and places in the British Isles that they might be linked with those present on Eron.

A short time of silence and meditation followed. The actual ceremony began at 2.30 pm (Irish time). Of the ceremony itself, little can be said. A staff was placed at the highest point on the hill and a circle made around it. Miss M and WTP stood inside the circle. WTP deposited near the staff stones and sand from Avalon, Iona and St Michael's Mount. Both were conscious of a mighty event taking place in which their own part was very humble, and both Miss M and WTP felt themselves lifted in consciousness to a very great height. A little while later the Hymn of the Archangels was chanted. A period of silence was followed by the sprinkling of salt upon the ground and a turning outward and praying to the four quarters of the Earth.

So far as Miss M and WTP were concerned they took little part in the

Devenish Island (or Eron, or 'The Holy Isle of the West') in
Lough Erne, with abbey ruins in the foreground and round tower behind

events which followed. At a certain moment WTP was instructed to leave the circle and go down the hill to the Abbey ruins and to pray and work for the knotting and tying up of threads connected with the Ecclesiastical dispensation now closed (or closing).

(From a 17 page document hand-written by TP, enclosed with a letter to David Russell on 6.10.30)

TP conveys the impression here that a spiritual, or at least 'Ecclesiastical', age was ending. In keeping with such an occasion TP had brought along the Glastonbury Cup (or Blue Bowl), which he mentions as the narrative continues:

It must have been about 3 pm (Greenwich sun time) that the two pilgrims became aware of a great Light that seemed to shine down in countless rays upon Eron and from there to be thrown out over the world in all directions. At the same moment WTP became aware that the three principle centres Avalon, Iona, Eron had become reunited and were re-consecrated for their holy mission in the New Time. Early in the ceremony, prayers for this end had been offered and the Glastonbury vessel had been held out toward each centre and to the four winds.

Some Cosmic Purpose was being fulfilled before the pilgrims' eyes. It was as if a great trumpet had been blown and as if St Michael and his company of Angels had appeared. The invisible Choir took up their chanting and the heavens seemed to be filled with an immense multitude.

It was as if a Voice had spoken:-

'It is Finished. It has begun!'

St Michael took the golden key and opened a new Door.

A dispensation was closing, a new one had dawned.

The effect of these events upon the pilgrims was so overpowering as to be beyond description. After kneeling in prayer once more, they descended to the Lough side, entered their boat and returned to the mainland. It was now 4 pm (Greenwich) or 5.30 (Irish time).

(From a 17 page document hand-written by TP, enclosed with a letter to David Russell on 6.10.30)

Such is the sincerity of the writing that one feels it must somehow be true. However, as TP acknowledged to Russell, 'it may take centuries for the fulfilment to manifest widely and leaven the thought of the Race' (letter to Russell, 14.10.30).

This long account was not written straight away. TP wasn't up to it. Instead he sent shorter, astonished letters from Lough Erne Hotel while he tried to digest it all (and gritted his teeth against the sciatica). Here is one written on the 1st October, although TP was so stunned (by pain or rapture) that he wrote the date as 1.9.30 (which would involve some unlikely time travel):

> *It has been uplifting and wonderful beyond anything I have yet experienced; and yet I have been in intense physical pain since Thursday last and never expected I could manage to get here at all. But that seems as nothing when set against the almost terrible privilege of being allowed to take part in an event of which it is quite beyond my power to realise the full significance or ultimate effects. We are asked to tell those who were watching and praying on St Michael's Day and yesterday to give praise and thanks for the successful fulfilment of a great undertaking; and to draw to themselves a ray from the Michael splendour that was released on St M Day 1930 on this sacred isle.*
>
> *The peace of this place is so deep that it must come from what has just happened and as I watch the Lough I can see processions of 'invisible' beings on pilgrimage toward the holy isle, drawn by the great illumination here to make obeisance and prayer.*
>
> (Letter from TP to David Russell, 1.10.30)

When he did get round to writing the full account, it was the 6th October, and he was just about realising what month he was in. We have seen his view of events. Now let us see his view of their significance:

> *Three strands of experience seemed to be knitted together for me on St Michael' Day 1930 and it is not easy to deal with them independently.*
>
> *First there was the witnessing of what appeared to be a very immense Cosmic event, seen and felt in time and place on the holy isle of Eron.*
>
> *Second there was the relation of this event to Avalon, Iona, Eron and other shrines, and to the countries and peoples of the world.*
>
> *Third there was the taking place of an initiation personal to myself.*
>
> *This third experience undoubtedly purified my inner perceptions in some way which made it possible to understand faintly what was going forward and to take some infinitesimal part in the events of the day and the hour.*
>
> *But what were these events?*

So far as I am able to understand the purport of St Michael's Day 1930, I should say that in some manner, mysterious and almost unintelligible, the keynote was sounded of the new Spiritual Dispensation for this earth. And that the death knell of the old order was sounded immediately previously and on the same day.

Is there any way by which proof might accumulate showing that some Cosmic event did take place then? Yes, I think there is a good possibility of this.

(As I was writing the last sentence, Jean came to the door and said, 'Daddy, it's all right.' She did not know what I was doing nor does she know of recent events. And so I asked her what was alright and she replied:- 'Everything, I felt somehow I ought to let you know.')

(From a 17 page document hand-written by TP, enclosed with a letter to David Russell on 6.10.30)

And those lovely, uncomprehending words from TP's sixteen year old daughter can round off the episode.

Back to Normality

They can also return us to normal life, which, of course, was never all right, for remember this was 1930 and Britain might be escaping the worst of the Great Depression for now, but TP was not. He was still struggling to earn a living, especially since the acrimony over the CPP crash estranged him from George Leavey, the financier. On the other hand, he was still alive, albeit wincing with pain, which was more than could be said for one member of the Quest group:

We heard on Saturday night of the passing of Dmitry Sissoëff in Paris.

(Letter from TP to David Russell, 20.10.30)

The timing seems almost too precise to be co-incidental. Two months earlier, just when TP was arranging to meet Miss Mellor, Sissoëff had been struck down with serious kidney trouble. Now, at the culmination of the Eron work, Sissoëff had gone:

It is sad that poor Sissoëff's passing should come when we are nearing the end of our long journey but the sweep of power released at Eron seems to

have required the severance of the BB channel (for the time being anyway);
their work was done; and apparently the removal of one of the instruments
from earth has been one of the consequences.
(Letter from TP to David Russell, 20.10.30)

Of the original Quest Group that left two Russians, Bergengreen and
Pojidaiev, both living for now in Paris. Frederick Leveaux went across to
them right away to help arrange the funeral and defray expenses, but TP's
business troubles kept him in London.

His own personal portion of the Great Depression, the CPP crash, was
far from remedied. The fact that some of its mills were based in Germany
would not help, with the Nazis and Communists indulging in street warfare,
as Hitler brawled his way to political power. Bruno P, the master mind of the
CPP scam, may not have been such an eminent villain as Hitler, but TP had
no good to say of him:

CPP Ltd: German industrial conditions are so black that all the
Mills (save Rube) have become liabilities and not assets. Bruno P and his
associates have succeeded in their robberies.
(Letter from TP to David Russell, 4.12.30)

Such calamity and dishonesty might induce despair in some people,
but not TP. At Christmas 1930 he wrote:

On the whole I feel that 1931 augurs more cheerfully than 1930 did and
I refuse to tolerate all these alarmist rumours about 'War in the Spring',
'German Default', 'More American Crises' and so on. The world is not
out of the Wood by any means but light is on the way and we must reflect
it and get people to abandon their gloomy ideas and beliefs.
(Letter from TP to David Russell, 25.12.30)

For himself, he had plenty of projects on the go. Indeed, he made a
list of 'Activities, January 1931', comprising sixteen different items. Several
concerned Italy, especially the ongoing Gargano and Aureliana businesses.
Two were about Algeria and his work for Russell's paper mills. But others were
newer projects, ranging from monoplanes, to railway systems, to road making
processes, to roller blotters (for ink pens), to a waterproofing paper invention.
By the law of averages, some of these should have succeeded—surely—but
his own personal business cloud was still tenaciously casting gloom, whether

he wished to acknowledge its potency or not:

> *Curious how and why so many negotiations seem to go so far well,*
> *and then fall down for reasons quite apart from the intrinsic merits of the*
> *inventions concerned.*
>
> (Letter from TP to David Russell, 30.3.31)

Looked at from a 'War in the Spheres' angle, it sounds suspiciously like his old adversaries, 'the Antipodes', were at it again. Had TP been doing anything to alarm them?

> *Unexpectedly, on New Years Eve, among the impressions and*
> *instructions received for 1931 was the intimation to 'stand by' in regard*
> *to Q events. Quite definite and detailed methods for the preliminary*
> *expedition were given.*
>
> *I did not expect any developments just yet, despite the events on Eron,*
> *and this mainly because the economic crisis would seem to render any*
> *expedition impracticable during the present year. However I 'stand by'.*
>
> (Letter from TP to David Russell, 16.1.31)

The Quest Revived

Yes, the Quest was about to be revived, and it was Gertrude Mellor who got things moving again, via a friend of hers called Janson:

> *I think the hour is about to strike for the Q. Mr E.W. Janson, who is*
> *so interested in Irish centres, has a suitable yacht and would be ready to*
> *co-operate. He is 50, English with Danish forebears; lives at Grosvenor*
> *House and is a business man. Implicitly believes in Miss Mellor and her*
> *powers and she is responsible for bringing him into the picture.*
>
> (Letter from TP to David Russell, 2.3.31)

The idea of a yacht was important, for approach to Constantinople by sea still seemed necessary. Turkey, under Mustafa Kemal, might be in the process of modernisation, but the transition was incomplete, and permission for land-based investigation was almost certain to be refused. The tactic therefore was to sail along as tourists, anchor off the coast, and achieve as much as possible without stepping on dry land.

The physical aspect of the Quest began to look promising, but TP, as man of two worlds, would want the discarnate aspect to be similarly positive. Fortunately, he felt he was getting back in contact with the Sage and at 11 a.m. on the 28th of March he felt sufficiently in touch to act as amanuensis for the following:

> *All your old friends have now reassembled under the guidance of our Master known to you as the Sage. Amongst us is Jack [Cheape], several messengers who have spoken to you from time to time since 1903, guides who have been personally associated with FL [Leveaux], DR [Russell] and yourself in times gone by and many others hitherto unknown to you. We are unifying the various groups and individuals over here into one Council under the pure inspiration of the Christ power directed by the great being known to you as St Michael.*
>
> (Manuscript, TP's handwriting: 'Messenger from the Sage', 28.4.31, London SW1, 11 am)

Mention of 'Christ power' and 'St Michael' would ease any residual qualms about the non-appearing Sixth. The Quest no longer felt like the pedantically occult thing it had become in the 20's. The horizons were expanding upwards, and the effects were energising:

> *Frederick Leveaux and Michael Pojidaiev are at Tackley re-reading all details and making a summary of the necessary tackle, tools, chemicals, clothes, rations, etc.*
>
> *Janson is having all plans etc enlarged and co-ordinated. He is also enquiring re yachts through Lloyds.*
>
> *Those actually 'going in' to the tunnels will be Leveaux, Bergengreen, Pojidaiev, Janson, WTP, and possibly two young Cornish miners of Janson's employ who are also fishermen and used to the sea and to all underground problems.*
>
> (Letter from TP to David Russell, 29.4.31)

Soon the cast had grown further, a certain Henry C.M. Hardinge having joined, and the group as a whole made its spiritual preparations on Sunday May 17th 1931 at Tackley, Frederick Leveaux's home:

> *At 9.10 pm the members of the Quest Group gathered together in the Michael Chapel at Tackley to pray for the blessing of God upon the Quest Crusade and upon all those seen and unseen who were to take part in this*

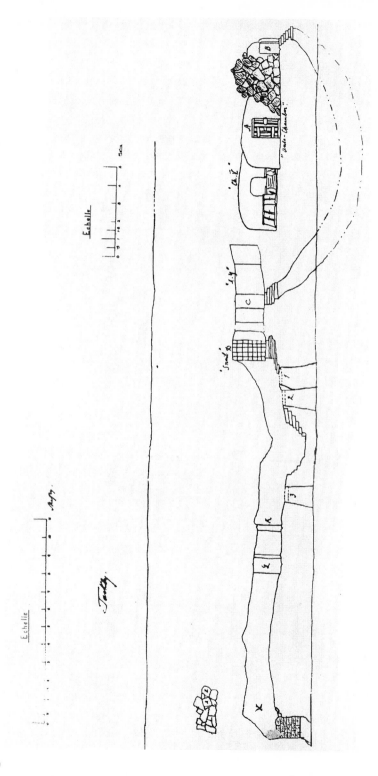

work. Present were Miss Mellor, Frederick Leveaux, E.W. Janson, Anatole Bergengreen, Michael Pojidaiev, Henry C.M. Hardinge and Wellesley Tudor Pole.

(Pencil manuscript, TP's handwriting, 17.5.31, copies in both Russell and Leveaux archives)

It is noteworthy that TP called it 'the Quest Crusade'. Doubtless he was referring to the idealistic aspirations of the group. However, it is well to remember the original crusades were actually wars and are remembered as such in the Near East. TP would not anticipate earthly conflict this time round, but experience warned him of unearthly conflict. Hence a spiritual dedication would be a wise preliminary:

The Glastonbury vessel lay upon the altar and also the Stone of Destiny or Power used by Miss Mellor in her work at Avalon, Iona and Eron.

Those present were aware of a descent of great power and felt that the Quest Crusade had been initiated in its outward form from that moment. The Chapel was filled with unseen presences. Indeed most of those were present who have been working for the Quest ideals from the wider world. WTP could sense (but not see) a number of Angelic beings with wings outstretched above the Quest group as if in protection.

During the service a light rose from within the Cup and spread its rays upward and also over all who were gathered in the Chapel. WTP saw the Michael Sword in the central ray with the shining blade pointing heavenwards.

(Pencil manuscript, TP's handwriting, 17.5.31, copies in both Russell and Leveaux archives)

The sense of impending drama was shared by many at the time. Mrs Firth (mother of the redoubtable Dion Fortune), had been a quiet ally of TP's for many years 'working actively on the inner Quest from a metaphysical and spiritual standpoint'. Now she wrote to TP, (20.5.31) 'My dear Friend, your news is very thrilling. You know that you will have my best thoughts, and constant work with you, and I feel that your mission will not return void, but will accomplish that unto which it is sent.'

Meanwhile the travel arrangements were nearing completion. They

[Opposite Page] The Quest: portion of the underground tunnels shown in cross section: sea level marked by horizontal line; Chamber V to the right; exit (into Sea of Marmara) at left; man traps at 1,2 and 3

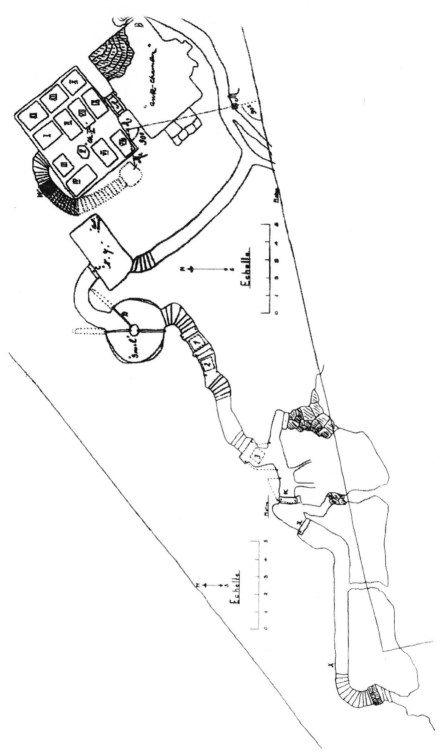

would use a hired yacht (not Janson's) large enough for the group and the equipment, and it didn't come cheap:

> *We have now got the yacht and must take her as from Brindisi on*
> *3rd June, charter one month with 14 days extra as option. £700 per lunar*
> *month and we have been in competition with Charlie Chaplin for her!*
> *Everyone except Hardinge and myself (who join her at Naples) will proceed*
> *to Ajaccio and join her there on June 5th as BB won't allow the party and*
> *material to travel down through Italy to Brindisi. This fact adds a week to*
> *our expenses but seems unavoidable.*
>
> (Letter from TP to David Russell, 16.5.31)

Here we might pause. BB is not just back in the picture but, typically, requires complete obedience. In the early twenties he had wrecked much of TP's life with his dictatorial insistence on waiting for the no-longer-necessary Sixth — and now he was being no less dictatorial about routes of travel. In his defence, we might say he had given some impressively detailed information via the planchette (board) about the catacombs, treasures and necessary preparation. But not everyone was impressed. It may be coincidental that the name of the hired yacht was 'Tyrant', but as coincidences go it is somewhat symbolic:

> *When I joined the Tyrant at Naples I found some dissension in the ranks. FL*
> *and the two Russians were insistent that the Board's instructions should be followed*
> *in every detail; hour for start from each port, exact course to be steered and details of*
> *preparing paraphernalia etc. Miss Mellor and Janson took the view that BB and the*
> *Board were for giving clairvoyant instructions on the spot underground, and that*
> *the course pursued, hours of sailing and ports of call were matters for the Captain*
> *(and for Janson) to decide.*
>
> (Letter from TP to David Russell, 'Off Messina', 11.7.31)

The Fourth Quest Attempt, 1931

When TP joined them, most of the group had been together for four days, time enough to establish some sort of group atmosphere, and unfortunately it was a strained one. Nonetheless, the trip seemed good in terms of scenic locations, as the diary relates:

[Opposite Page] The Quest: the same tunnels and chambers seen as ground
plan (n.b. the point of entry would be some way east-northeast of this section)

June 11th The yacht left Naples at 6.55 p.m. Beautiful scene, sunset,
Capri and a brigantine in full sail. Sea very calm
June 12th: They passed Strombóli at 8.30 am
They passed Etna and arrived at Syracuse at 8 pm
June 14th 8 a.m. off coast of Calábria. Sea calm, nice breeze.
June 15th Yacht arrived at Corfu at 12.45 am. Left the port in a calm
sea for Patras at 10.45 am
June 18th Left Patras at 6 am. They passed into the Corinth Canal
1.30 - 2pm. They reached Phaleron about 6 pm
('The Quest', ps. 28-30, Renee Nicol, 1958)

However, the sea did not always remain calm. Nor did the people on
board. BB had insisted on an eccentric route, which involved pilgrims going
ashore to touch 'necessary places', such as the Temple of Artemis at Patras:

> *It seems a zigzag course but we are following a special magnetic route*
> *at BB's desire. There is a certain amount of tension, and of course it's very*
> *hot, and we have rolled a lot coming down from Naples.*
> (Letter from TP to David Russell, 'From Syracuse', 13.6.31)

Here was the culmination of 25 years work and aspiration for TP, and the
humans involved—as ever in vital enterprises—seemed beset by squabbles.
He wrote to Russell, apologising for failing to keep him up to date:

> *Somehow I am feeling and living too deeply just now to write much.*
> *There is a lifetime's thought, emotion and aspiration hanging in the*
> *balance.*
> (Letter from TP to David Russell, 'From Patras', 16.6.31)

Eventually the disagreements came to the boil, though it was not BB
who set everyone off. Indeed he seemed to have gone missing again, as in
1922. It was another member of the discarnate 'Council', Crookes—allegedly
the same Sir William Crookes, now deceased, who had been part of the Cup
story back in 1907, along with TP and Archdeacon Wilberforce (see page 19).
His instruction was that the boat should take a specific route for Mt Athos,
to get the best of the weather and to avoid hostile 'spherical conditions'. For
board-believers, this might seem weighty advice. However, to the Janson-
Mellor point of view it was unacceptable:

20th June The Tyrant left Phaleron at 6 am. Unfortunately the course indicated for going to Mt. Athos was not followed, and the route by open sea, past Skyros was taken. Miss Mellor, for reasons of an occult nature which she believed to be imperative, had expressed the wish that the yacht should go by the open sea to Janson who, acting under her instigation, took advantage of the Captain's hesitation to go by the Euboea-Chalcis channel, to order the change in the route, and later, when the Captain expressed his willingness to take the course of the narrow channel, adhered to his decision. He only informed the others afterwards, and they, being in the presence of a 'fait accompli', did not care to insist that he should change again the orders he had given to the Captain.

The 'conditions' were felt to be very difficult in the 'sphere', and when work with the board was begun that evening the conditions for writing were extremely difficult.

('The Quest', p.31, Renee Nicol, 1958)

This was a crucial moment. The cruise was no longer a matter of a yacht taking an eccentric course between desirable locations. It was about to become war.

Up till now, in the absence of BB, the board scripts had featured the friendly but rambling script of 'Crookes'. However, that evening Latin capitals in ferociously packed order announced the presence of MR (Murcius Robustus) and he was in emphatic mode. 'QUO USQUAM TANDEM SERVITORI DEI NOLLI ATTENDERE VOCEM SUPERIOREM AMICUM VOSTRUM?' he demanded ('how much longer will you servants of God fail to take heed of the Higher Voice of your friends?') His message continued in thunderous fashion: 'FORCES INIMICI CIRCUMSTANT CASTRUM NOSTRUM. DE OMNIBUS VENTIS SAGITTANTES BALLISTANTES AREAM NOSTRAM SUNT' ('enemy forces surround our camp; from all sides they throw arrows and stones in our midst.') While all this was coming through, the planchette operators were Bergengreen and Leveaux, whilst TP, Pojidaiev, Hardinge and Miss Mellor looked on as the trenchant Latin capitals continued:

There are some of us who have been wounded by them. There are some of us who have been sent to the other world. The wounds are without blood, the going without death. They are looking for each undefended place in our walls. Defend the gates, defend the walls. Victory is a capricious goddess. MR

(Original script: 'M.Y. Tyrant at sea, 20th June 1931, 9.45 pm')

Murcius Robustus was clearly a spirit who went in for military metaphors. Reading this, of course, a sceptic might suspect that Leveaux and Bergengreen, operating the board, were annoyed at the Janson-Mellor tactics, and so, subconsciously, fabricated attacks in the Beyond. TP, however, with his long training in separating the genuine from the bogus, was not inclined to doubt the message. Nor did future events suggest MR's dramatic communication to be any storm in a cranial teacup. Indeed, one of the first things MR did after this message was to fall silent.

BB had already gone silent, and the group on the yacht must have felt alarmed. What was going on? Had the battles in the 'sphere' gone badly for their friends? With no discarnates able to produce any written script, Leveaux and Bergengreen fell back on the default tactic of a letter grid. Numbers 1 to 6 formed the horizontal axis, and 1 to 5 the vertical axis. 'A', for instance, being the first letter horizontally and vertically, was spelt out as 1/1. Thus a struggling communicator could give one tap followed, after a suitable pause, by another tap.

The messages for the next few days are all 'taps' from a new communicator identified by the initials MM. He had apparently been a saintly friend of Bergengreen's and Pojidaiev's but was now discarnate. How he survived the onslaughts that removed BB and MR is not clear, but it did not seem easy. 'They hunt me like a rabbit,' he tapped, laboriously and dramatically, in Russian, on the 25th June. When asked where the yacht should go, he continued, again in Russian:

> *I am not entitled to say anything whatever because I am not a member*
> *of the Council. My personal advice is to go to the Marmora Sea. MM*
> (Original script: 'Castro, Island off Lemnos, 8.20 pm 25.6.31)

It sounds from this as though all members of the 'Council' had fallen casualty. Not so, not yet. The yacht sailed through the Dardanelles, passing such war-scarred locations as Gallipoli and Chanak, till it moored at Light House Isle in the Sea of Marmara, not far from their ultimate objective. That evening, at 10.10 p.m., a last member of the Council succeeded in getting through, although not firmly enough to form written script. It was a matter of taps and numbers again with Bergengreen and Leveaux touching the board whilst this time TP, Pojidaiev and Janson looked on. What emerged gradually was an English message in Russian characters. The first five letters were, more or less, KRUKS, a simplified spelling of 'Crookes'. Sir William had returned, albeit briefly, and the message he had to give was a desperate one:

Kruks speaking: The forces of the enemies overwhelmed us. All working members of the Quest group are incarnated or blocked. Our friend MM was a little too quick to send you in the Marmara Sea. A torrent of antipodal forces is concentrated here. K

(Original script, 'Lighthouse Isle', 10.10 pm, 26.2.31, Leveaux archives)

The earthly weather outside the yacht, meanwhile, was unseasonably vicious, heavy wind and rain paralleling the psychic conditions around Crookes. Next morning, the board desolately tapped out numbers from MM, beginning 2/4, the number for 'K' It was a message about 'Kruks', and the news was unsettling but not yet catastrophic:

Crookes was taken yesterday by a maelstrom. He will come to you about ten o'clock.

(Original script, 'Sea of Marmara', 27.6.31, 9.50 am, Leveaux archives)

At 10.20 am Crookes returned from whatever maelstrom had whirled him away, but he was not out of peril, and desperation seems to have lent him strength to operate Leveaux's and Bergengreen's hands. The resulting script is wild, spidery, as though hunted across the page by unseen enemies:

Crookes is writing. I fighting one to legions. The position is uncertain and nearly hopeless. I giving providential directions. Follow them in Godsname. Only exactness can save the Q.

(Original script, 27.6.31, 10.20 am, Leveaux archives)

Twelve hours later, at 10.00 pm, MM got back in touch, tapping out Russian letters. The first five were the now familiar: KPYKC (Russian version of KRUKS). The translation emerged, culminating in:

Kruks was attacked. What happened to him is unknown. In the morning go to 3ST. MM

(Original script, 10 pm, 27.6.31, Leveaux archives)

3ST, the reader may remember, was code for Trieste (which in turn was code for Constantinople—modern day Istanbul). So the next morning the Tyrant left its island mooring at 7.40 am for the last crucial portion of the journey.

At this point it is best to leave the planchette despatches and allow TP to take up the story. In several letters afterwards he summarises events, conveying the struggles and frustrations they encountered:

> *Finally we reached Trieste where storms of wind and rain met us and made physical investigations extremely difficult. The Russians were not allowed to land and the yacht was watched because they were aboard. (They must get naturalised). BB and his group could not 'speak' but the Board tapped out short code messages to the effect that conditions were bad and that we ought to get into a quieter zone.*
> (Letter from TP to David Russell, 'Off Messina', 11.7.31)

If problems in the Beyond were bad, they were worse in the physical, the most disastrous being:

> *The entry is under deep water.*
> (Letter to David Russell, 'Off the Dardanelles', Sunday 5.7.31)

That should not have been! The whole point of the approach by yacht was to enter the catacombs from the sea, and TP's 1922 surveys had shown the entry could be used. The sea level must have changed drastically since 1922.

> *We could sink a shaft into the passage at the point where it passes under the Beach and under the Justinian sea wall; we know the exact spot and everything accords with the BB plans except the sea levels.*
> (Letter to David Russell, 'Off the Dardanelles', Sunday 5.7.31)

What had happened since 1922? Enquiry of the planchette produced vague surmises (from MM) that earth movements were responsible, maybe in 1927. As the expert on terrestrial conditions, BB might have been able to say more, but BB was not around, whirled away in the Borderland conflicts just as he had been in 1922. His absence was yet again crucial, especially as detailed scrutiny on the spot began to suggest that BB had got most of his data correct:

> *Indeed we have seen under the water and between the rocks, the Byzantine brick archway exactly at the spot shown by BB, and the position and shape of the rocks is identical with the plan. But to sink a shaft 8 to 10 feet through the beach at that spot and above sea level could not be done secretly. It would take 24 hours continuous work and there are barracks*

etc on the high ground above this section of the wall and overlooking the spot.

We penetrated the walls privately and examined ancient well shafts in the foundations. If the place were more isolated, 48 hours work and we could have sunk a shaft into the passage at the spot where it passes under the walls and goes inland. Under existing circumstances that proved impossible. Why were we not warned of this, seeing that so many other conditions and places 'seen' on the spot by the invisible helpers have proved so accurate?

(Letter to David Russell, 'Off the Dardanelles', Sunday 5.7.31)

The whole expedition was going wrong. With BB gone, all they could do was make reconnaissances, a process hampered by especially hostile weather:

So far as we could check up BB's plans inland, from an above ground survey, all is as stated and in order. Miss M stood at a spot in the ancient Serai gardens (above the 'Chapel' marked in the plan) and felt a remarkable uprush of power and was quite satisfied that the buried 'things' are there. [This is where TP felt a similar uprush back in 1907, ed.] Then in regard to the exit, a mile down the coast but still below the sea walls, here again we made a thorough investigation by sea and land and all was according to the BB data. But the exit is walled up (as we knew all along) and we could not enter that way through the sea, although if we were inside and wanted to come out it would be practicable to deal with the wall from the inside.

(Letter from TP to David Russell, 'Off the Dardanelles', Sunday 5.7.31)

As he had stated before, the planned entry was 'under deep water.' They might have tried to find an alternative, if only BB had been available.

Quite possibly there is another feasible entry inland and via one of the innumerable catacombs in S: itself; but BB had disappeared; there was a magnetic storm raging, wind rain and thunder for three days running, and it seemed as if the very elements were leagued against us.

(Letter from TP to David Russell, 'Off the Dardanelles', Sunday 5.7.31)

It must have been fiercely perplexing. Why should all this apparent opposition occur when nothing of the kind had been foreseen? There again, why were they not forewarned about the sea level? Discarnate failures of perception were multiplying alarmingly:

Reaction and Reappraisal

It was time to take stock and assess both the expedition and its personnel:

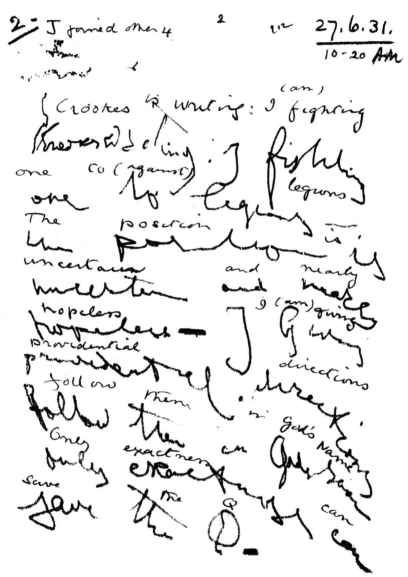

Planchette writing: 'I fighting one to legions'; spidery scrawl attributed to 'Kruks'; translation added above his words

Two contradictory facts stand out:-

(a) We are all more than ever convinced that the papers are there and the passages in accord with the plans.

(b) We are shaken in our faith as to the power of all or any of our unseen helpers to actually conduct the outer details of the work, using us as instruments. Apparently they cannot see all the conditions as they exist today from a distance and have to use our presence on the spot in order to psychometrise salient details.

(Letter from TP to David Russell, 'Off the Dardanelles', Sunday 5.7.31)

In TP's 1922 expedition it had seemed that physical eyes on the spot could act as x-ray cameras, enabling distant beings (dimensionally speaking) to see through the ground. However, those distant beings were no longer around, so who else could help? How about Miss Mellor?

Another problem: the effort to mix the oil of Miss M's vision and advice with the water of the Board work has not succeeded. From the first she has intimated that no Board or BB work was necessary and that she could receive direct all that was necessary. She and Janson and Hardinge frequently formed a clique and none of them behaved in a very selfless manner. 'I hold the keys and without me nothing can be done' was Miss

Three Quest members stand over the entry point which has become too deeply under water to be feasible

191

M's constant cry on the outward voyage; yet when we arrived, found the expected entry in deep water and tried to find a quick entry elsewhere, she could not help and seemed to hold no keys, and her Michael messages led nowhere although worded as if all power had been granted to Miss M and her alone. I think she should have stuck to her plane of work as a protector and channel for spiritual inspiration and not attempted to usurp the functions of the BB group, who have shown such a remarkable knowledge of local conditions (with the one vital exception of the sea levels). Her attitude now is as follows:- 'The BB group are unreliable and the work should now be carried on on practical lines and without any further reference to them.' However, she can give me no satisfactory explanation of why her guides prophesied complete success all the way through and never warned her of difficulties which they implied did not exist.

(Letter from TP to David Russell, 7.7.31)

This was an expedition that foundered on disharmony, and, as such, can be taken to exemplify much that was to happen, privately and politically, in that doomed decade, the Thirties. Not all of the trouble, however, was self generated. Much appeared to come from 'the Antipodes' who, as ever, seemed more potent than anticipated.

Undoubtedly (apart from thunderstorms etc) we were surrounded by very adverse psychic conditions and so we up anchored and made for Yalova on the South Marmora coast, seven hours away. Here we regained contact with 'Crookes' and he said there had been a big battle during which BB and those who could calculate time and space in our group had been compelled to withdraw and were imprisoned. FL and the Russians were inclined to say that as we had not obeyed BB implicitly as to route on outward journey we were partly responsible for his enforced absence at this vital time.

We stayed a day or two at Trieste, having returned from Yalova meanwhile, then Janson and Lovelock returned to London overland, Janson being full of the idea of forming a small London syndicate to prosecute the work. I begged him to take no action of any kind at present. We then started on our homeward way and the tension between FL and Miss M continued, FL considering that her presence and method of work impeded the Board. Probably it does.

At Patras, Crookes and several others 'returned' (not BB who is said to be unavailable for another 14 days) and gave us various explanations for what had happened. According to these, a great battle raged in the middle spheres during our passage out and came to a crisis at Patras on the outward journey, when the Quest attempt on this occasion was definitely defeated (viz four days before we even reached our destination).

Crookes also stated that the work must be lifted out of the sphere where it could be held up by antipodal attack in future, and on behalf of the Michael Council, instructed me to consult you [David Russell, ed.] as to the best method for proceeding officially to secure a Concession, using some Society as a figurehead.

(Letter from TP to David Russell, 'Off Messina', 11.7.31)

That last paragraph was vital for the future of the Quest. From now on the seaborne route would be abandoned and the Quest would be pursued above ground and in semi-official fashion. David Russell, once enlisted, would bring in the Walker Trust of St Andrews University (although, in fact, he would quietly do the funding himself) and along with him would come James Baxter, Professor of Divinity at St Andrews University. It all makes an amazing story and one symbolically typical of the Thirties, but it requires consideration all to itself so will not be pursued in this chapter.

TP Enters the Tunnels

However, TP had not yet told the full story of his Quest, for, in his view, he had actually got into the tunnels and chambers—including the fabulous Chamber 5, laden with boxed treasures of every kind. His method of entry, however, was not one that could be shared by others, as it was not entirely physical. The story he tells is a long one, and TP begins it at the point when the 'Trieste' expedition appeared utterly defeated:

When all progress seemed impossible and we seemed to be checkmated in all directions, I retired to my cabin and asked for light and guidance. The Sage's messenger, the Sage himself and another guide whom I did not know by name or remember having seen before, came to the rescue. The upshot of the conference was as follows.

'Certain work has to be done now. You should do it. The Quest cannot be fulfilled outwardly at this juncture for various reasons to be gone into later. Plans have miscarried on several planes and the methods so far employed will not be employed further. Another page will turn. Meanwhile you must pass into the garden of Quest fulfilment.'

I was told to go into the silence, being careful to shake off the gloom that

193

had descended upon the group on the yacht and to await instructions. *Very soon afterwards I found myself sitting on the brick archway in the sea at the closed entry. The projection was so complete that I could feel the water lapping at my sides and the breeze against my body. Then I sank down into the passage below, which seemed to be nearly full of sand and refuse and had a very bad smell! I crept along going up inland, sometimes grazing myself against the sides of the tunnel so badly as to feel considerable pain!*

I saw a light ahead and thought it came through some crack from above, but when I had crawled nearer, I realised that it was the light from the guardian of the centre, who was waiting to receive me. When I reached him he gave me his hand and lifted me on to my feet. I could just stand upright. The strange fact emerged that I was subject to the limitations of the tunnel and seemed in a semi-physical and sensory body, whereas the guardian was quite unaffected by these limitations and although tall, he could stand upright as if there were no tunnel limitations!

I ought to say here that during the whole experience I felt at peace and completely free from all the friction and opposition that seemed to surround the Q group on the yacht. Though apparently fettered by the narrow surroundings (as if I really were in a sense body) I was aware of spiritual presences whose light filled the tunnel and was reflected in the light which emanated from the Guardian of the place.

I cannot remember all that happened. The Guardian took me by the hand, saying I had been expected, and we visited the Chapel, two other chambers and finally chamber 5. On four separate occasions during the journey, the Guardian (whom I believe was the chief of three) made a search and then handed me an object to carry. In one case this object was a heavy metal tube, in another a wooden box, another seemed to be a book with wood or hard hide covers, and the fourth was a roll of parchments wrapped in a kind of skin. The total weight of these things in my arms made progress very slow.

I told the Guardian I should have to pass out through the sea and feared damage to the precious scripts. He replied, 'You have been entrusted with the living originals of the four most important 'Key' parchments and of which the physical counterparts are deposited here. These writings are for the Christian world. They must be taken to safe sanctuary in your own country, for wherever they are taken their earthly counterparts will follow.'

There was more conversation as we returned to the entrance (not the exit) and I remember the Guardian saying that our voyage had relieved considerable tension and pressure on the spot and that in some way we had made the task of guarding the sacred relics less arduous and that a danger of their physical destruction had been averted. When I said goodbye, he kissed me saying, 'You and yours will come again. Be at peace.'

I passed through the roof of the archway once more, up through the water on to a rock, and then back to the Boat. When aware of being fully awake and in my cabin again, I heard the Sage's voice saying 'You are now in the garden of Quest fulfilment.' I looked down and saw my arms and hands still held their precious burden. I asked what to do with what I held and was told to carry on until shown clearly to whom the 'documents' should be transferred for safe custodianship and meanwhile not to speak of the matter to anyone.

(Letter from TP to Frederick Leveaux, 9.9.31)

One bizarre consequence of the whole incident was that 'wherever I went my hands and arms were weighted with their precious burden' (letter to Leveaux, 9.9.31). So, while the MV Tyrant was sailing away to calmer waters, and the discarnate communicators were getting back in touch (and Frederick Leveaux and Miss Mellor were getting on each other's nerves), TP was secretly and invisibly carrying guarantees of future success.

It was in Italy that the next step in the story of the 'Key parchments' took place. TP, as a businessman, called in on important clients on his way back from the East, and the road to one of them went past somewhere with a remarkable name:

The origin of the name Stigliano (Stygis, Styx) hinted at what this centre stood for in the transition between the two worlds.

(Letter from TP to Frederick Leveaux, 9.9.31)

The River Styx—or, in this case, the mountain-crater Styx—was the legendary division between this world and the next.

I motored out and up to that strange place. Stigliano is a natural crater in the mountains, surrounded by woods and containing hot radio-active springs. On arriving I was unexpectedly met by the Guardian of the place who told me I was expected. He said that Stigliano was a very ancient holy place with Atlantean origins, or rather that Atlantean relics of wisdom had been brought there for safety at the time of the Deluge.

The Sage appeared and told me to hand over my burden to this

Guardian who was destined to carry it safely to the sanctuary prepared for it in England 'under the direct protection of the holy reunited triangle'. I gathered that the actual spot was not Avalon, nor Iona, nor Eron, but elsewhere.

I handed the living writings over to the Guardian of Stigliano and saw him cover them with his cloak and set out for England along the Michael route through Southern and Eastern France and then through the two St Michael Mounts.

Since this experience, BB upon being asked, has given it as his view that the prepared sanctuary is at Winchester, but the actual place at present is veiled and possibly may remain so until the material counterparts rejoin their living originals.

(Letter from TP to Frederick Leveaux, 9.9.31)

Return to the Mundane

Of course, the Quest still had to be pursued on a mundane level, but so did many other matters. Soon TP was back in London, dealing with the workaday world of international business and politics. It must have been a baffling transition, although as a man of two worlds, he would be habituated to such bafflement.

Having just returned from Italy, he passed on to David Russell his latest impressions of that country and the financial rumours surrounding Mussolini's regime. Immersion in such topics would confirm to TP that the Quest attempt was truly over and other considerations had come to the fore:

Italy
All this talk is exaggerated. Nevertheless Mussolini has a hard struggle to keep the country loyal to his regime because of the economic stringency. I have discussed politics quite openly and in public places with members of Mussolini's cabinet and with prominent fascisti; but there is much discontent at present.

(Letter from TP to David Russell, 9.10.31)

Also that year TP passed on opinions about Germany, opinions which demonstrate to us the contemporary, pre-Hitler view, that Communism was the only evil to be feared:

196

> *Germany may follow in Italy's rather than Russia's footsteps. Her*
> *people have not the Slav outlook and are at bottom too law loving to*
> *welcome Communism.*
>
> (Letter from TP to David Russell, 1.8.31)

This attitude was scarcely surprising in view of the information emerging from Stalin's regime at the time. TP's 'Appeal for the Russian Clergy' was still in full operation, raising funds, campaigning discreetly and gathering information. Thus he was in a position to tell Russell about the latest sufferings of the 'Kulaks':

> *Concerning Russia: Sir Bernard Pares gave us a review of current*
> *conditions at our meeting this week. He says that the unrest amongst*
> *the peasants was greater than ever, mainly owing to the fact that over*
> *five million households had been uprooted during 1931 and the farmers*
> *and their families spread all over Russia and Siberia, often in the greatest*
> *poverty, having been dispossessed of all their belongings.*
>
> (Letter from TP to David Russell, 5.12.31)

Such sufferings would be scarcely imaginable in Britain, although life was far from comfortable there. TP could 'never remember such a situation, national, economic or personal; undoubtedly we are in for some turbulent times' *(letter to Russell, 1.8.31)*. Indeed, he felt that 'everyone will have to pull in his belt this winter, and the discipline should help national and individual character' *(letter to Russell, 27.8.31)*. Throughout it all he believed that the British Prime Minister was trying his best:

> *Yes I heard Ramsay Macdonald on the wireless. He sounded very*
> *tired but inspired by great ideals. I hope he can hold his team together,*
> *and I believe we shall emerge into better times. Meanwhile there is much*
> *debris to be cleared away.*
>
> (Letter from TP to David Russell, 9.10.31)

The debris that got cleared away would eventually be Macdonald himself, allowing his old partner in alternation, Stanley Baldwin, to step forward again. Baldwin inherited a major problem in the shape of a Great War (nay Boer War) fossil who kept insisting another war was on the way. His name was Winston Churchill, and he was finally about to find the right dragon. Hitler was not yet in power, but once he arrived, Churchill would saddle up his invisible steed, polish up his invisible lance, and set off across the murky political landscape of the Thirties, eventually enlisting the help of a fellow dragon-slayer, one Franklin D. Roosevelt.

All that was a decade away, and perhaps—who knows?—need not have happened. Back in September 1931, however, the Japanese military lost patience with their economic restraints and set about invading Manchuria. And thus the countdown to World War Two began. It was as though some fantastic law dictated that seeds of militarism in the East should be carried by the Earth's rotation to germinate in the West.

Yes, the Thirties were to be a low, dishonest decade. Despite TP's hope of a New Dispensation being ushered in on Eron, it seemed more as though a new Curse of Babel was descending on mankind. People from now on might speak the same language but fail utterly to understand each other. The centre could not hold, baffled friends would fall apart.

The test case was Mussolini. If he could stay sane then perhaps the decade might stay sane as well. Alas, the essential Mussolini was already burning out. Over in Turkey, over in the territory of the Quest itself, there was another test case, another long-term dictator, Mustafa Kemal. Could he stay sane where Mussolini could not? And the answer, mercifully and amazingly, was that he could.

As the new Quest adventurers set out East, this time backed by archaeological respectability, would they share Kemal's rugged pragmatism, or would they be infected by the new Curse of Babel, going Mussolini's way, sheering off into egotism, confusion and ultimate self-defeat? Whatever the answer, surely TP and Russell had gained enough hard-won wisdom to avoid divisiveness. Hadn't they?

As decades go, the Thirties were going to be very odd indeed.

10. Conclusion—What Was Going On?

In 1931 Wellesley Tudor Pole was 47 years old, a ripe old age compared to much biography fodder: rock stars and poets, for instance, not to mention the odd world conqueror. TP filled the years with plenty, but a cut off point must come somewhere, and the 1931 Quest attempt is the obvious place to end Volume One.

At that stage, he had accumulated a substantial C.V: managing director of the family firm, Constantinople adventurer, published author, public speaker, decorated war hero, prophet rescuer, director of occupied enemy territory administration, unpaid counsellor to the impoverished and distressed, business entrepreneur, land reclaimer, roving esparto agent, pilgrim site pioneer and, of course, husband, father, son and brother.

All of these come under the heading of This World. As for the Other World of Wellesley Tudor Pole, the most potent link was the Cup. For instance, when TP told the Dean's Yard Meeting of 1907 about its finding, he also reported (a) he had 'received instructions' (b) to predict, amongst other things, 'a Divine outpouring of the Holy Spirit into the world'.

And there we have two consistent themes in his life: (a) alleged contact with discarnate mentors, (b) bulletins on the Second Coming.

After that the Quest for evidence on the Cup's origins became a Quest for 'the release of the Forces focalised' beneath Constantinople—because TP understood, 'through the Sage', that this would help prepare for the Second Coming. Such things he considered 'a great Mystery, one which I vowed to solve when the Cup first came to light at Glastonbury in 1906.' (All quotations from letter to Russell, 2.8.22)

If, therefore, the Cup appears to melt away from the narrative at times, its influence does not.

What can all this mean to us? Considering such data, we might react in one of three ways: dismiss it as preposterous, accept it as illuminating, or examine it as data.

If we follow the third option, the word data must include, of course, 'statements made in all conviction'. It cannot mean 'items that are true in all respects' (if such ever exist). Their 'truth' must consist in some people believing them to be true.

It would be useful to correlate such data with outside information to clarify it by example. So, as a beginning, let us put it all in a scientific context. In June 1930 TP wrote to David Russell:

> *You will probably have noted Einstein's latest statement to the effect*
> *that what he calls 'space' has now become the sole theoretical representative*
> *of reality, having swallowed up ether, light, corpuscles and the gravitational*
> *and electro-magnetic fields.*
>
> (Letter from TP to David Russell, 17.6.30)

If 'space' is—or seemed at the time—the only reality, then that would relegate matter to unreality. TP's conclusion was:

> *It is the physicist who is now undermining Materialism, after having*
> *been its bulwark for so long.*
>
> (Letter from TP to David Russell, 19.6.30)

Nowadays physicists who undermine materialism are scarcely big news. They tell us about quantum entanglement ('spooky action at a distance,' according to Einstein), strings (too small to physically detect), multiple dimensions (ten or even eleven). But perhaps the biggest shocker is that most of the universe is missing. Only 30% of it is matter, the remaining 70% being 'dark energy'. Furthermore, of that 30% matter, a massive 90% is actually 'dark'. Consequently, if we do the sums, we find our own reality (sometimes known as baryonic matter) comprises something like 4% of the total.

In this context, 'dark' means undetected, hidden, or—here comes a provocative synonym—occult. A similar definition applied back in the 1600's when Galileo described prototype musings on gravity as 'occult fancy' (because while the effects were observable, the cause was hidden). This did not seriously disturb Isaac Newton, though, as he sat before his alchemical crucible peering ever further into what he called 'the great ocean of undiscovered truth'.

A Universe Full of Life

So what might be happening in the undiscovered, nay occult, 96% of Reality? Plenty of action, if TP and his communicators are to be believed. For instance, in 1924 TP let David Russell have the latest information on their own patch of unseen Reality:

> *BB said there are now 18 persons in the Council and 321 servitors*
> *around them and that the actual unseen helpers ran into thousands.*
>
> (Letter from TP to David Russell, 19.5.24)

That is, thousands of beings in the Beyond were apparently helping out on the Quest, a project that appeared to extend way beyond the recovery of certain documents. The Council was known as 'Tous' (or 'All') and communicated using various symbols and languages:

> *A member of each of the 18 groups who form the Council ('Tous')*
> *spoke to us one after the other giving the design or motto of the group in*
> *each case. The messages were in Greek, Latin, French, Italian, English,*
> *Hindustani, Russian and Egyptian Hieroglyphics.*
> (Letter from TP to David Russell, 12.8.24)

If we are willing to credit such things, then the Universe changes from the empty, cold thing of Post Reformation Science, and returns to something like the old Medieval Universe, thronging with all sorts of life. Back in the times of Dante, Thomas Aquinas, Chaucer and Roger Bacon, the universe was both glorious with light (only dark where Earth's shadow fell), and harmonious with the music of the spheres:

> *The Primum Mobile, The Stellatum and Leaden Saturn*
> *Shining Jupiter, Iron Mars and Golden Sol*
> *Coppery Venus, Quicksilver Mercury, Silvery Luna*

In the spheres above silvery Luna soared the angelic hierarchies:

> *Seraphim, Cherubim, Thrones;*
> *Dominations, Powers, Virtues;*
> *Principalities, Archangels, Angels.*

More interestingly for our present purpose were the sublunary regions (below Luna, the moon) where Daemons rode the air, beings who in Classical thought could be either good or bad, as indeed could those TP was getting involved with. Some of the most unusual data on these came in a letter to David Russell in December 1924:

> *BB says: 'Upon our path we have met a gigantic complex of souls,*
> *some who have finished their cycle of incarnations, others who have not*
> *yet begun them. All these souls belong to angles [i.e. directions, ed.] which*
> *are antipodal to our work.'*
> (Letter from TP to David Russell, 18.12.24)

(Here, as we have seen before, the word 'antipodal' suggests intentions opposed to the broadly Christian intents of 'Tous'.)

We might note that some of these 'antipodal' beings are old enough to have finished their incarnations. Does this mean they are wise enough, even perfect enough? Or do other rules apply? This is not a question we can expect to answer, but it does provide strange data for anyone pondering reincarnation.

The strangeness becomes more marked when we hear in a letter dated 18th December 1924 that Rome is the 'greatest antipodal centre' in the world, and are told later that incarnate antipodes are indeed in action there:

> When I was in Rome BB said I met several antipodes but as they were out of touch with their Guides, no harm could result (i.e. they had no power). Is that true of all who are not linked up with unseen guides or helpers?
>
> (Letter from TP to David Russell, 5.6.24)

Who were these Roman antipodes, we might wonder? Could they have been some of Mussolini's Fascisti, or, perhaps more alarming, Vatican power-grabbers?

Once upon a time there used to be a heresy called Manichean Dualism, based on the Zoroastrian outlook of continual conflict between the force of light (Ahura Mazda) and the force of dark (Ahriman). The Cathars of Southern France, for instance, favoured such an outlook round about 1213, so the humorously named Pope Innocent III pronounced that any Crusaders were forgiven in advance for whatever they might do to Cathars. Burning struck the Crusaders as a favourable tactic, along with standard interview tortures. And such responses put paid to any serious speculation about discarnate realities for a few centuries. (Protestantism, of course, did not help: merely narrowed the outlook a bit further.)

So what are we left with as we begin the new millennium? A somewhat Manichean world, we might suspect, with good and evil finely balanced. If God is in charge, says the honest sceptic, how come He (or She, if you prefer) allows things to go on as they do? It is a crude question, which receives the subtle answer that free will must operate freely, even if the free will happens to belong to, say, that noted antipode, Adolf Hitler. Subtle answer or no, we persist with our crude line of questioning: who's in charge then, God or the latest antipodal psycho?

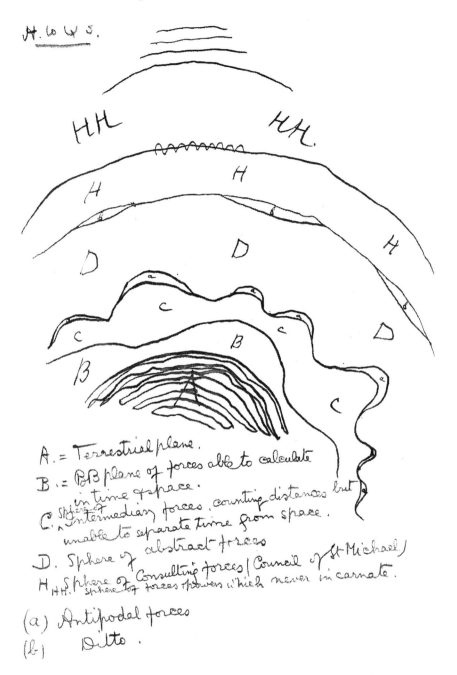

A. to Q.S.

HH   HH.

H   H

H   H

D   D   H

C   C

C   B   D

B   C

A. = Terrestrial plane.

B. = BB plane of forces able to calculate in time & space.

C. Sphere of intermediary forces, counting distances but unable to separate time from space.

D. Sphere of abstract forces

H. HH. Sphere of Consulting forces (Council of St Michael) powers which never incarnate.

(a) Antipodal forces

(b)   Ditto .

Sketch map of discarnate forces, friendly and antipodal,
in relation to the 'Terrestrial plane', following battle over Quest group

If we refer to TP's diagram, 'A. to Q3', we can see something like the old fashioned medieval spheres surrounding planet Earth (labelled A), including places for BB, intermediary forces, abstract forces and so on, as well as little pockets (small 'a' and 'b') where the 'antipodes' lurk.

The conclusion it offers is an interesting one. If you are on Earth or close by (in what TP called Borderland) then things would indeed appear to be Manichean. As TP wrote to his sister, Mary, in December 1920:

> *Our unseen friends do not dwell in the spheres of omnipotence, but in the Borderland of Conflict, battling to save the Soul of the World.*
> (Letter from TP to Mary Bruce Wallace, 3.12.20)

However, and here is where the answer to who is in charge becomes rather elegant — the further away from Earth you go the more it appears that God is. (So Pope Innocent didn't need to burn the Cathars; just tell them they were referring to a limited portion of Reality).

Perhaps this can suffice for a general view of TP's universe.

The data we have, then, is that numerous friendly entities are in continual, quasi-Manichean conflict with numerous 'antipodal' entities in nearby Borderland 'battling to save the Soul of the World'. Further away are 'the spheres of omnipotence' where Divine Power is unassailable.

All this seems to have affinity with the classical/medieval picture of the universe, where good and bad 'daemons' mingle in the 'sublunary' sphere, but ultimate power resides with the 'Primum Mobile'.

A Meta-Biography of BB

The next information we require concerns the discarnate characters. Some readers will naturally view them as figments of overheated imaginations, but such views will inhibit any data gathering. So we must suspend judgement, at least temporarily. Let us, then, with due open-mindedness, begin with a brief meta-biography of BB. As we have already heard, the initials stand for Boris Bavaiev, an early nineteenth century Russian poet and philosopher. That, however, was not his most recent incarnation. In 1926 TP asked David Russell:

> *Did I tell you that BB has revealed his (earthly) identity? He was Prince Olege son of the Grand Duke Constantine, cousin of the Czar and King George, a rebel against his caste, a student of occultism, killed in October 1914 on the Eastern Front. His sword being broken, he drew his*

revolver whilst at the charge and accidentally shot himself through the groin, dying the same day. Prince Olege is of course an identifiable person and known to have existed. He died at 24.

(Letter from TP to David Russell, 1.1.26)

There seems much symbolism in this account. BB does indeed appear the sort to go charging boldly onward, whether adequately armed or not, and the resulting possibility of error is something TP experienced only too acutely. However, the gripping interest about BB is his continuing imperfection in the Beyond. Forget clouds and harps; if we can get things wrong down here, we can get them wrong up there. For instance, TP and Russell agreed that:

He ceased to become a mouthpiece for a higher power when the temptation of personal authority crept in.

(Letter from TP to David Russell, 22.10.30)

This exercise of personal authority was arguably at its most annoying in the matter of the 1931 sea level. Apparently, there had been a suggestion that TP might check on such things first:

On 1.1.31, amongst other things I received 'A visit to the spot by two members of the Group should be undertaken to definitely locate and mark the spots and sea entry.' When this was put to BB he said it was 'not necessary'. Had it been undertaken we should have been saved the 1931 yachting fiasco.

(Letter from TP to David Russell, 5.1.33)

This is damning evidence, but if we are putting BB on trial we ought to provide defence material too, so let us consider Solovetsky Island (somewhere west of Archangel in northern Russia). When BB was asked where the Quest group might seek back-up information, he cited an obscure monastery there which had been founded by two paragons of obscurity:

I have now heard from a trusted correspondent on the Solovetsky Island, confirming the fact that the Monastery there was founded in the 14th century by Saints Zosima and Savaty (the names given by BB). Interesting because none of us (the two Russians included) knew the names of these out of the way Saints (or of the Monastery there).

(Letter from TP to David Russell, 17.10.32)

This sounds like precise, and therefore evidential, information. There again, we must remember that BB seemed extraordinarily accurate in the matter of the Quest (apart, of course, from the crucial detail of sea level):

> *Everything accords with the BB plans except the sea levels. Indeed we have seen under the water and between the rocks the Byzantine brick archway exactly at the spot shown by BB and the position and shape of the rocks is identical with the plan.*
>
> (Letter from TP to David Russell, 5.7.31)

It appears then that BB as a source of information might perhaps be defended. However, we will not have completed our brief examination of this fallible (and therefore oddly endearing?) figure till we consider the question of how he allegedly got in touch. The answer is provided in a document dated 19.8.23, entitled Methods of Communication. Here is part of what it says:

> *When a sitting takes place BB draws the etheric fluid from the two mediums on his side and draws the magnetic fluid from AB and DS [Bergengreen and Sissoëff, ed.] on your side. These fluids interpenetrate, creating a spherical cloud in which the invisible machine on our side, and the planchette on yours, are enclosed.*
>
> *The invisible instrument, of which your wooden planchette is a replica, or shadow, is now contained within the etheric vacuum. The ideas to be expressed are whirled into this vacuum by BB in the form of spiral columns of kinetic etheric current, which set the real, and to you invisible, machine in motion. Your planchette responds to the activity of the unseen machine.*
>
> (TP typescript, 'Method of Communication: Notes from Memory. The Sage, 19.8.23'.)

Once again, if we are seeking data, here is something to consider: machinery on the Other Side! But where does this information come from? And the answer—inevitably in TP's case—is his own personal source of uplift and information, 'The Sage'. So now we move onto our next character.

The Sage

We can actually get a word picture of the Sage so long as we remember we are dealing in subjective metaphor. If we listen in on a Family Group meeting at Letchworth in July 1922, we find Mary breaking the awed and atmospheric silence to report on interesting guests from Beyond. (As usual in these meetings, we might remember, TP is 'objective' — neither seeing nor hearing — whilst Mary is 'subjective', tuned in). She describes the leader of the guests who is, according to her impressions:

> *Very venerable-looking. He is clad in a brown garb, has a rosary round his waist, sandals on his feet and a staff in his hand. A bluish light surrounds him. He is a very gracious personality — a shorter figure than our Family Guide, and broader. He looks old, while the F.G. looks young. He is like 'the Sage' whom I have seen before behind Wellesley. Accompanying him are a band of disciples or fellow-workers. Around them is a yellowish light. There are six or seven of them, forming a circle. They approach the earth boundary. Looking down, one says:*
> *'Is the time ripe now?'*
> *The leader answers: 'Not yet.'*
> *They ask: 'How long?'*
> *Answer: 'After a short interval.'*
> *Question: 'Will the revelation be sudden?'*
> *Answer: 'Yes, if the chaos does not intervene.'*
> (Family Group transcript, Tudor Cottage, 28.7.22)

There is data here, but there is also, if we wish, food for the imagination. The picture of six or seven discarnates approaching the earth boundary, peering down, and discussing prospects is one that may appeal to some temperaments. Remember again, though, that this is subjective metaphor (i.e. the characters may look that way to Mary but probably not to each other). As for a job description of the Sage, here is what TP was told later on:

> *Although a member of the Council of St Michael, my own place is a modest one. You call me the Sage, I am sometimes known as the Unifier. Power reaches the Quest group on earth in three qualities: Cosmic, Spiritual and what is sometimes called Psychic. My task is to unify the manifestations of this the Christ power as it passes through the Michael Council in the unseen and through the Quest group on earth. Help me with this work. Nothing can be more important.*
> (From the Sage through his Messenger. Noon 7.5.31 London SW1)

It does not sound anything like the 'modest' work he calls it, but 'modest' seems a key word in spiritual self descriptions (probably for good reason, pride in high places tending to produce Paradise Lost scenarios.) As for the Sage's work in relation to TP, it was, in a way, irritatingly vague and, in another way, eminently sensible. That is, he would not say much of practical value about the Quest, but he did say plenty of moral value, and in the end (one might argue), morality is practicality, because otherwise everyone wastes their time posturing and quarrelling. Here is the Sage's mission statement for TP:

> *My desire is to help you to strengthen your own vision and inspiration*
> *so that you may place complete reliance upon these and become independent*
> *of communications from outside sources.*
> (Manuscript, TP's handwriting, 6 p.m. 13.9.31)

The Sage's job as regards TP, therefore, was to render himself more or less redundant which, arguably, may be the goal of every good teacher. We might notice, by the way, that the quotation above was written down in TP's own handwriting. That is the way he preferred receiving messages from his discarnate friends. And at last one of those friends, Jack, agreed with him.

> *When I have been 'talking' to Jack, he always seems pleased if I record*
> *in writing the conversation as it goes along; the writing seems to strengthen*
> *the psychic link that keeps the contact going and when the link snaps,*
> *through noise or interruption, the exchange of ideas immediately stops.*
> (Letter from TP to David Russell, 14.6.29)

We are not talking anything spooky here, no planchettes, no automatic writing, just a jotting down of ideas to help the flow (one step up from doodling perhaps).

Jack

And now let us cross examine Jack. He had been a ward of TP's, the reader may remember, before the Great War, and since his death on the Somme in 1916 he had been able to return the favour by looking after TP. Here is his own summary of usefulness during the difficult days of Quest frustration:

> *I am the only worker in the Quest on this side who knew you in the*
> *flesh during your present earth life. For this reason I can reach you more*
> *easily at this juncture than is possible for others over here.*

> (Manuscript, TP's handwriting: 'From Jack from memory. Received early
> a.m.' 8.9.24)

Because of this, it was Jack who was able to give TP a perspective on
the whole BB situation, and once again we are presented with some very
unusual data:

> *I have had a long talk with the Sage, and he allows me to talk to you*
> *about it. As you know, the Council or group, whose instrument BB is, have*
> *been working out an experiment in occultism. It is the first time for many*
> *centuries that such an experiment, on such an important yet intricate scale,*
> *has been attempted in the Western World. Work of similar character has*
> *been undertaken many times in the East, in India and China and in what*
> *you term prehistoric times in Persia and Egypt. Such work calls for the*
> *training of a group on our side who can function at will within the Astral*
> *envelope of the Earth. I use your terms to help you understand better. When*
> *the unseen group have reached a certain point in their training, a group*
> *of souls on earth, who have been associated with the unseen group in the*
> *past, are brought together for training and discipline.*
>
> *At a given moment the two groups are linked together for the purpose*
> *of carrying out the work jointly.*
>
> *In the present instance the Quest and all that follows from it is the*
> *work ordained.*
>
> (Manuscript, TP's handwriting: 'From Jack, London NW11, Early a.m.',
> 13.9.24)

So that is the first point: the whole BB thing is a rare and intricate
experiment. The next point will be that the Sage does not like the experiment
much. From a data-gathering point of view, this is noteworthy. Disputes
in the Beyond may not be what we expect, but they are what TP and his
communicators offer. Here is the inside story from Jack:

> *The Sage and those surrounding him are not members of the unseen*
> *group of BB and Tous, although they are represented. The Sage has been*
> *close to TP since 1904. It was his intention that the Quest should be carried*
> *out by the use of other methods than those now being employed.*
>
> *In 1922, on the 'Rubicon' night [presumably of decision in the*
> *Beyond, ed.], co-operation between the two unseen groups was decided*
> *upon finally. The Sage, through TP's personal guide, instructed him to*

obey the suggestions communicated through BB, so far as outer details of the Quest were concerned. This has been done.

During 1922, 1923 and 1924 there have been occasions when the leaders of the two unseen groups have differed as to the methods to be employed for completing the group formation on Earth. The principal disagreement developed during the summer of 1923. In order to carry out the occult project elaborated by BB's group, it was necessary for the

Jack (Cheape) in uniform; killed on the Somme in 1916

vibrations of the five on earth to be attuned to a certain keynote. When the five were thus attuned, work through planchette was easier and it was hoped that the 6th could be drawn into the circle more rapidly.

(Manuscript, TP's handwriting: 'From Jack, London NW11, Early a.m.', 13.9.24)

Here, perhaps, we need to pause or our data will dwindle out of intelligibility. The best analogy for what follows is to consider radio broadcasts. Let us say the keynote of BB is something equivalent to 198 kHz long wave, and the Sage is on, say, 909 kHz medium wave. TP will have difficulty keeping his receiver tuned to both at the same time, as Jack goes on to say:

Each time that TP raised his mental rate of vibration in order to receive guidance from the Sage and his guide, the BB system was interfered with. Sometimes TP fell between two stools, neither holding the BB note nor reaching the higher note. Messages from the Sage and others (including myself) were misinterpreted and at times not 'heard' correctly, and the strain on TP became so great that it was decided to concentrate upon the BB note until the group on earth had been completed.

You have already been told that the Sage agreed to hold his group on one side while Tous' plan for the drawing in of the 6th had been worked out to completion. This plan failed in its object and has been abandoned. What we consider to have been unnecessary mental and physical suffering has been caused to the workers on Earth. We have done all we could to mitigate this.

(Manuscript, TP's handwriting: 'From Jack, London NW11, Early a.m.', 13.9.24)

Whether one regards this as ripe imaginings or descriptions of reality, it offers perspectives unobtainable elsewhere. War in Heaven has been a familiar concept since the Fall of Lucifer, but now we have Disputes in Heaven—even Botched Plans in Heaven. Are these more credible, more incredible, or—tantalisingly—both?

Whatever the answer, it is Jack who has provided the data (or, of course, TP's subconscious masquerading as Jack, a patronising theory but one we must not entirely discount).

TP was also open to other sources of information, such as the planchette scripts involving BB and such other personalities as Murcius Robustus, who, as we saw in Chapter 9, could step in, indignant Latinate capitals and all.

This, of course, is as perceived by TP, and—in their own ways—by Leveaux and the Russians.

The Russians, David Russell, Gertrude Mellor

It is time now to consider these perceivers, so now we move from discarnate characters to corporeal ones. Were they all mad, fantasising, self-deceiving—or did they actually perceive something real?

The best defence witness for the Russians seems to be one Renée Nicol, a French academic, who joined the Quest group in the 1930's. She testifies that when TP first met the Russians 'their transparent honesty impressed' him 'as favourably as their exceptional automatic writing' ('The Quest', Renée Nicol, 1958). She came on the scene too late to meet Dmitry Sissoëff, who died in October 1930 but had much to say about Michael Pojidaiev (in her second-language phraseology):

> Besides, of being a real seeker of Truth, MP has done several marvellous pieces of sculpture according to his sensations and the Other World. I know him sufficiently well to assure that he is most reliable and works only for an IDEAL. I had never met before anyone sacrificing himself entirely for an IDEA. All his life is—THE OTHER WORLD. I may add that since I met MP in July 1932, my life seems to have changed tremendously.
>
> (Letter from Renée Nicol to Prince Frederick of Saxen-Altenberg, 19.2.38)

TP and his family also had much to do with Pojidaiev (TP's daughter, Jean, referring to him as 'Podgy' the reader may recall)—and there was nothing in their amiable enjoyment of him (and his silver teeth) to suggest he was regarded as anything other than sincere. This is an important point. Sincerity does not guarantee accuracy, but it may help dispel doubts (if any exist) as to the motivation of the Russians who, being asylum seekers, were consequently impoverished.

Michael Pojidaiev died in Paris in March 1950. As for the third Russian, Anatole Bergengreen, he gave up the struggle to get a work permit and left Paris with his daughter, Madame Ouchakoff, in August 1935 for Paraguay where he died in December 1949. (TP, ever friendly, kept in touch with Madame Ouchakoff, during the 1950's, arranging presents of magazine subscriptions for her on an annual basis.)

One more witness for the Russians may be called forward: David Russell. Nowhere in the extensive TP/Russell correspondence is there any hint that he mistrusted the honesty of the Russians, and Russell was a man who had his own mind on matters.

It would be good to look at that mind now.

David Russell had been TP's closest friend since 1912, and with the change in Quest work he looked set to be TP's closest collaborator. Before committing himself, though, Russell wanted to make his attitude perfectly clear:

> *My first close personal contact with mediumistic powers and trance conditions was in 1911. The medium in whom I was particularly interested then had very unusual powers and I am satisfied that he was absolutely sincere, but I came very definitely to the belief that the mental and other conditions surrounding the medium influenced at times the messages received.*
>
> *That belief I might say is a fundamental conviction and applies equally to what might broadly be called intuitive guidance.*
>
> (Typewritten statement by David Russell, 13.9.31)

Here is an example of what we might call open-minded scepticism. Russell is not ruling out 'unusual powers' but he is ruling in contamination via 'mental and other conditions':

> *If we are to rely on intuitive guidance, we have to make sure that the intuition is true, i.e., that we ourselves are masters of the conditions through which these intuitions reach us. I believe that through faith and concentration we can secure this. I hold equally strongly that we cannot divide what might be called our loyalties without losing that sense of absolute reliance and certainty.*
>
> *For this reason I can never accept guidance that intuitively I do not feel to be right. If I fail to get guidance, or if the guidance I get is not of the highest, that is my fault and is a matter for myself to deal with, but I do not feel that I can ever submit willingly to other guidance.*
>
> (Typewritten statement by David Russell, 13.9.31)

Let us be clear about what Russell has just said. TP, or anyone else, may have marvellous and mesmerising things to say, but Russell will not accept a word of them unless his own intuition says so. More than that, he insists on being master 'of the conditions through which these intuitions reach us.' This is a man who intends to be nobody's dupe:

I am willing to consider any facts or suggestions that may be put before me and these may be obtained from any source, but the conclusions to be drawn from them, so far as I am concerned, must always be left to myself and to my own inner convictions.

(Typewritten statement by David Russell, 13.9.31)

This self-reliant attitude applied not just to psychic matters but to business, offering a clue to the man's success as the owner of one of the largest and most progressive paper mills in Europe:

This statement is in general terms and applies not only to any particular interest, but to my whole life.

(Typewritten statement by David Russell, 13.9.31)

Alert readers may perhaps sniff trouble brewing. TP was clearly the leader of the Quest, but if Russell was asked to take over the official aspect of it then Russell would do whatever he thought right, regardless of whether TP agreed. Two such long-standing friends could surely be trusted to maintain harmony and unity of vision in ideal, or even fair, circumstances, but the Thirties were no time for things to go ideally or fairly. Throw in a couple more personalities, say Frederick Leveaux, sincere to the point of apoplexy, and James Baxter, the nominated archaeologist for the new Quest attempt, and the plot might thicken in a way that deserves a Second Volume for its exposition.

Russell's opinion of Russian honesty is worth noting, but more important is his opinion of TP's various qualities, because, of course, TP is the perceiver on whom we must chiefly focus. And the positive news here is that Russell trusted TP's perception most of the time. For instance, Russell's letter of May 1918 to James S. Hyslop (see Chapter 1 for a fuller version) gives clear testimony of TP's faculties:

W.T.P. has from the age of 16 or 17 had abnormal vision, but since leaving school he has, until he joined the army, led a strenuous business life, and the development of his psychic powers has been natural.

Since the outbreak of war he has come into touch with many soldiers killed in battle. Practically all his experiences have been in the homes of friends or of a personal nature, and the vision is direct and he seldom makes written records of experiences. Speaking generally, he lives a perfectly normal life and sees abnormally while in a perfectly normal state.

(Letter from David Russell to James S. Hyslop, May 1918)

There we have back-up for TP's psychic faculty, and soon we will consider that faculty in more detail. However, we must delay. There is another character to consider first, that vital catalyst of disharmony, Gertrude Mellor. There will be no sense of completion if we do not know what happened after the Eron and Constantinople ventures.

A star of 1930, Gertrude Mellor had been a flop in 1931 — an illustration, if illustrations be needed, that in spiritual journeys an ego is excess baggage. To be fair, TP had known all along about her 'strength and in a certain sense, insensitiveness' and had realised 'she is not a mystic but is trained to withstand great shocks' (letter to Russell, 9.5.31). Unfortunately her 'insensitiveness' seemed largely directed towards her Quest companions and the 'great shocks' she withstood were their resultant opposition. Teams only succeed if there is team spirit, and it was time to drop her from the Quest line-up. Moreover, TP felt her whole approach was incompatible with his:

> *In regard to Miss Mellor's work and outlook, she works on occult and even magical lines, hence comes to grief at times. Her activities draw down upon her head, active occult opposition, as on the occasion of Quest work in 1931, and her methods are not ours.*
>
> *My approach to the sacred centres is a mystical and not an occult approach; anyway one tries to make it that. My thought turns to prayer and meditation and not to any ceremonial ritual or invocation. It is the latter which might bring about the opposition to which Miss Mellor refers in her letter.*

(Letter from TP to David Russell, Eve of St Michael's Day, 1934)

The 'letter' in question had warned about hostile entities on Devenish Island (also known as Eron or the 'Holy Isle Of The West'), where she and TP had encountered friendly entities in September 1930. However, she no longer regarded the island as a healthy location:

> *I should advise you to leave Devenish alone. Some very retrograde Atlantean forces are about. All that is good of the old magic forces has been released. We are all especially warned not to revive or contact these old fading forces.*

(Letter from Gertrude Mellor to TP, Sept 21st, year unspecified, 1934?)

Her verdict on Eron/Devenish is a disappointing one, but one that TP came increasingly to share. Writing in 1966 he described it as 'riddled with unattractive elementals' (letter to Rosamond Lehmann, 1.10.66). As for Gertrude Mellor herself, she faded from the TP correspondence and is heard of no more.

TP as Man, Mystic and Psychic

And now the main topic must be TP, but we can lead into it by briefly considering his attitude to another psychic lady. It seems fair to assume that mystics need a way of keeping a grip on reality, and for an example of due scepticism, we can observe his reactions to Helena Handcock (née Humphreys), a long term collaborator, friend and recipient of TP's practical help (for instance, with overdue rent). Back in 1906, when she was still single and Helena Humphreys, her dramatic reactions to the Cup helped set him off on the Quest. However, that did not mean he swallowed everything she subsequently uttered:

> *I saw Mrs Handcock yesterday and she foresaw a short journey for me and then a long one, said all would be well financially and that the Quest would succeed. One wonders whether unconscious mind reading plays a part in her vision?*
>
> (Letter from TP to David Russell, 11.7.23)

This, of course, is very much what Russell suspected about his test medium back in 1911, so thus far we find the two friends at one in their caution.

We could look at plenty more examples of such scepticism, but let us see how far TP balanced it with open-mindedness. For an instance of this we can see him in 1924 speculating to Russell about how reincarnation might work:

> *What do you make of the idea that we can 'choose' our own bodies when the time comes to reincarnate? I suppose this only refers to souls who are developed and highly individualised. I wonder how the Law works and whether one can resist a new gravitation earthward?*
>
> (Letter from TP to David Russell, 17.4.24)

Apparently he is no expert at this stage, and it is interesting to note the contrast between this and later certainty. As we saw in Chapter One, George Trevelyan, the New Age pioneer, called TP 'one of the great seers and adepts of this epoch' and Rosamond Lehmann went further, calling him 'a Master'. Clearly, though, he was neither of these in 1924, and here we have one of the benefits of his lifelong letter writing: we possess a unique record of an alleged Adept (or even Master) in the process of development.

He could sense something of this process himself. For instance, on New Year's Day in 1925 he wrote to tell his mother about a supernormal experience in Rome, then went on to make a fascinating observation:

> *I stopped to watch a crowd of young people saying Goodbye to a peasant lad who had evidently driven his horse and cart into Rome with vegetables and was about to return. A voice said: 'That boy drives to meet his Fate'. I crossed the street with a vague intention to speak some warning but again the Voice: 'You must not interfere'. So I walked on. Fifteen minutes later when nearing my hotel in the Via Bambuino I came upon another crowd. A tram had run into a horse and cart, horse safe, cart smashed and my boy... quite dead.*
>
> *Now what was the use of warning me if I were allowed to take no action to avoid a tragedy? And if I had spoken would it have had any effect? I have been trying to find the boy since but so far without result. Such a nice handsome, sunny lad and yet his time had come and he could not escape. The problem of fate and free will is not easily solved.*
>
> *It is a pity, perhaps, that I have never kept a diary record of such experiences as these; they are so common to me that I forget that they are unusual. However, I doubt whether they possess any permanent interest or value for others, although they go to build up within me what I shall ultimately become.*
>
> (Letter from TP to 'Darling Mother', Grand Hotel De Russie, Rome, New Years Day 1925)

It is an anecdote full of interest: whose is the voice, and why the useless warning (as he says)? There again, if TP is trying to find the boy, it cannot be in this world, so he is clearly trying some of his 'rescue work' in the Beyond. However, the main thing to note is that he feels he is 'becoming'. That is, he feels he will in future be more than he is at present.

Nor was this an isolated incident, as his niece, Monica, relates (simultaneously mentioning something tantalising about TP's home life, to which we will return later):

In his ordinary daily life, and in his travels, he was constantly having abnormal experiences, of every kind, about which he would tell us and Katharine, but we all knew that they were not to be mentioned to Florence (or in his home).

(Letter from Monica Bruce Wallace to Patrick Benham — author of 'The Avalonians' — 24.2.88)

It seems, then, that if we are willing to credit psychic powers at all, TP had plenty, and these were developing just as were his spiritual powers (a quite different kind of ability). Discipline is often reckoned crucial in spiritual matters, and this is where the Quest might, paradoxically, have been most successful. It provided him with plenty of opportunity to learn through suffering, to mould success out of failure, to be tested and disciplined—all the bracing and annoying things a discarnate adviser might say. For instance, back in 1932 TP was shaking his head in wonder at it all:

I seem to have been tested, in material matters anyway, up to the hilt these last years and one wonders whether external perplexities etc do lead to purification.

(Letter from TP to David Russell, 19.8.32)

It did seem to be a material testing, but beyond that it was a test of tenacity and belief—in fact a test of faith:

Sometimes I feel as if I were doing nothing of any value with my life, and time goes on and the best years pass, and still there is nothing worth while to show for it. I suppose patience really is a virtue?

(Letter from TP to David Russell, 32.10.31)

Was all this suffering needless? Or was it valuable training? Consider the example of Milarepa, an eleventh century mystic revered in Tibetan culture. In the 'Ordeal of the Towers' he was ordered by his spiritual master to build stone towers in various unsuitable places then tear them down, half complete. It seems a mad method of teaching spiritual enlightenment, but that was the end result: spiritual enlightenment. Was TP similarly building the 'obedience muscles', albeit unintentionally, for future enlightenment?

So far, then, we might be willing to credit TP with (a) unusual talents, (b) due scepticism and (c) adequate discipline. However, that still does not make him a reliable receiver of alleged messages. He might, to put it bluntly, be a nutter. How do we address the problem?

Social relations are a good indicator, and here TP seems to enlist strong support. Friends made were frequently friends for life. For instance, Christine Allen, one of the 'triad of maidens' back in pre-war years, was still a friend and accomplice fifty years later, re-emerging as 'Sandy' (after a South African marriage to a Colonel Sandeman) and acting as first on-site warden to TP's recently purchased Chalice Well Gardens in 1959.

There may perhaps have been a further component in TP's goodwill towards Christine, though it involves a bit of gossipy speculation. In pre-war, and unmarried, years he may have noticed she was the right age, highly attractive and very psychic. Indeed, her haste in upping and marrying John Duncan, the artist, in Edinburgh (her first marriage) seems to suggest something had uncomfortably stirred her feelings. That something may well have been the arrival on the scene a few months earlier of one Florence Snelling, who was soon to become Florence Tudor Pole.

Why did TP marry Florence and not Christine? Here we have, perhaps, another argument in favour of his basic sanity.

If TP was a man of two worlds, he would need a secure environment to keep him earthed in this one. He had many challenges to meet and couldn't afford to stray too far from everyday reality. It seems likely, therefore, that he instinctively selected Florence as someone strong minded enough to support his imaginative projects (offering hospitality to Russian psychics, Hindu seers and the like) whilst also retaining her own independence of outlook (remaining carnivorous, for example, and even tempting TP away from unduly strict vegetarianism). Looked at in that light, she was just what he needed — along with his business suits, military experience and precision of speech — to keep him 'grounded'. And hence, we can see why, as Monica (rather gleefully) reported, his 'abnormal experiences, of every kind were not to be mentioned to Florence (or in his home)'.

So far so good, but there are deeper sources of quirkiness than making the right or wrong friends and marriage choices. Biographies often delve into a subject's sex life, so perhaps we should ask if there is anything of note in TP's case? 'Not much' is the answer, although there is a rather interesting letter he wrote in 1919 to an unnamed colonel who was apparently having difficulty keeping his flies buttoned. Fair enough, acknowledged TP, it is not easy:

> *Don't think I am going to preach; I have as hard struggles as any man and have by no means reached a final haven in this direction. I simply attempt to practise what seems by experience to show the way out into*

clearer regions of thought and conduct. First one must be sure that one wants to find a way out of the sense jungle.

Then one must cease to regard the sex urge within one as an enemy to self respect and decency; something unclean. This Urge is the physical expression of Divine Creative potency within the mind.

Welcome one's (apparent) enemy as a friend, a true messenger from the Creator to the Created, a Divine instinct that has become temporarily uncontrolled and misdirected. Don't try to stifle and destroy a friend; without the true creative instinct nothing great can be achieved by man.

When the Tide comes surging through your mind do not surround its inner expression with sensual thoughts and wishes, but on the other hand immediately turn the Tide inward and upward rather than downward and outward. If you are working on a healing case, or for greater strength of being, or for added faith and purity, or for inner illumination, this is the moment when all your efforts should be put forth. If lying or sitting down, rise up and praise God, welcome his messenger, harness the Power waiting to be used and pour all your effort into the particular mental task on which you are engaged.

(I am speaking now of course of sensual sexual practices and not of natural normal sex intercourse between man and wife.)

(Typescript, 'Dear Colonel' crossed out at top, copy sent to David Russell, 23.7.19: 'I send this for what it may be worth; it was written in answer to an enquiry')

TP was no expert on sex: his mind was on other matters, and we can see above how he kept it there. As for the bracketed bit at the end about 'natural normal sexual intercourse between man and wife' that is as much as we are ever likely to find out about TP in the bedroom. Outside that room his daughter, Jean, described him and Florence as 'a devoted couple', and TP's letters after Florence's death in 1951 show just how bereft he felt.

Lest anyone wishes to invent covert liaisons, however, consider the following. Each year in the early 1920's the 'Family Group' would meet, and discarnate communicators would offer words of encouragement and advice (via Mary). Although sceptical about the insights of F.G. and A.B. (the Family Guide and a departed friend) TP did not query their existence. Hence, he accepted there were intelligences who were not only capable of observing his every action but of fully discussing them. As a prophylactic against misbehaviour, the Family Group would seem unusually potent.

This is not to say TP's mind was closed to the topic of sex. For instance, he wrote to David Russell in 1923 about a manuscript by Violet Firth (later to be known as Dion Fortune):

> *If I sent on Violet Firth's MSS on Sex Psychology, if you thought it worthwhile, could you have them copied for our private use? The MSS consists of a short preface and four short 'communicated' lectures, some of the ideas are worth consideration.*
>
> (Letter from TP to David Russell, 2.10.23)

The 'ideas worth consideration' can be found in Esoteric Philosophy of Love and Marriage by Dion Fortune, and in general they agree with TP's position (do not deny natural force; harness it for higher use). David Russell, by the way, did not consider the MSS worthwhile. Having been born deeper in the Victorian age than TP (1872) he objected to the word 'sex' in the original title.

This leads us to consider what social relations TP had with women other than his wife. Here is his view as expressed to his mother in 1925 (when he was forty years old):

> *I go to Viareggio on Saturday to stay the night with Lady Paget's funny but interesting old ladies, Contessa Campello and Miss Lister. I seem to specialise in old ladies from Mrs Bourne onwards, but of course my two principal friends (D.R. and F.L. [David Russell and Frederick Leveaux, ed.]) are men, still in the prime of life but neither of them is very masculine.*
>
> (Letter to 'Darling Mother'; Grand Hotel de Russie, Rome: New Years Day 1925)

Perhaps he sensed older women were a safer bet. His daughter, Jean, interprets the not 'very masculine' comment as a bit naughty. Maybe. Or maybe TP and his ilk acknowledged the feminine side in men seventy years before the concept entered the language.

This has been a somewhat rambling look at TP's social and sexual life, but sometimes a ramble is what the situation requires, and nowhere on our ramble have we been able to spot anything furtive going on behind bushes. Therefore, in testing TP's sanity (and hence his reliability as psychic and spiritual perceiver) we can find no evidence against him.

To this we might add the very powerful point that he never made a penny from his psychic powers. In fact, he was beset by financial problems all his life even whilst raising money for others via his charitable concerns.

To exemplify the sort of psychic powers under discussion let us return to the testimony of Israel Sieff, previously recorded in Chapter 6:

> *One day he said to me suddenly: 'Israel, I'm sorry to have to tell you, but shortly there is to be a tragedy in your life. Somebody you know and love is going to die. I wish I could tell you who it is; I can't.' Two weeks later there was a telephone call from Algeria. It was Tudor Pole. 'Israel,' he said, 'I must tell you that your sorrow is about to fall on you.' That was all, he said, he could say. The next morning, one of my sons died in an accident.*
>
> (Israel Sieff, 'Memoirs', Weidenfeld and Nicolson 1970, p.102)

How could TP possibly warn of an accident that happened the next day? Struggle all we will, there is no satisfactory answer. It just could not happen.

Are we then to accept TP's paranormal faculties? — because if we do we may find his paranormal universe demanding acceptance too. His own view on this appears in the foreword to The Silent Road (1960):

> *I have no desire to bring conviction to those who may regard what I have written as being incredible or the product of a fertile imagination. However, it is well to remind ourselves occasionally that in almost every field of research the so-called fantasies of yesterday often become the facts of today. The horizons of the mind are not fixed: they are expanding ceaselessly. Therefore it is suggested that what I have recorded should be read with a mind free from preconceived ideas or set opinions.*
>
> (Foreword, 'The Silent Road', 1960)

It is perhaps right to finish with words that TP wrote in the 1960's, because, of course, his story is by no means finished in this volume. In leaving off at 1931, we leave out many highlights of his life as a whole. They could amply fill a second volume: his struggles in the 1930s, his extraordinary 'Silent Minute' movement in World War Two, his post war researches, his dramatic resumption of the Quest, his purchase of Chalice Well, the books he published in the 1960s, and even a successful outcome to his Quest.

But for now, it may be best to let the last, elusive word rest with his younger son, writing in 1973:

> *He was a seer responding to requests made upon him by others. He taught but he was not a teacher. He wrote but he was not a writer. He acted but he was not a man of action.*
>
> (From 'The New Messenger' by David Tudor-Pole, private document sent to Patrick Benham, 13.3.73)

What was he then? David Tudor-Pole does not—or cannot—tell us. There again, a man who lived simultaneously in two worlds could not, by definition, be pinned down into one.

Timeline

1884: Born 23rd April (St George's day) in Weston-super-Mare.

1902: First visits Glastonbury, following a dream.

1904: Managing Director, aged 20, of Chamberlain Pole & Co. Had his first inner contact with 'The Sage'. Recruits 'Triad of Maidens'.

1906: Cup (or Blue Bowl) found near Bride's Mound, by Brue Stream, on the edge of Glastonbury, following a vision by TP.

1907: Dean's Yard Meeting on Cup. Daily Express report mentions Holy Grail causing great but temporary interest. First and second Quest attempts are made in Constantinople.

1910: Meets Abdul Baha at Ramleh (near Alexandria). Subsequent journey to Constantinople abandoned. TP and Triad take the Cup to Iona to revive island as a spiritual centre.

1911: Abdul Baha comes to England, stays with TP in Bristol.

1912: TP marries Florence Snelling, and first meets David Russell.

1914: Outbreak of World War One. TP's daughter Jean born (February).

1915: Son Christopher born (May). The Great War published.

1916: Enlists as private in Marines and documents brutal training conditions.

1917: Publishes Private Dowding. Posted to Near East as a 2nd Lieutenant with the Devons. Wounded in action near Jerusalem.

1918: Director of Occupied Enemy Territory Administration. Arranges rescue of Abdul Baha. Receives Zionist Commission. Meets Frederick Leveaux. World War One ends (November).

1919: Treaty of Versailles (often blamed for helping cause World War Two). TP leaves army with rank of Major. Awarded O.B.E. Returns to England and severs ties with Chamberlain Pole & Co.

1920: Sets up W. Tudor Pole & Co. in London.

1921: Son David born (April). Meets Bergengreen and Sissoëff.

1922: Meets Pojidaiev. Quest Group convenes in Cairo, receiving detailed information from BB. Third Quest attempt at Constantinople. Sets up Appeal for the Russian Clergy on his return.

1923: Frustrating problems over enlisting the 'Sixth' member of Quest Group.

1925: Sets up land reclamation company (SACI) in Gargano peninsula, Italy; visits Padre Pio. Sets up esparto grass company in Algeria (EAAN). Spiritual experiences at Tintern with 'Brother Brighill'.

1926: Sets up land development company in Rome (Aureliana). Writes The Cosmic Touch (unpublished). Deaths of father and mother.

1928: Family living on a houseboat. Spiritual experiences at St Michael's Mount with a 'guardian of the Mount'. Sets up groups to work for Sacred Centres. Aids publication of The Scripts of Cleophas (Geraldine Cummins).

1929: Wall Street Crash. TP battles with CPP and other defaulting companies.

1930: Dramatic experiences at the Holy Isle of the West (Devenish/ Eron) with Gertrude Mellor.

1931: Fourth Quest attempt in Constantinople. Subsequently decides to invite David Russell and the Walker Trust into the Quest.

1933: Hitler comes to power in Germany. Roosevelt comes to power in U.S.

1934: TP dangerously ill, rescued by surgery.

1935: Visits Constantinople. Increasing strain and conflict with Baxter, the Walker Trust archaeologist. Baxter uncovers Great Palace Mosaics. Considerable publicity results.

1936: Forms Wellesley Holdings Ltd to transform town waste into organic fertilizer.

1939: TP puts together the British Byzantine Archaeological Committee to find an alternative method of pushing forward the Quest. Outbreak of World War Two.

1940: Churchill becomes Prime Minister. Dunkirk, Battle of Britain, Blitz. TP sets up Big Ben Silent Minute.

1943: TP concerned about moral effect of bombing campaign over Germany.

1945: Atomic bombs dropped on Japan. End of World War Two.

1947: Churchill's 'Iron Curtain' speech, Cold War beginning.

1948: TP attempts to bring natural products via Emion Ltd into a market dominated by synthetic drugs.

1951: Death of Florence Tudor Pole.

1953: Fifth Quest attempt in Constantinople (now known as Istanbul).

1955: Major speech, 'Some Spiritual Issues Underlying World Problems', at the Palace of Het Oude Loo in Holland.

1956: Death of Sir David Russell.

1958: Death of Frederick Leveaux.

1959: Purchase of Chalice Well for the nation. Setting up of Chalice Well Trust.

1960: Publishes The Silent Road.

1965: Publishes A Man Seen Afar with Rosamond Lehmann.

1967: Opening of Upper Room in Little St Michael, the retreat house at Chalice Well. So far as TP's 'far memory' allows, the Upper Room duplicates the room of the Last Supper.

1968: Publishes Writing On The Ground with Walter Lang. His 'final withdrawal' on 13th September (n.b. TP considered 'death' a misleading and destructive concept).

1979: Rosamond Lehmann publishes My Dear Alexias, a selection of TP's letters to her.

1993: Patrick Benham publishes The Avalonians, giving information on TP, especially his earlier years.

1994: Lorn Macintyre publishes biography of Sir David Russell, including information on TP as businessman and originator of the Quest.

2008: wellesleytudorpole.com website: with information, articles and comprehensive photo galleries.

2009: Fiftieth anniversary celebrations at Chalice Well.

Bibliography

Brief comments are included so the interested reader may select appropriately. At the present time, however, (2010) most of TP's works are out of print, but one can always hope.

1. BOOKS BY WELLESLEY TUDOR POLE

The Great War: Some Deeper Issues (G. Bell and Sons, 1915)
With a foreword by Stephen Graham.
The main headings on the 'Contents' page can give an idea of the scope of this book:
PART 1: THE GREAT WAR, SOME DEEPER ISSUES (Being the substance of an address given at the Caxton Hall on 28th November 1914)
PART II: THE PASSING OF MAJOR P. (This article is reprinted from the Quest for July 1911, by the courtesy of the editor, Mr. G.R.S. Mead, M.A.)
PART III: LEAVES FROM THE NOTEBOOK OF A VISIONARY, INCLUDING EXTRACTS FROM PRIVATE LETTERS, CHIEFLY TO MY MOTHER
* The Great War: Some Deeper Issues has been out of print since World War One, so can only be accessed via the British Library, or - if lucky - via a private owner.
* See Chapter 5 for extracts.

Private Dowding (John M. Watkins, 1917)
(Fifth expanded edition 1943; Sixth Edition, Neville Spearman, 1966; Seventh edition, Pilgrims Book Services, 1984)
* In the expanded edition (and thereafter), TP added (a) The Return of Private Dowding (further material dating from 1919) and (b) The Passing of Major P (from The Great War: Some Deeper Issues). Hence, it became, like all TP's books, a collection of different pieces.
* See Chapter 5 for extracts.

The Cosmic Touch (1926, unpublished)
* This exists only as a set of disorganised carbon copies in the Russell papers at St Andrews University Library. Watkins, the publisher, rejected the manuscript, and although a certain Herbert von Krumhaar wished to publish a German translation in 1931, there is no evidence that he went ahead.
* See Chapter 8 for extracts.

The Silent Road (Neville Spearman, 1960)
(Sixth impression, C.W. Daniel, 1987)
With an Introduction by the Hon. Brinsley le Poer Trench.

* Probably the best book for a new reader, this is a collection of thoughts and experiences—ranging from, say, 'An Aftermath of Suicide' to 'Thinking from the Summit', and from 1910 to the late 1950's.

* See Chapters 1, 4, 5, 6 and 8 for either verbatim extracts or earlier versions of extracts.

A Man Seen Afar (Neville Spearman, 1965)
(New Edition, C.W. Daniel, 1983)
Written in collaboration with Rosamond Lehmann, with a foreword by Sir George Trevelyan, BT. M.A.

* Purported memories of the life and time of Jesus, along with supplementary material, most notably 'Man and his Relations with the Kingdoms of Nature'.

* See Chapter 2 for an extract under the heading 'Credo'.

Writing On The Ground (Neville Spearman, 1968)
(New Impression, Pilgrims Book Services, 1984)
Written in collaboration with Walter Lang, with a foreword by D.F.O. Russell.

* Further 'glimpses' of Jesus, along with much supplementary material, including a substantial section on the Baha'i Faith.

* For a brief extract relevant to the latter, see Chapter 6.

My Dear Alexias (Neville Spearman, 1979)
Letters from Wellesley Tudor Pole to Rosamond Lehmann, edited by Elizabeth Gaythorpe, with a foreword by Rosamond Lehmann.

* TP at his most unguarded (and humorous); hence, much 'way out' material, as well as gossip and anecdotes.

* Extracts can be found throughout the present volume.

2. OTHER WRITINGS BY WELLESLEY TUDOR POLE

Editorials and Articles in 'The Race Builder' (1906)
'Mind and its Mysteries: How to Develop and Control Thought Power' appeared as a series of four monthly articles, beginning in February 1906.

Some Unrecognised Arguments In Favour Of Vegetarian Diet (1909)
'Being a synopsis of an Address delivered by W. Tudor Pole at the Colston Hall, Bristol on May 4, 1909.'

The Mastery of the Citadel (1910)
Published in 'The Great War: Some Deeper Issues' (1915), reprinted in 'The Messenger of Chalice Well' (Issue 1, Christmas 1966).

The Passing Of Major P. (1911)
Published in 'The Quest' magazine, July 1911. Reprinted in 'The Great War: Some Deeper Issues' (1915), and in later editions of 'Private Dowding' (1943 onwards).

Some Deeper Aspects of the War (Taylor Bros, Bristol, 1914)
'Being the Substance of a Public Lecture given at Caxton Hall, Westminster, on Saturday, 28th November, 1914, by W. Tudor Pole. Mrs. Despard in the Chair.'
An altered version of this was used in PART I of 'The Great War: Some Deeper Issues'
* See Chapter 5 for extracts.

You Can Help To Protect Those At The Front (John M. Watkins, 1915?)
Advertised on the inside cover of 'The Spiritual Significance of the Hour'.

The Spiritual Significance of the Hour (John M. Watkins, 1916)
'Being the substance of an Address delivered in London on 5th March 1916, by Wellesley Tudor Pole, with a foreword by Lady Portsmouth' (On 18th March he delivered a similar talk in Edinburgh, 'The Deeper Meaning of the Hour'.)

March 1917 Notebook

A collection of supernormal anecdotes and interpretations probably intended for publication but superseded by 'Private Dowding'. Published posthumously in two parts in 'Light' magazine, spring and summer 1978.

* See Chapter 5 for extracts.

St Michael's Sanctuaries (1928)

Article on locations associated with St Michael, published in 'St Silas-the-Martyr, Kentish Town, 21st Anniversary Number, September-October 1928'.

* For a brief extract see Chapter 8.

Light On The Horizon (1930)

Article on approaching spiritual revelation, published in 'Light' magazine, 21.6.30.

The Shadow Doctor ('The Listener', 5 January 1938)

Article by 'Major W. Tudor-Pole' under a magazine heading of 'Things I Cannot Explain'.

* For an edited version, see Chapter 6.

The Spiritual Front (Andrew Dakers Limited, 1940 onwards, numerous editions)

TP's wartime booklet promoting the Big Ben Silent Minute, carrying endorsements from Churchill, the King and various religious leaders.

The Light Is Come (Andrew Dakers Limited, 1941)

Eleven page pamphlet on the arrival of spiritual light.

A Lighthouse Set on an Island Rock (Big Ben Council, 1942 onwards, numerous editions)

Pamphlet: 'Big Ben Silent Minute Series. (2)'

'Being the substance of an address given at the Oddfellows Hall, Worthing, on Sunday September 13th 1942, by W. Tudor Pole.'

Memory Time and Prevision (St Christopher Press, 1943)

'Being the substance of an Address given by W. Tudor Pole at 16 Queensbury Place London, S.W.7 on September 9th, 1943.'

Reprinted in 'The Silent Road', 1960.

Round the World at Nine O'clock (Big Ben Council, 1945 onwards, numerous editions)

Successor to 'The Spiritual Front', carrying the original endorsements and including much retrospective material on arguably miraculous aspects of World War Two.

Michael: Prince of Heaven (1951)

Anthology on St Michael, put together by TP, with contributions from other writers and including two articles of his own: 'The Archangel Michael' and 'Preparing the Way for the New Age'.

After 1951, TP published numerous other short writings, such as:

Meditation (1956)
The Mind Set Free (1959)
A Mansion in the Mind (1960)
Notes on Healing (1961)
A Message for the Coming Time (1962)
God Is Love (1967)
The Second Coming Is Here (1967)
What Does the Coming Mean? (1968)

These, however, fall outside the scope of the present volume.

3. LETTERS AND UNPUBLISHED WRITINGS

Sir David Russell Archives, St Andrews University Library

This vast correspondence starts in 1913 but picks up momentum in the 1920's, letters passing back and forth at the rate of approximately one a day (each!). Many concern their business interests, but many also address their wider interests. Sir David Russell died in 1956, and TP carried on writing to his son, D.F.O. Russell, but those papers are at present (2010) closed to the public.

Chalice Well Archives, Chalice Well, Glastonbury

TP set up the Chalice Well Trust in 1959, and most documents in the archives are relevant to that period or thereafter. There is, however, a collection of TP's shorter writings (made by Oliver Villiers, probably with intent—unfulfilled—to publish them) and these have been extensively drawn on.

Frederick Leveaux Archives

Two tin trunks contain large amounts of Quest-related material, including photographs and original planchette writings.

Letters to Rosamond Lehmann from WTP

The originals of these are still extant (and considerably more numerous than those quoted in 'My Dear Alexias') although they have been little used in this volume. The account of the Deans Yard Meeting in July 1907 (see Chapter 3) does, however, come from this collection.

Private Letters

Various people, especially Lady Jean Carroll, have made available private material in their possession. Patrick Benham has been particularly generous in sharing his researches for The Avalonians (see below).

4. OTHER PUBLICATIONS

Mark Twain, a Biography, the Personal and Literary Life of Samuel Langhorne Clemens, by Albert Bigelow Paine (3 volumes, Harper & Brothers, New York, 1911)

    * See Chapter 3 of the present work for Paine's 'Holy Grail' account, involving TP, Clemens, Archdeacon Wilberforce and the Blue Bowl.

The Thinning of the Veil, A Record of Psychic Experience: Mary Bruce Wallace (Watkins, 1919)

    The revised edition published by Neville Spearman (1981) incorporates her later book, 'The Coming Light'. Mary was TP's oldest sister. He and Russell published this book (via Watkins) in their 'Deeper Issues' series.

Two Incidents Concerning Glastonbury: Leslie Moore (article in 'The Month', May 1920)

    Reprinted in 'The Messenger of Chalice Well', issue 14.

    * See Chapter 3 for extensive quotation from the second of these 'Incidents', which helped set TP off on his Constantinople Quest. (The first concerns Bligh Bond.)

The Coming Light: Mary Bruce Wallace (Watkins, 1924)

    The second book by TP's sister, later incorporated by Neville Spearman into the 1981 edition of 'The Thinning of the Veil' (see above).

Memoirs: Israel Sieff (Weidenfeld and Nicolson, 1970)

    Pages 101 and 102 of Sieff's book include the reminiscences quoted in Chapters 7 and 10 of the present volume.

Wellesley Tudor Pole, Appreciation & Valuation: Oliver G. Villiers (Bells of Canterbury, 1977)

    This 48 page booklet offers a tribute to TP and includes much useful material, such as some articles by TP, as well as photographs and a bibliography. It would appear from Chalice Well Archives that Villiers hoped to publish a larger volume incorporating an anthology of TP's shorter writings, but was unsuccessful. Hence this reduced version.

The Avalonians: Patrick Benham (Gothic Image Publications, 1993)
(Second edition: Gothic Image Publications, 2006)

Glastonbury characters form the focus of this book, amongst them Dr Goodchild, Dion Fortune, Bligh Bond and Rutland Boughton. About a third of its pages concern TP, his family and friends, although after the First World War TP moved from Bristol to London and hence largely out of Patrick Benham's chosen range.

Sir David Russell, a Biography: Lorn Macintyre (Canongate, 1994)

The material for this book is derived entirely from the Russell papers at St Andrews University Library (see above) and it focuses largely on the business and other activities of Sir David Russell. TP is extensively mentioned, although his other-worldly side is not emphasised. There is much of interest concerning the Quest, however.

This Enchanting Place, Facets of Chalice Well: edited by Ann Proctor (Chalice Well Trust, 2006)

The purchase of Chalice Well for the nation in 1959 was one of TP's greatest triumphs. Consequently this short book (112 pages) is of considerable interest. Most notable for present purposes is a chapter on TP himself by Paul Fletcher (Chalice Well archivist) focusing largely on TP's thoughts concerning the Well.

Chalice Well, the Story of a Living Sanctuary (Chalice Well Trust, 2009)

This is a large impressive volume, collated and largely written by Natasha Wardle and Paul Fletcher, full of diverse information and sumptuous photographs. Chapter 3, 'A Life of Wellesley Tudor Pole the Founder' by Paul Fletcher gives a 17 page survey of TP's life, including much material that falls outside the scope of the present volume.

Afterword on Chalice Well

TP's most tangible legacy is the Chalice Well Trust. The Chalice Well site nestles comfortably in the dip between Glastonbury Tor and Chalice Hill, fed by an ancient spring of red chalybeate water, always flowing at a similar rate and always at the same temperature (52 degrees Fahrenheit). Over the decades and centuries this water has been credited with many physical healings—skin conditions, for instance, and eye problems—although perhaps its greatest effect is mental: calming stress, realigning the outlook, refreshing the spirit.

Around Chalice Well a garden has accumulated, ingenious with nooks and pathways, thronging with shrubs and flower beds, stately with yews, beeches and ash. Around the gardens sits a yet further layer—three orchards and a cress field—acting as buffer against the everyday world, so that what remains inside—apart from delight—is peace: peace of the ambient life, peace of the slowing mind, peace of the emerging soul.

The whole area is managed by a dedicated group of trustees, workers and volunteers, poised between the urgency of administration and eternity of waters. They welcome visitors to the gardens and the Trust Shop. They maintain Little St Michael and Chalice Well House, the two guest houses. And they host events throughout the year—solstices, concerts, retreats, community celebrations—an array of activities exemplifying the underlying philosophy: Many Paths, One Source.

But it is the Well itself that beckons. Back in TP's day there were around 1,000 visitors per year, whereas now the figure is between 40 and 45,000 per year. As arrivals move from the Entrance Archway they can overlook the Vesica Pool with its dancing waters before passing between the Entrance Yews en route to King Arthur's Court and its Healing Pool—then, skirting the Waterfall, they can drink from the Lion's Head Spout, before moving beyond the Angel Seat towards the Sanctuary, and up to the Well Head itself.

For each the experience is unique yet sufficiently similar to engender lasting enthusiasm. Back in TP's era there were only a few hundred Companions, nowadays the figure is well over 3,000. A four-monthly magazine, 'The Chalice', links Companions in America, Australia, Asia and all parts of Europe, giving news, reviews and information. And when Companions visit Glastonbury—perhaps on holiday, perhaps on pilgrimage—they can stay at Little St Michael, experiencing the numinous atmosphere of the Upper Room, or wandering the gardens in the calm of evening.

Perhaps one day you too will become a Companion. There again, perhaps you are already.

Index

About the Author

Gerry Fenge has been Head of English, History, Music and Drama departments in schools around Africa and the U.K. Having lectured extensively on esoteric subjects, he now concentrates full time on writing. He has two grown up children and lives in Yorkshire with his wife.